Dr. Tim Me...
Best Wishes.
N.P. Badlai
Aug. 2, 2021

Best Wishes-God Bless
Dr. Hiro Badlani
www.hinduismpath.com

Hinduism: An Evolutionary Religion
ISBN-13: 9781986981651
ISBN-10: 1986981657
Copyright © 2018 Dr. Hiro G. Badlani
hgbadlani@aol.com

Cover Page Photograph:
Mahamandapam inside Kauai's Hindu Monastery Temple, USA

HINDUISM

AN EVOLUTIONARY RELIGION

Dr. Hiro G. Badlani

Proofread and Edited by Mansi Motwani

Sri Ramakrishna's Message to the Modern World

"Do not care for doctrines; do not care for dogmas or sects or churches or temples. They count for little compared with the essence of existence in each man, which is spirituality; and the more a man develops it, the more power he has for good. Earn that first, acquire that, and criticize no one; for all the doctrines and creeds have some good in them. Show by your lives that religion does not mean words or names or sects, but that it means spiritual realization."

Swami Vivekananda

(The above excerpts from "Ramakrishna As We Saw Him" authored by Swami Chetanananda are reprinted with the permission of Vedanta Society of St. Louis, USA.)

**B.A.P.S.
SWAMINARAYAN
SANSTHA**
PUBLIC CHARITABLE TRUST REG. NO. A/2500/AMDAVAD
HEAD OFFICE : DHARMA SADAN, SHREE SWAMINARAYAN MANDIR, SHAHIBAUG, AMDAVAD-4.

TEL: (91-79) 2562 5133,2562 5151
FAX: (91-79) 2563 3815
WEBSITE: www.swaminarayan.org
Email: festival@akshardham.com
info@swaminarayan.org

BLESSINGS

7 July 2007
Ahmedabad

Respected Shri Dr Badlani,

On behalf of HDH Pramukh Swami Maharaj I would like to convey my profound commendations and congratulations to you in writing this book, *Hinduism – Path of the Ancient Wisdom*. It is extremely difficult to write a comprehensive book on Sanatan Dharma because of its wide spectrum of beliefs, philosophies, customs and denominations that have flourished for over 11,500 years. Despite this, your immense effort is a matter of inspiration for all.

To diligently read over 100 books on Hinduism and distilled its essence to produce this book requires acumen, patience, enduring enthusiasm and faith. May all Hindus and true seekers of spiritual knowledge take a leaf from your efforts and read the vast treasure house of Hindu shastras. Daily reading of the Upanishads, Ramayan, Mahabharat, Shrimad Bhagvat Gita and other shastras imbues personal peace and happiness, and pride for Hinduism. The spiritual knowledge of Sanatan Dharma helps all remain in good stead amidst the uncertainties of joy and misery in life.

My heartfelt prayers to Bhagwan Swaminarayan and Guruhari Pramukh Swami Maharaj that may they grant you good health, happiness and inspiration to serve society through more such inspiring works.

Jai Swaminarayan

Sadhu Swayam Prakash Da

Sadhu Swayamprakashdas
(Dr. Swami)

BAPS NGO IN CONSULTATIVE STATUS WITH THE ECONOMIC AND SOCIAL COUNCIL OF THE UNITED NATIONS
www.swaminarayan.org

Editors' Notes:

"With its powerful narrative and roots in spiritual storytelling, this book is perfect for anyone who desires authentic information on Hinduism. Engaging with this book will not only educate you, but imbue you with personal peace and happiness, becoming an experience both elegant and empowering."

"Working on this project has been a joyful surprise. I say surprise because I did not expect to enjoy a book on religion as much as I enjoyed reading "Hinduism: An Evolutionary Religion." The chapters are short, yet captivating. Each chapter leaves the reader with a little more understanding of the topic than the previous one. The easy-to-understand language is another aspect about this book that is appealing. Being a 23-year-old, I would strongly recommend the youth to read this book, as it exceeds what one would expect from a book on religion."

Contents

Blessing and Opinions

This book is like a map of Hinduism, which shows from where one should start his or her spiritual journey and where the journey ends.

Baba Hari Dass
Mount Maddona Center, Santa Cruz, California

Your book is definitely written in a way that presents abundance of information about Hinduism in easily readable format and style that will clearly appeal to the Hindu youth Diaspora.

Satguru Bodhinatha Veylanswami
Publisher of Hinduism Today
Head of Himalayan Academy and Kauai's Hindu Monastery, Hawaii

Each subtitle is like a rung of ladder, systematically leading the reader into the depths of our ancient wisdom. Whosoever reads this book will be surely benefited from its beautiful and penetrating insights. This book will also certainly do justice in imparting correct and more comprehensive about Hinduism to those settled abroad and have forgotten its lofty principles.

Swami Vagishananda
Head of Ramakrishna Math and Ramakrishna Mission, Mumbai, India

In this retired life when most Indians enjoy, you did painstaking research on Hinduism for ten years like tapasya. Fruit of that *tapasya* is evident in this beautiful book from which many readers will benefit. Your work will be treasured by the community.

Swami Tathagatananda
Sri Ramakrishna Vedanta Society, New York, USA

You have comprehensively dealt all different aspects of Hinduism that a Hindu or non-Hindu needs to know to get a good idea of Hindu religion, society and family. May the God who got this book done from you shower His choicest blessings on you.

Swami Yogatananda
Sri Ramakrishna Vedanta Society, Providence, USA

You have wonderfully expressed your ideas in very lucid English, which has made it more readable by those who will otherwise not read such text. You have given enough references to substantiate your points-that is also helpful for the readers.

Swami Sarvadevananda
Head of Sri Ramakrishna Vedanta Society, South California, U.S.A.

The get-up, cover design, and everything is nicely planned. It is your hard work for a long time. ...I found you have contacted so many swamis of our order other great scholars and devotees and institutions, and liberally drawn material for your book, and that has made it rich and wide in its content.

Swami Tanmaynanda
Sri Ramakrishna Vedanta Society, India

You really worked hard and brought so many things of Hinduism which many Hindus do not know. ....found your presentation and language are wonderful.

Swami Chetanananda
Head of Sri Ramakrishna Vedanta Society, St. Louis, U.S.A.

You have done a beautiful job in setting forth our ancient faith. The text, the cover, the printing, everything is well-done.

Swami Atmarupananda
Sri Ramakrishna Vedanta Society, South California, U.S.A.

The book will receive a great appreciation from the most critical persons. It has all that is needed for the newcomer in this faith or for the well- rooted person. Your efforts in putting things together are wonderful and deserve congratulations. The scientific minded you is distinctly reflected in your treatment to the vast subject on Hinduism.

Swami Anubhavananda
USA

You have done a great service to Hinduism by providing such a readable and balanced account that people in the West will be able to make profitable use of. It breathes the spirit of the Sanatana Dharma, universal tolerance, the underlying oneness of all paths. In reading this book, a non-Hindu will gain a comprehensive understanding of Hindu history and spirituality, while a Hindu will be inspired to live his or her faith proudly and dynamically. I don't think there is another book that does as much justice to the almost infinite complexity of Hinduism.

Swami Shankarananda
Mount Eliza, Australia

Something that makes it very attractive is that it contains many brief topics but written with great knowledge and a wide array of bibliographic data that allows the reader to continue searching that line of thought on their own.

Dasavatara Das
Argentina, South America

Dr Hiro Badlani's book is an excellent introduction to Hinduism for lay people. Dr Badlani, a lay person himself, conducted extensive research into the history, philosophy, and ethics of his own religion, including interviews with many leading Hindu leaders and scholars. He distilled his findings and his carefully thought out and perceptive conclusions into a readable volume that makes Hinduism come alive for lay people.

Nicholas Piediscalzi, Ph.D.
Professor Emeritus Religion
Wright State University

The book offers a comprehensive insight for the reader wanting to understand the sprawling complex religion. Covering a number of topics that comprise the corpus of the world's oldest religion, Dr Badlani has reduced Hinduism's intricate philosophy to engaging, simple-to-understand explanations.

Robert Arnett
Author of India Unveiled

We have reviewed the book and find it full of fascinating information about Hinduism. It is pretty comprehensive and can be a useful resource for studying Hinduism.

Jay Lakhani
Hindu Academy, U.K.

The book contains excellent and easy to understand information, which I am sure will be of particular interest to the Youth Diaspora across the World.

On behalf of the Hindu community here in the UK, we hail this noble effort and do hope to see a wide circulation and readership of the contents of this magnificent work.

Sanjay Jagatia
Hindu Council, UK

.... it seems very thorough and comprehensive, especially for those looking into Hinduism and wanting to learn more about it. You have certainly covered many important topics and aspects of Vedic culture.

Sri Nandanandana dasa (Stephen Knapp)
Vedic Scholar and Author
Detroit, USA

The Sindhi Sammelan Organizing Committee has recommended for you "THE PRIDE OF SINDHI COMMUNITY" Literary Award for your writing an outstanding book Hinduism. We feel proud of your dedication and hard work in publishing this much needed book for new generation of Hindus and for seekers of knowledge about ancient Indian religions.

Sindhi Association of South California SASC
Los Angeles

...The clarity of content is just incredible. The chapters are organized well and you did something that I truly appreciate, you got to the key points without excess wordage or fluffy descriptions.

It belongs to every practicing Hindu's bookshelf, and it is a must for anyone even remotely curious about our faith. This book should be in every book store.

Sheree Bice
Florida, USA

This book is like a mini-encyclopedia of Hinduism.

Mohan Dadlani
Los Angeles USA

The book, in my opinion, is suitable for almost anyone interested to learn about Hinduism that has shown the path for co-existence based upon human experience of many thousands of years.

Navin Doshi
Businessman and Philanthropist
Los Angeles, USA

With availability of vast literature on Hinduism, your book fulfills the need of quick reference and source to number of questions that Hindus encounter particularly in the minds of children born yearning to probe their heritage.

Dr. Shiv Navani
Radiologist, USA

The book consists of short chapters (easy reading) covering myriads of topics including the birth of Cosmos, evolution of mankind, and appearances of Consciousness, spirituality and religion. Author also painstakingly traces the history of Hinduism through a long period during which India went through changing dynasties of rulers. Author detailed discussions on Hindu way of life, Hindu society and its various customs, traditions and rituals.

Dr Gopal Das
Cardiologist
Las Vegas, USA

The author has harvested many of profound and beautiful quotations from this ancient and vast spiritual heritage under various organized themes and chapters. The reader gets the intellectual roller-coaster ride through ancient cultures of India, the Vedas, the Vedic philosophies and is eventually zapped to awareness by cosmic consciousness of intelligence of Divinity-the Soul.

Mani Matta
Dentist
New York, USA

It is a monumental effort testifying to your extensive study and admirable research. I sincerely wish that our youngsters keep it on their table & periodically read a chapter or two. They will benefit greatly.

Rada Krishna
Los Angeles USA

I urge all Indians, particularly youth, who are seeking to know more about their religious roots, to read this book. Dr. Badlani's book will show you the path you need to walk to reach your roots.

Chandru Mirchandani
Los Angeles USA

...and found the book very interesting and very in-depth and yet very easy to read and understand. I like the way you start with the origins of the universe, man, religion and time, this is basically the beginning of everything. I am sure that I will produce some great sermons for my Sunday morning service from this book.

Ganesan Gramanie
Hindu Priest, South Africa

You have very carefully and beautifully treasured all the customs, culture and religion, we had all most forgotten in your beautiful book.

Pandit Bhagirath
Los Angeles USA

I admire the way in which he has simplified the whole thing in fine English language. He has done justice to the subject matter so beautifully. And it throws light on the vast spectrum of Hinduism right from the Vedas!

Vijay Karripal
India

The path helps the beginner to move forward step by step gaining more and more enlightenment. The path laid down by Dr Badlani is clear and straight. Sign-boards carry thoughtful quotations to guide all sorts of pilgrims who seek knowledge about Hinduism...Dr Badlani systematized the vast subject of Hinduism in a gradational and authoritative manner.

G. Shankara Bhanu
Hyderabad, India

Preface

At the very outset, I wish to make it clear that this volume is not a new book; it is rather like a new edition of the previous book. I have also decided to change its name from *"Hinduism: Path of the Ancient Wisdom"* to *"Hinduism: An Evolutionary Religion"*, and have added significant new passages, especially in reference to the new subtitle, to justify and explain the change. Indeed, it has been rather hard for me to part with the old name for that was very relevant and even more close to my heart. After good deal of deliberation, I decided to make the change, hoping that it work out for the better.

Hinduism is now regarded as the oldest living religion of the world. It is ancient, with its roots going back to almost 10,000 years. Even so it has remained dynamic, as the American philosopher J. B. Pratt has aptly put: *"The reason for the immortality of the Vedic religion of Hinduism is that while retaining its spiritual identity, it has been changing its outward form in accordance with the demands of the time; and particularly it is the only religion which has been able to meet the challenges of science, which governs the thought and life of the Modern age."* This vibrant character, in fact, is also the reason of its survival through millennia, when most other prehistoric religions have almost disappeared. More importantly, the changes have taken place in a subtle manner, without any serious protest and bloodshed. Often there is some resistance observed at the onset of "change"; this is natural. Some changes are however unavoidable, and also very necessary; we may therefore keep an open mind, and accept these serenely and amicably. In Hindu culture, the old are always revered and not openly defied and antagonized. Old philosophies, rituals and customs have sustained alongside new ones, leaving individuals to decide for themselves as per their personal choices. It is not uncommon in a Hindu family for members to worship different deities. Differences also exist in choosing various rituals and religious practices.

At the end of each chapter is a small write-up by me, which elaborates on the changes that have taken periodically through the centuries.

It is imperative to realize that Hinduism was not started by one single founder. It is rather like a conglomeration of the spiritual wisdom of many ethnic tribes that inhabited the Indian subcontinent in the ancient period. Thus it absorbed the "pluralistic" character at the very beginning. In accommodating the opinions and beliefs of many, it also acquired the character of becoming non-dogmatic and unbiased. This attitude has been maintained in the Hindu psyche throughout centuries. Religious masters and "*Rishis*" have repeatedly prompted us to maintain harmony and peace, and to look at all beings as creatures of one divine family - "*Vasudhaiva Kutumbkum*". In the earliest of the Hindu scriptures, the Rig Veda, another foremost principle has been inscribed, "*Ekan Sat, Viprah Bahuti*", which translates as "There is one Truth, the paths leading to it may be many". The book repeatedly emphasizes the essential unity and homogeneity of all religions. With this eternal principle in mind, at no time has any Hindu religious leader ever claimed that Hinduism is the only way to salvation or God-realization. Over a long period spanning many centuries, Hindus have also refrained from using any kind of pressure tactics to convert others into Hinduism. It is rather unique that in many Hindu scriptures and hymns (*bhajans*), names of other religions and messiahs are freely used with utmost reverence and devotion. In this book, I have strived to uphold and support that universal philosophy, which according to me is also the greatest asset of Hinduism.

Of late, there has been an undue and rather unnecessary discussion regarding Religion vs Spirituality. Some persons claim that they are "spiritual" but not "religious" intending to mean that they are moral and virtuous, but do not belong to any religion. This new thinking, however, has also created some confusion and misunderstanding, creating doubts whether religion and spirituality are antagonistic to one another! This is not true. All religions basically teach us to live moral and virtuous life and shun vice and wickedness. Without the spiritual teachings, what other role does a religion have to play?

Hindus have undoubtedly suffered to a great extent, especially at the hands of those who have wrongfully invaded and exploited them, often very mercilessly and ruthlessly. Feelings of hatred, revenge, and acquiring justice are very understandable in such conditions. Even so, our spiritual masters have always taught us to be compassionate, to strive for peace, and not to indulge in a tit for tat plan. We may always endeavor to do everything possible to dutifully defend our land and our people, but we may not part with our divine values of moral and ethical living. History is witness that people who have remained committed to such spiritual ideals have always survived and succeeded. Hindu society has paid dearly for becoming rather docile and passive in the face of unjust aggressions in the past; those mistakes and missteps may be avoided in future. Ramayana and Mahabharata provide with truthful and appropriate guidance.

This book also contains a lot of unique information that I hadn't included in the previous version. Hinduism is a vast, almost infinite database; whenever I come across any new and important piece of material about Hinduism, I have made an attempt to update my writings with the same.

In writing this book, I claim nothing original. I have taken the help of many religious scriptures, met and communicated with a number of Reverend Swamis and learned scholars, and gone through scores of books. I have acknowledged them properly in the earlier volumes of my work and also uploaded the same on the website of the book. I have maintained the same chronological pattern in the book, from the very earliest to the present day endeavors. The earlier book has been appreciated by many, who kindly endorsed it as a "mini encyclopedia" of Hinduism. I take this opportunity to thank everyone with all my heart for their generous comments and opinions, some of which are also published in this edition as well as on the website of the book www.hinduismpath.com. I invite all my readers to note down their relevant positive remarks and queries in the "Reader's Column" on the aforementioned website; I shall strive to reply individually as suitable, and also include any new valuable information suggested by them in the future version of the book. It is also my earnest wish to create a permanent editorial board, which will oversee the periodic update and other aspects of this manual in the future.

I have also uploaded the entire edition of this book on the website, free of cost for anyone to read. It is my earnest wish that the youth, both in India and abroad read and acquaint themselves with the worthy and glorious attributes of our religion and culture; the book is dedicated to them.

In compiling this new edition, young editor Mansi Motwani has put lot of sincere efforts; I sincerely appreciate and thank her. My old friend Eric Esquivel and my wife Kamla have continued to remain the strong pillars of personal support; I simply cannot thank them enough.

The Influence of Hindu Philosophy on Thinkers throughout the Ages

I found a race of mortals living upon the Earth, but not adhering to it,
Inhabiting cities, but not being fixed to them,
Possessing everything, but possessed by nothing.

Apollonius Tyaneus, first century CE
Greek thinker and traveler

Among all nations, during the course of centuries and throughout the passage of time, India was known as the mine of wisdom and the fountainhead of justice and good government, and the Indians were credited with excellent intellect, exalted ideas, universal maxims, rare inventions, and wonderful talents.

Qadi Sa'id, 1029–1070
Arab Muslim scientist of Cordova, Moorich

It does not behoove us, who were merely savages and barbarians when the Indians and Chinese people were civilized and learned, to dispute their antiquity.

Voltaire, 1694–1778
French author and philosopher

The motion of the stars calculated by the Hindus before some 4500 years vary not even a single minute from the tables we are using today.
[Cassine and Meyer tables used in the nineteenth century]

Jean-Sylvain Bailly, 1736–1793
French astronomer

The Sanskrit language is of wonderful structure, more perfect than the Greek, more copious than the Latin, and more exquisitely refined than either.

Sir William Jones, 1746–1794
British jurist and Indologist

In the whole world, there is no study, except that of the original Vedas, so beneficial and so elevating as that of Upanishads. It has been the solace of my life; it will be the solace of my death. They present the fruit of the highest knowledge and wisdom.

Arthur Schopenhauer, 1788–1860
German philosopher

The Indian teaching teaches to speak truth, love others, and to dispose trifles. The East is grand—and makes Europe appear the land of trifles.

Ralph Waldo Emerson, 1803–1882
American poet and philosopher

In the morning I bathe my intellect in the stupendous and cosmological philosophy of the Bhagavad Gita, in comparison with which our modern world and the literature seem puny and trivial.

Henry David Thoreau, 1817–1862
American poet and philosopher

If I were to look over the whole world to find out the country most richly endowed with all the wealth, power, and beauty that nature can bestow, in some parts a very paradise on earth, I should point to India.

Friedrich Max M. Muller, 1823–1900
Renowned German scholar and Indologist

Tolstoy not only read the Vedas but also spread their teachings in Russia. He included many of the sayings of the Vedas and the Upanishads in his collections.

Alexandra Shifman on Leo Tolstoy, 1828–1910
Russian author and philosopher

India is the cradle of the human race, the birthplace of human speech, the mother of tradition. Our most valuable and most instructive materials in the history of man are treasured up in India only.

Mark Twain, 1835–1910
American author and humorist

The Indian way of life provides the vision of the natural, real way of life. On the face of India are the tender expressions, which carry the Creator's hand.

George Bernard Shaw, 1856–1950
Irish author and literary critic

If there is one place on the face of earth where all the dreams of living men have found a home, from the earliest days when man began the dream of existence, it is India.

Romain Rolland, 1866–1944
French author

The history of India for many centuries had been happier, less fierce, and more dreamlike than any other history. In these favorable conditions, they built a character—meditative and peaceful and a nation of philosophers such as could nowhere have existed except in India.

H. G. Wells, 1866–1946
Sociologist, historian, and author

When I read the Bhagavad Gita and reflect about how God created this universe, everything else appears superfluous.

Albert Einstein, 1879–1955
German scientist and humanist

India was the motherland of our race, and Sanskrit the mother of Europe's languages; she was the mother of our philosophy; mother, through the Arabs, of much of our mathematics; mother, through the Buddha, of the ideals embodied in Christianity; mother, through the village community, of self-governance and democracy; Mother India is in many ways the mother of us all.

Prof. Will Durant, 1885–1981
American author and historian

It is already becoming clear that a chapter, which had a Western beginning, will have an Indian ending, if it is not to end in the self destruction of the human race

Arnold Joseph Toynbee, 1889–1975
British historian

India conquered and dominated China culturally for twenty centuries without having to send a single soldier across her border.

Hu Shih, 1891–1962
Former Chinese ambassador to the United States

The Bhagavad Gita] is one of the clearest and most comprehensive summaries of the perennial philosophy ever to have been done.

Aldous Huxley, 1894–1963
English novelist

Access to the Vedas is the greatest privilege this century may claim over all previous centuries.

J. Robert Oppenheimer, 1904–1967
American nuclear physicist (father of the atom bomb)

About a thousand of their [the Jews'] forefathers fled from Palestine to India after the destruction of the second temple in 135 CE, and were welcomed by the Hindu ruler of the time, who allowed them to settle wherever they pleased. The governing factor in politics was dharma (righteousness), rather than any panth (denomination).

Geoffrey Moorhouse, 1931–
Travel author

Says Swami Vivekananda, "Like the gentle dew that falls unseen and unheard, and yet brings into blossom the fairest of roses, has been the contribution of India to the thought of world."

Adapted from the slide show "Mera Bharat Mahan"
Presented by Indiatimes (www.indiatimes.com)

1 The Cosmic Calendar

Unlike the Western concept of linear time, the Hindus accept time as cyclical, with neither beginning nor end. Hindu Rishis have stated that there are eternal cycles of evolutions (*srshti*), and dissolutions (*pralaya*) taking place in the cosmos. The modern scientific opinion suggests that the whole cosmos was created by a "big bang" about 18 billion years ago. Our solar system was created 4.5 billion years ago. The solar system is a part of a larger galaxy of stars, the Milky Way. If we were seated in a spaceship zooming at the speed of light—186,000 miles per second—it would take 100,000 years to traverse from one end of the Milky Way galaxy to the other.[1] There are billions of other galaxies of stars like this one. Many modern scientists including the famous physicist Stephen Hawking now tend to discredit the theory of "big bang" in favor of the Hindu concept of cosmos being eternal, without any beginning.

Hindu scriptures have given stunning descriptions of these infinite, countless solar systems (*brahmands*) in the cosmos. Hindus have two concepts of time periods: mythological and historical:

Mythological Concept: in this cosmic concept, Hindu Rishis conceived the largest measure of time as *kalpa*. One kalpa consists of 1000 smaller unite *mahayugas*. The current mahayuga is further divided as:

Satyuga period: 1,728,000 years

Tretayuga period: 1,296,000 years

Dwaparyug period: 864,000 years

Kaliyuga period: 432,000 years

Historical Concept: According to R.C. Majumdar, as described "Vedic Age" in the book, "*The History and Culture of the Indian People*" (1951:316) compiled by him, the four Yugas or periods of the Indian history are as follows:

Kritayuga-------Manu------3100 B.C.

Tretayuga-------Rama------1950 B.C.

Dvaparayuga---Krishna---1400 B.C.

Kaliyuga-------------------- (after Mahabharata war)

Hindu Rishis also recognized the cosmic phenomenon, and they called it *Brahman*—the transcendental, the supreme, the eternal divine soul, which pervades everything, everywhere, at all times. The concept of universal Brahman sowed the seeds of spiritual unity. The ancient Rishis recognized the utter vulnerability and weakness of man. They recognized the futility of man to depend upon his own ego. They compared man to a wave of the ocean; it rises and moves because it is with the ocean. Separated from it, the wave will perish in a moment. They compared the man to a whiff of air, to a bubble of water, to a speck of dust, and to a grain of sand. They teach that man must accept God in his own best interest. Pramukh Swami, the previous spiritual head of the Swaminarayan sect, was asked how he managed to do so much, despite his advanced age. He replied, *"I completely trust the Supreme Lord. As I trust that the sun will rise in the morning and set in the evening, I trust that all things of life will be done with His grace. I don't take any responsibility of the doer-ship on my shoulders. I simply work as per His instruction."* This in essence is the Hindu concept of religion—the Dharma as it is preferred to be called. It denotes cosmic unity of all beings, purity, righteousness and orderliness as ordained by the Supreme God.

Hindu Rishis conceptualized "evolution" from a very early age; the perception of eternal cycles of evolutions (srshti), and dissolutions (pralaya) taking place from the infinite period, suggesting the everlasting movement of the changing cycles, forms the basis of Hindu doctrine and philosophy. It is incredible that Hindu Rishis made stunning descriptions of these countless solar systems (brahmands) in the cosmos over 5000 years ago, a time when technology was non-existent! Although the "big bang" theory is widely accepted by contemporary science, many, including the great physicist Stephen Hawking, are now inclined toward the ancient Hindu concept of the cosmos being eternal i.e going through recurring cycles of evolutions and dissolutions without an origin.

2 Evolution

Earth and its solar system started to form around five billion years ago. Life came into existence soon after, first in the form of plants. The earliest living creature on Earth was a single-celled organism. Then more complex aquatic and land animals appeared. The Indian subcontinent was formed from glaciers about forty million years ago. Where there are now the mighty Himalayas, there once were oceans—there is evidence of fish fossils on the rocks of the Himalayas.

Man descended from apes around six million years ago (proto-human-*orrorin tugenensis* species). This is the time he started to walk on his two hind limbs; that is, he became a biped. The first appearance of man was in the Sahara region of the African continent. From there, man moved to the east, west, north, and south. Modern human (*Homo sapiens*-thinking man) originated about 200,000 years ago, reaching full maturity around 50,000 years ago.

Man is superior to other beings because of his highly developed brain. This organ has billions of specialized neurons and neurological pathways with which we think and can use our free will. Before this development, beings functioned only through instinct. The main feature that differentiates the modern brain from that of our early ancestors is its capacity to restrain the instinctive behavior—the activity of the lower brain—by its voluminous gray matter, which is much less developed in lower animals. The modern human brain has over hundred billion nerve cells, called neurons, mainly in the grey matter cortex. It is believed that only 10 to 20 percent of these are ever used. This in itself offers a great potential for further human development.

Hindu Rishis seem to have acquired an intuitive knowledge of this evolutionary process. Many of God's emissaries, or *devtas*, also have been depicted in other animal forms, such as cow (*gaoo-mata*), bull (*nandi*), cobra (*naag*), bird (*garud*), and monkey (*Hanuman*), etc. When understood in context, although it might have looked comical to an outsider, worshiping these animal gods is, in fact, pertinent and even rational. They are all our ancestors and forefathers in a way! A Hindu is taught to see God in all beings. As a symbolic gesture, he is asked to keep a portion of his food aside to be served to animals and birds every time he sits for his meals. Millions of Hindus perform this ritual religiously, even today. What appeared to be so awkward—to bow before a passing cow—now has earned a grand dignity. Hindu thought recognizes that all creatures have a divine connection.

Hindu scriptures have many sacred hymns in which God is worshipped for showering His bounty on all the beings of the universe. One such hymn reads:

Om Sarve Bhavanthu Sukhina- May all be happy
Sarve Santhu Nira Maya- May all people be healthy
Sarve Bhadrani Pashyanthu- May all see only auspicious
Ma Kashchith Dukkha Bhaag Bhaveth- May none suffer

Even as the theory of evolution is wholly endorsed by science- right from single-celled organisms to the proto-human-orrorin tugenensis species that finally came to be known as "man", from the lowest to the highest forms of life, Hindu Rishis went one step further and recognized this concept in a spiritual way by understanding lower animals as the virtual ancestors of human beings and propounding the awareness of cosmic unity at the highest level. Hindu theology believes in the celestial unity of all beings.

3 The Origin of Religion

The first proto-human beings walked upright as far back as six million years ago; that is, man walked on his two hind limbs instead of on all fours, as his ancestors had. Religion, however, came into being less than ten thousand years ago. Hindu Rishis even so had an ingenuous approach toward religion, or *dharma*, as they would call it. They conceived that when a thing or being is created, its dharma is imbedded in it. For example, the dharma of fire is to burn. Hindu sages then meditated long to discover the dharma of man--*manav dharma*. They conceived dharma as the inherent duty in accordance with the laws of the cosmos. Dharma has been described as God's divine law to steer people on righteous path.

Evidence of proto-religious activity in the form of rituals, though, probably dates back to a much earlier period. In fact, the caveman made his first attempt at healing and guiding others possibly as early as one hundred thousand years ago. Before the written word came into existence, all such ideas and activities were passed by word of mouth or through cave paintings.

Man's earliest encounter with religion would have been in the form of viewing natural phenomenon as magical and mystical occurrences. His thinking brain might have posed questions such as "*Who brings the sun in the morning?*" Man started to attribute superior powers to an unknown command, beyond his strength and energy. He considered the sun, the sky, the fire, the wind, and other natural elements as gods, the supreme authorities. Man responded with many thoughtful reactions, and in the process, he built a treasure trove of wisdom to guide him. The earlier tribal groups later merged into larger racial or ethnic divisions. Thinking man gradually understood his humble place in the vast cosmos of God. The Godhood became established. Ancient Hindu sages, much like the saints of other faiths, linked the vast infinite creation of the universe with the Creator! As man was searching for God, the supreme power above everything, he visualized God in different forms in different places. Thus evolved many different religions; each with its own set of rules and regulations. In this diversity, however, there would also be a factor of unity. All religions professed faith. All religions accepted the invisible supreme power of God Almighty. All religions also advocated that man should live a life of virtue and morality, while abandoning vices and selfishness. In all religions there would be God incarnations, messiahs, or simply godly or divine persons, who would lead others on the path of spirituality and divinity. Religion and spirituality would teach man to give more than to take; to help and care for others; to love and nurture the beings and non-beings. These divine qualities would also usher in the progress and prosperity of human civilization; without these special qualities, there would be no real progress. Man would be like a lower animal! In all religions, there also would be an element of mysticism; religion is not exactly like science. All religions function by the element of faith; one person's utter faith may appear blind faith to the other person! We may also not comprehend all the infinite nature of God and religion. Scientists in some places are now searching for more concrete evidence about the religious developments. Some believe that the humans may have been hardwired by evolutionary forces to believe in God. "God" gene too has been named!

God also created in man the fountain of inner joy, within his own self. Whenever man did a righteous or virtuous act, he would feel peace and bliss. In the long voyage of religious evolution, this fountain of joy would sustain and inspire him more than any material thing ever could do. Indeed, it would be the search for this bliss, or *ananda,* as it is described in Hindu philosophy that would keep people on this path in the face of the most severe obstacles. God endowed man not only with a physical body, mind, and intellect but also with a higher faculty, the spiritual soul. As man advanced in his evolution, he became gradually more mind oriented than body oriented. Later, he would reach for higher peaks of growth. He would become more spiritual in nature. He would imbibe the spiritual or divine qualities. He would be a loving, nurturing, forgiving, and helping creature. He would do all these things, of which the lower creatures are not capable. He would eventually find the treasure of inner joy, irrespective of whatever the outward conditions of his body might be. He would be beyond the pain and sorrow of the physical and the mental worlds. He would see God in all beings, and he would be blessed with eternal joy!

Said Dalai Lama, "*Relying on the dharma (religion), we will be able to generate happiness and eliminate suffering.*"[4] Simply put, religion enhances the quality and merit in all our deeds, and in the process creates more success and joy in our lives. In human history, religion became the great unifying force of culture and the guardian of tradition.

The Hindu concept of evolution goes beyond the bonds of the modern scientific concept. Science recognizes "human intellect" as the highest potential whereas the concept of "Higher or Spiritual Consciousness" as perceived by Hindu theology identifies the soul qualities of "virtue" and "divinity" as the highest stage of human development. All religions have similar codes about moral and virtuous values. Hindu theology urges all humans to strive for that higher goal through eons of life cycles, to fruitfully accomplish their evolutionary soul journey till they attain full transcendental maturity.

Note on "Aryans"

"Aryan" is originally a Sanskrit word meaning "noble", and indicates more cultured people. Aryan people are associated with the creation of the Vedas and other scriptures. According to Prof. D.R. Sardesai, Aryans originated in India in the pre-historic period. It is believed that in the beginning, there was no hereditary caste. There were only classes or varnas not castes or jatis. Later some of them went out of India to propagate the spiritual knowledge to other lands. (Personal Communication)

In late-19th and early-20th century, Nazi ideology in Germany adopted "Aryan" name for its inhabitants, the "Nordic peoples" to emphasize their pure and superior culture. The "master race" and anti-Semitic attitude of the Nazi "Aryan" name has no bearing whatsoever with the Indo-Aryans.

A similar movement in America, the White Aryan Resistance (WAR), had no connection with the Indo-Aryans.

4 Roots of Hinduism in the Ancient Cultures of India

Hinduism has been compared to a growing banyan tree; spreading its roots on the earth and sprouting up in many directions. In Hindu faith, there are no set parameters, no fixed rules, and no rigid schedules. Hinduism is a vastly liberal religion. In fact, it openly and fervently encourages and tolerates differences of opinion, use of discretion, and interpretation based on one's own circumstances and perceptions. At the same time, there are some strong ethical principles and rituals that characterize this religion. The great Vedas and Upanishads affirm these principles in an organized compilation. Belief in the authority of these ancient scriptures is one of the chief prerequisites of Hinduism.

Although Hinduism recognizes the Vedic teachings as its basic principles, the roots of this religion go back a long way. The excavations of the Sindhu-Saraswati civilization (more commonly known as Harappan or Indus civilization) show evidence of the carvings of Shiva in his proto form as Pasupati, the lord of all animal kingdoms, and also in the yoga asana, or yoga positions. There are also carvings of exuberant feminine deities, which would later be known as various forms of the Mother Goddess, Shakti. The naked figurines, in meditative poses of the lotus position and standing *kayotsarga* (relaxation with self-awareness), are very similar to those later adopted by the Buddha and the *Tirthankars* (humans who achieve enlightenment) of the Jain religion. These carvings are said to point toward the concepts of God as prevalent in that period. Evidence suggests that the Saraswati and Sindhu (also known as the Indus) rivers originated at the end of the great Ice Age, about ten thousand years ago. It is believed that the colossal civilization along this verdant belt was more widely spread than the civilizations of Egypt or Greece. The Saraswati River ran parallel to the Sindhu River, about two hundred miles east of it. The huge mass of land between the two great rivers developed as the Sindhu-Saraswati civilization. Names of these two rivers are mentioned repeatedly—perhaps more frequently than other rivers—in the most ancient Hindu scripture, the Rig Veda. More than fifteen hundred cities developed on the banks of these two great rivers. Sindhu-Saraswati civilization is called the Harappan civilization after Harapa, the first of its sites excavated in 1920, followed by Mohenjo-Daro. Gujarat too shows large concentration of Harappan sites, which include the important excavations of Lothal and Dholavira. This great civilization came to end due to the gradual drying up of the Saraswati River because of some structural changes in the north at the Himalayas. New evidence with satellite imaging and limited excavation by a French team has revealed the course of the prehistoric Saraswati River, earlier mentioned in the Rig Veda. It was hitherto considered as myth only!

India, on the other hand, continued to march ahead and, in fact, remained the wealthiest country in the world until the seventeenth century, despite repeated invasions from outsiders, who plundered and looted her repeatedly.

One more equally ancient and great civilization was established in the south of India. This became the home of the Dravidian culture, which incorporated Tamil, Telugu, Malayalam, Kannada, and other languages of this group. Dravidian culture has its own distinguished history, literature, fine arts, and spiritual heritage. The Dravidian community adopted the emerging Hinduism thought, translating it into its own languages and script. Later, the idol and the temple concepts of the southern Dravidian culture were assimilated in the emerging Hindu religion. Indeed, adaptation and modification would become the hallmark of the Hindu philosophy. Some also think that there is a link between the Sindhu-Saraswati civilization and the Dravidian culture, the exact extent of which has not been fully assessed; others consider the Dravidian a separate ethnic entity. The acceptance of the Vedas as the supreme authority, however, eventually became the melting point of many diverse ethnic cultures toward the formation of Hinduism.

The terracotta seals and sculptures of the Sindhu-Saraswati civilization indicate the introduction of Neolithic culture, which has remained very dominant in India as seen in the temple sculptures through millennia. Strong association of Dravidian society with the stone sculpture is suggestive of a close link between these two ancient civilizations. The history of Indian civilization begins in the Neolithic cultures dating back to the late eighth millennium B.C. Advancing from the hunter's life to the agriculture and vegetarianism in India brought about the major cultural pursuits. The stone cutting techniques were modified from hunting tools toward sculpture, which became a great obsession with Indian people in the past and has continued to be an artistic passion even now.

The ancient scriptures of the Hindu religion, the Vedas, are recognized as the earliest documented literature of mankind. It is affirmed that the Vedas are the very first Hindu scriptures, but the flow of the written word would never stop in Hindu philosophy. In the beginning, many spiritual and moral concepts were devised to help man overcome his fears and problems. Initially, this doctrine was called the *Manav Dharma*, or the preferred duties of mankind. Later, the name *Sanathan Dharma*, the eternal religion, came to be associated with it and is still very popular in many places. It has also been described as *Vaidika Dharma*—religion based on the Vedas. Hindu sages in fact, perceived religion, or dharma, in a wide sense. Universal or cosmic religion is called *rita*, which denotes order and harmony; social religion of a community is named as *varna* dharma, which describes the laws governing a section of people according to their customs and culture; and religion of an individual, *swadharma*, guides a person to lead life in conformity with one's personal situation. A Hindu is thus prompted to consider the righteous duty—*dharma*--as a guideline for all his actions.

Dharma itself has a wide spectrum of meanings. Literally, it means "something that sustains." Religion in Hindu philosophy concerns with the rules and regulations that hold the society together. It is based essentially on ethical considerations so that we may hold and nurture each other. Without the ethical principles, the society would fall apart, hurting and destroying each other in the process. Thus, dharma is closely linked to its application in our everyday life. In Hindu philosophy, dharma has come to uphold the cause of righteousness and moral duty.

Until the fourteenth century, none of the earlier scriptures have any mention of the word Hindu. Hindu was first mentioned in the fifteenth century in Persian as a geographical concept in reference to the people and territory across the River *Sindhu* (Indus). Strangely, the term Hinduism became popular only around the nineteenth century.[7]

The concept of Hinduism thus has grown out of the mergence and union of many sects and cultures of different origins, joining together with greater freedom to pursue their individual customs, manners, practices, and languages. It is like a mighty ocean of thought, which has risen from the confluence of many small and large, old and new rivers of philosophy and doctrine. The origin of Hinduism fixedly belongs to India, without contest. Max Muller also confirms, "*The Vedic religion was the only one the development of which took place without any extraneous influences.*"[8]Hinduism was born in the cradle of peace; "*religious persecution was rare*" in its historical growth.[10]Civilizations grow with the manure of peace and cooperation, not in the brutalities of war and bloodshed.

There have been some interesting new discoveries regarding the ancient Indian symbol Swasika; it is now regarded as much older than believed, older than the Aryans and even the Sindhu-Saraswati Civilization. The researchers say the Swastika dates back at least 11,000 years. In tracking the antiquity of the Swastika, the researchers came across a staggering discovery -that the Rig Veda, generally associated with Aryan civilization, existed much before that, dating back to the pre-Harappan times in the form of Shruti that were orally handed down through the Indus Valley civilization. With passage of time over millennia, the Swastika did travel across many countries in Asia and Europe. Its use by Hitler as anti-Semitic weapon of destruction bears no relation to the original Indian symbol of peace and auspiciousness. (Source: timesofindia.indiatimes.com)

The prehistoric ancient history of proto-Hindu religion is truly vibrant, with its origin dating back to over 10,000 years. Relics of the Sindhu-Saraswati (Harappan) civilization include many sculptures, terracotta seals, paintings etc., which would later mold the future religions of Indian origin such as Hinduism, Jainism and Buddhism. The Dravidian culture co-mingled with plenty of temple structures. From the very beginning, proof of Hinduism's open-arm methodology has been found in the assimilation of concepts and designs. Indeed, Hinduism is a conglomeration of many ethnic and tribal sacred concepts, which blended and coalesced peacefully in search of the highest truths of the divinity.

5 Ancient Hindu Scriptures: An Ever-flowing River of Knowledge

For Hindus, scriptures have most powerful influence in everyday life: *"The man who rejects the words of the scriptures and follows the impulse of desire attains neither his perfection, nor joy, nor the Path Supreme. Let the scriptures be, therefore, thy authority as to what is right and what is not right."* (Bhagavad Gita, 16: 23–24). The spiritual richness of the ancient Hindu scriptures is simply unmatched, but the volume of these scriptures is even more amazing. The very first scriptures were the four Vedas. These scriptures comprise the divine revelations, the *Shrutis*. As such, they have been considered the basis and command of Hinduism. The Upanishads, which are the essence and final culmination of the Vedas, also form part of the *Shruti* scriptures.

Two great epic scriptures, the Ramayana and the Mahabharata, soon followed the Vedas/Upanishads. These scriptures and others that followed were formed as *Smritis*, the ones that were remembered. The Vedic scriptures had a strict code of finality. The Smriti scriptures of the later period had no such compulsions. One example may explain: Vedas teach that no violence be done to any being. This, however, would prove to be an impossible position in certain circumstances. The *Smriti* scriptures, on the other hand, encouraged modifications as the situation demanded, according to place and time. *Smriti* scriptures are derived from human experience and are the bedrock of tradition, continuing from the ancient and into modern. The *Smriti* scriptures may be varied according to the sect (*sampradaya*), and may be written in languages other than Sanskrit.

The earliest written script for the Hindu scriptures was the Vedic Sanskrit *Brahmi*, as early as the seventh century BCE. Classical Sanskrit, which is also associated with the proto-Indo-European languages and is considered the mother of many Indian as well as European languages came to become prominent in fourth century CE. It adapted the present *Devnagri* script in the tenth century CE. It is said that Sanskrit is phonetically the most accurate language. Its grammar is also most correctly built. Its constitution was so perfect that no word could have any variation of pronunciation or meaning and denotation.

Each syllable (*akshara*) in the Vedas is endowed with significance and purpose, imparting to it a cosmic energy in a spiritual manner. Many experts suggest that it would be the most ideal language for computer technology.[11] Says Swami Vivekananda, "*The vast ancient literature of India was written in Sanskrit, which was never a spoken language! It was only used for writing the scriptures, epics, and dramas, etc.*"[12] It thus became truly a classic language of India. In the absence of paper, the ancient Hindu scriptures were originally written on dried palm leaves. Sir William Jones first established its relationship with other European languages in 1789.[13]

Different ethnic groups, however, retained much of their original linguistics and folklore, apart from influencing the mainstream Sanskrit. India today has nearly thirty languages and over five hundred dialects in use. All these languages originated from four important groups: Austro-Asiatic, Tibeto-Burman, Dravidian, and Indo-Aryan. The earliest was the Austro-Asian, which group passed by the Indian subcontinent from Africa on its way to Australia about fifty thousand years ago.[14] In the long history of existence—over six million years— mankind perhaps began the journey of writing only around five thousand years ago or little earlier!

Apart from the Ramayana and the Mahabharata, the *Smritis* recognize a number of other important texts. The Bhagavad Gita, which forms a part of the Mahabharata, is considered the authoritative vehicle of Hinduism and its philosophy. The *Dharma Shastras* are specialized manuals that deal with different subjects such as law, politics, and economics. *Manu Smriti*, the Book of Manu, gives exhaustive details of the codes of conduct for all occasions. Even though there now may be some areas of disagreement, this treatise has long held its powerful influence in framing the laws for Hindu society. Manu, who is the mythological son of Lord Brahma, is thus considered the origin of mankind in Hindu philosophy. Manu literally means "thinking mind" and is therefore regarded as the symbolic beginning of higher thinking in human beings.

Niti Shastra, written by a clever prime minister of the Maurya dynasty named Chanakya (329–297 BCE), has been hailed as an authoritative treatise on politics and administration. *Artha Shastra* and *Kautilya Shastra* deal with economics, law, politics, and the like. *Vastushastra*, Hindu science of architecture, gives details of construction activity, and is closely associated with thousands of ancient as well as modern Hindu temples.

The *Darshanas* are texts that explain and comment on the main Vedas/Upanishads:

The *Sankhya*
The *Purva Mimamsa*
The *Uttara Mimamsa* or *Brahama Sutra*
The Yoga Sutra
The *Nyaya*
The *Vaisheshika*

Different philosophies do not reflect opposing views. More likely, they portray different aspects of Hindu theology, complementing each other to present the full picture.

Apart from these different philosophical codes, there was yet another one: The Charvaka philosophy, which has been known as Hindu materialism. It is a philosophy that promotes pleasure seeking and is contrary to the Vedic teachings. Even though this philosophy was never accepted by mainstream society, its existence and endorsement without any serious opposition indicates the extent of freedom of opinion in Hindu culture.

Agamas are the *Smriti* scriptures that were written as operating instructions for Hindu worship in the three main sects of Hindu faith. These scriptures are the manuals for the construction of temples and installation of the idols, and for conducting various rituals, worship ceremonies (*pujas*), and festivals.

There are three different sets of these scriptures:

Shaiva Agamas—worship of Lord Shiva
Vaishnava Agamas—worship of Lord Vishnu
Shakti Agamas—worship of many goddesses

Puranas literally means ancient. The Puranas have been described as the Vedas of the common man. The complex language used in earlier scriptures has been substituted with simpler and easy-to-understand descriptions. Hindu sages described the ancient tales and allegories in mythological style so that the ordinary person could understand the deep spiritual philosophy in a simple manner of faith and devotion. The Vedic concept of a formless and transcendental God was substituted by various images of the Divine, which could be more easily comprehended by the common person. Spiritual transformation through devotion (*bhakti*) became more popular in these scriptures. These scriptures also cut across the barriers of the caste system, as all sections of the society had access to them. There are a total of eighteen Puranas, in which the intricate philosophies are explained very candidly in tales and parables. Six Puranas each are dedicated to Lord Brahma, Lord Vishnu, and Lord Shiva.

It is through the Puranas that many Hindu religious practices like *murti-puja* (idol worship), *shradha* (worship ritual to propriate one's ancestors), *varna dharma* (religious ceremonies associated with different social categories) etc. have been properly explored. Puranas also contributed significantly toward the temple building activity. The exact date of the Puranas is not known, but it is likely to be in the early centuries of the Common Era. Amongst the Puranic scriptures, *Srimad Bhagavad* occupies a very special place in Hindu society. Few passages in the Puranic scriptures have been considered inappropriate. Some modern Hindu swamis have urged followers to ignore such writings and pay more attention to the real spiritual teachings.[15]

Panchatantra (five books)—a wise sage Vishnusharma wrote these scriptures around 200 CE. These scriptures contain stories of animals, through which human weaknesses and vices were portrayed very effectively. These books have now become popular for teaching children about morality.

Tantra—the Tantra scriptures are mostly dedicated to the *Shakta* philosophy of Hinduism, although there are also separate *Saiva* and *Vaishnav* scriptures of this tradition. There are sixty-four Tantra texts, which were written in the middle part of the first millennium and later.[16] These texts are devoted to many techniques, which have been formulated to invoke spirituality and divinity in man. Some of these Tantra techniques, like *Kriya yoga* and *Kundalini yoga,* have gained popularity in many different parts of the world, apart from India. The other aspect of the Tantra philosophy, however, in which the primordial energy is aroused by the practice of sexual techniques, partaking of meat and wine, and dubious methods of black magic, has been seriously questioned by many and has now become taboo mostly.

Commentaries on Hindu scriptures written later by Shankaracharya (700–740 CE), Ramanujacharya (1017–1137 CE), and Madhvacharya (1199–1278 CE) also must be mentioned for their great merit in relation to the ancient Hindu philosophy.[17]

There are many more supplements, commentaries, and manuscripts in other ancient languages, such as Pali, Tamil, and some regional languages. Most prominent among these are *Tirukural* and allied Tamil scriptures. Tirukural was written in the first century BCE and is regarded as the Holy Bible of Saivites. Tirukural, however, hailed the Vedas as the most superior spiritual guidelines.

If written word is any indicator of the level of civilization, the old Hindu scriptures certainly project a glorious and shining portrait of the culture of India during the ancient period. No wonder that ancient India became the chief hub of education. The first university in the world was established in Takshila in 700 BCE, where scholars from many other countries would come for higher studies. The University of Nalanda in the fourth century CE was one of the greatest achievements in the field of education in Hindu civilization. The ancient philosophy of India, the legacy of prehistoric oral tradition, also gave birth to the *Sramana* ideology of renunciation and meditation, which attracted scholars from many countries.[18] It is even probable that the Greek masters Plato (427–347 BCE) and Aristotle (385–322 BCE) had contact with Hindu teachings.[19]

Hindu scriptures have continued to grow till date; the important teachings of the most exalted seers have been regarded as the minor Upanishads as compared to the original major Upanishads, which were compiled before the Buddhist era (500BCE).

Hinduism does not have only one scripture as the sole authority; rather, there have been innumerable scriptures, each depicting its different ideas and viewpoints. This free flow of spiritual literature from a very early age provided abundant scope to change and modify itself, keeping up with time, circumstances, and individual aptitudes. Yet, the essential principles of the Vedas and Upanishads remained untouched. Different ethnic races and tribal groups that amalgamated toward what later became the Hindu religion were allowed to retain their individual identity to a very considerable extent. This freedom of thought and belief has remained the sheet anchor of Hindu theology over millennia, and has contributed immensely toward its evolution.

Some Important Glimpses into the Pre-historic

A group of scientists has identified two circular structures at Dholavira in Kutch district of Gujarat, which they say is the first identification of a structure used for observational astronomy during the Harappan Civilization. It is the first direct indication of intellectual capacity of people in the context of the civilization and their relation to astronomy."It is highly implausible that such an intellectually advanced civilization did not have any knowledge of positional astronomy. These (structures) would have been useful for calendrical (including time of the day, time of the night, seasons, years and possibly even longer periods) and navigational purposes apart from providing intellectual challenge to understanding the movement of the heavens," said the paper titled. (Hinduism Today, Kapaa, Hawaii: Himalayan Academy, Jan-Mar 2012)

6 Vedas: The Foundation of Hinduism

The most ancient scriptures of the Hindu religion, the Vedas, are recognized as the earliest documented literature of mankind. It is affirmed that the Vedas are the very first Hindu scriptures, but the flow of the written word would never stop in Hindu philosophy. The Vedas are regarded as *literature immortal*. The word Veda originates from the root *vid*, which means "to know." The Veda scriptures are considered to be the divine knowledge perceived by the ancient sages, *Rishis*. Regarded as the great truths and passed on by word of mouth from one generation to another, these scriptures attained supreme authority, which remains unchanged even today. Subtle transitions and modifications, however, soon became acceptable in Hindu tradition.

The Upanishads, which are the culmination of the Vedas, show abundant evidence of this attribute of ingenious change in the Hindu scriptures. The worship of the nature gods or deities, which occupied the prime place in the Aryan culture, was almost replaced by worship of one Supreme God, who was formless and transcendental. So, too, were the many lengthy and complicated rituals discarded and discouraged in the Upanishads.

Although there is evidence of significant religious activity in the prehistoric period of the Sindhu-Saraswati civilization, it would be correct to say that the real foundation of Hinduism was laid in the Vedic era. Most authorities consider that the first of these Vedas, the Rig Veda, was revealed around 1500 BCE. It is also considered the earliest scripture in human history. It is believed, however, that these psalms of wisdom were disclosed over many centuries, memorized, and orally conveyed from generation to generation within priestly families, then finally written down in the Vedic Sanskrit language, Brahmi, about a thousand years later. This would afterward develop into the classic Sanskrit in the earlier part of first millennium.[20]

As previously mentioned, one single individual did not create the Vedas. A series of learned sages, the *Rishis*, sat on the riverbanks, the mountaintops, and in the forests for extended periods of time. Thus, Hinduism was established by many an enlightened soul, spread across millennia. Rishis performed austerities, contemplated, and meditated, seeking solutions for the eternal problems of mankind. They would establish a spiritual union with the divine and be inspired with the revelations from their inner selves. These inspired thoughts and ideas were then passed on from father to son or from teacher to pupil, as *Srutis,* the revelations.

The word *sruti* is evolved from the root *shru,* which means, "to hear." It is said that the gods dictated the Vedas, and the sages first heard them internally and then passed them on. The authorship of these earliest scriptures is regarded as nonhuman (*apauarusya*) in origin.[21] Professor Max Muller has stated, *"One feels certain that behind all these lightning flashes of religious and philosophic thought there is a distant past, and a dark background of which we shall never know the beginning."* Recent evidence suggests that the Rig Veda may have been created in the form of spoken word *shruti* as early as 10,000 years ago, or even earlier. Hindus believe that only the spiritual seers of highest purity (*Rishis*) perceive these inspirational truths, *"almost as naturally as fruit is produced from a flower out of the mysterious center."*[22]

Ancient *Rishis* worshipped gods of nature in the Vedic era. Sun, or *Surya*, is the pivotal god. Hindu sages recognized the vital significance of solar energy in man's life. A most auspicious prayer, the *Gayatri Mantra,* also known as the *Savitri Mantra,* has been consecrated to *Savitra,* the sun god. *Savitra,* according to the scriptures, refers to the sun before the dawn, while *Surya* is the name to use when the sun is manifest. The word *mantra,* which has been adapted by Western society, is derived from *man* (mind) and *tra* (purity). Mantras are energy-based sounds. Saying any word with a deep sense of commitment produces an actual physical vibration. All mantras have meaning. Each syllable and word has a reason for being there. When produced correctly and with honest intent, the mantra comes alive. Repeating a mantra makes a groove in the mind of the person speaking it, until it is absorbed in the behavior and manner of everyday living. In the opinion of the learned Maharishi Mahesh Yogi, *"Vedic words are the words of the transcendental field, being the structuring dynamics of the transcendental field; they are not limited to space and time."*[23]

Special importance has also been given to god *Varuna,* the lord of order (*ruta/rita*). Hindu Rishis conceived the phenomenon of the cosmic order of the Divine as the *dharma,* or righteousness.[24] The celestial god *Indra,* the lord of thunderstorm and rain, also called the warrior god, has been acclaimed because of the many bounties associated with this god. The god of fire, *Agni,* also is given a very high position. All sacrifices are conducted through fire. Through the virtue of fire, the elements would disperse in all the cosmos and would come back to us in mystic refined way. In the Vedas there is mention of Lord Shiva as *Rudra,* the god of storm associated with destruction.

In ancient times, animal sacrifice was common. The highest type was the special ritual sacrifice of a horse (*asvamedha*), conducted by the king to express his power and authority.

Each Veda is divided into two parts: *Karma Kanda* and *Jnana Kanda*. Karma Kanda deals with the rituals and is again divided in two sections: *Samhita*, which contains the hymns or mantras in praise of the Divine; and *Brahmana*, which explains the meaning and the use of these hymns. *Jnana Kanda* deals with spiritual knowledge. It also has two divisions: *Aryankas*, which contains the spiritual knowledge learned in the solitude of a forest, and *Upanishads*, which contains the knowledge learned at the feet of a master, or *guru*.

Ved Vyasa compiled the Vedas—literally, the books of knowledge—into four parts:

Rig Veda: It contains the hymns of knowledge, the knowledge of the Divine, in the form of mantras and *ruchas*. The *ruchas* are the beautiful eulogies in praise of God. It has 1028 hymns set in more than 10,000 verses. Rig Veda is the *Jnana Veda*, the Veda of knowledge.

Yajur Veda: It contains more than two thousand verses, mainly focusing on the rituals. Sacrifice is one of the most important parts of this Veda. Yajur Veda is called the *Karma Veda*, the Veda of deeds or rituals. Performance of rituals sows the seeds of good deeds in life.

Sama Veda: It contains nearly two thousand verses, mostly from the Rig Veda, set to music. It is also called the Veda of *Upasana* worship. The worship ceremonies stabilize the ever-wandering mind toward divine thoughts and prayers. Classical Indian music originated from this Veda.

Athar Veda: It contains more than six thousand verses. It deals with science and many other secular subjects.

Each Veda has its own *mahavakya*, which narrates the grand truth of the Vedic philosophy:

Rig Veda: *Prajnanam Brahma*: "*Divine consciousness is the supreme reality.*"
Yajur Veda: *Aham Brahmasmi*: "*I am Brahman.*"
Sama Veda: *Tat Twam Asi*: "*That thou art.*"
Athar Veda: *Ayam Atma Brahman*: "*The atman, or soul, is Brahman.*"

The early Vedic scriptures were more occupied with mythological nature gods, such as the sun (*Suray*) or the moon

(*Chandra*). In later periods of the Vedic era (1000–700 BCE), there was a shift toward the *Brahmana* rituals and sacrifices that were devoted to the transcendental divine. The Upanishads (800–500 BCE) represent a subtle reaction to the glorification of the ritual philosophy, giving more attention to the mystical or transcendental thoughts, such as identity of the individual soul (*atman*) and the soul of the universe (*Brahman*).

Along with the main body of the Vedas, the Upavedas, or secondary Vedas, were created. These contain more secular sciences, such as the science of life (*Ayurveda*) and Vedic mathematics. Each Veda has its own Upaveda.

The Upaveda included in the Rig Veda—*ayurveda*, as it is called—deals with medicine and health. The Upaveda in the Yajurveda is *dhanurveda*, which is concerned with archery and the military. The Upaveda in the Samaveda is *gandharvaveda*, which deals with music. The Upaveda in the Atharveda is *sthapathyaveda*, which is concerned with astronomy, astrology, engineering, and mathematics.

The gandharva music of the Sama Veda may have been the beginning of this fine art by mankind. The classical notes of this period have remained an inspiration for all music lovers through the centuries. India became the first land to use the system of notations.[25]

Vedic mathematics is based on the harmony and perfect precision of the celestial movements. It has been observed historically that after the Muslim invasion, Hindu scholars were called to Arabia in the seventh to eighth century CE to demonstrate Vedic mathematics, which was later carried to the West and all over world. Aryabhatta (476–520 CE) was the first mathematician to try to explain the causes of an eclipse.

Astrology or *Jyotish Vidya* has occupied considerable attention in Hindu religion. Although there are no scientific evaluations about this study, some of the revelations are amazingly correct in detail.

In Hindu theology, the older scriptures and their teachings were never defied or contradicted. Albeit subtly modified, they were always revered. Never totally discarded, the old scriptures continued to remain in synergy with the new ones, as considered suitable. In this transition from the old to the new, violence remained absent and was discouraged in all forms. This gentle evolutionary change besides sowed the seeds of utmost respect for the elderly in the Hindu family culture-a trait that has become a unique feature in Hindu society.

7 The Spiritual Teachings of the Vedas

The Vedas contain a treasure trove of spiritual teachings in the form of *mantras* and *slokas*. The main philosophy of the Vedic teachings may be summarized as:

Shanti Karanam: the hymns of peace. These hymns are included in all the Vedas. Among the hymns of *Shanti Karanam*, the *Gayatri Mantra* undoubtedly occupies a place of prestige.

OM
Bhur bhuvah suvah
Tat Savitur varenyam
Bhargo devasya dhimahi
Dhiyo yo nah prachodayat
      —Rig Veda, 1.113.13

OM is the metaphor for the Divine Supreme. We meditate on the earth (*bhur*), the cosmic atmosphere (*bhuvah*), and heaven (*svar-suvah*). We meditate on the early morning sun (*savitra*) to grant us a good mind (*gayatri*). Hindu sages invoked all the gods and especially the rising, effulgent sunrise *savitra* for granting the noble mind, the sacred *gayatri*. They observed the symbolic but spiritual bond between the early rising sun and the (spiritual) augmenting of the human mind. They hailed the boundless supremacy of the sun (*suray*) in everyday life. They also recognized the prerogative of the early morning period on the development and creation of good mind (*sumati*).

Other hymns of peace—*Shanti Mantras*:
May our prosperity, prayers and wishes, elevated intellect and riches be auspicious to us. May our truthful speech based on noblest intensions bring us welfare. May those that are entrusted with the task of dispensing justice be men of wide fame and prove auspicious to us, and may the prayerful hymns of saintly persons give us peace.
      —Rig Veda, 7.35.3

Peace (*shanti*) and auspiciousness became watchwords in Hindu philosophy. Swami Vivekananda said, "*Every word has been spoken with a blessing behind and peace in front of it.*"[26]

After this period came the concept of the formless, transcendental, universal God.
May He, the Lord of the universe, bless our bipeds and quadrupeds.

—Yajur Veda 38.8

Hindu society started to become caring and benevolent to all creatures very early in ancient times.

O immortal Lord! Thou art my sustainer and shelter. May I, living under your protection, attain truth, good name, worldly prosperity, and spiritual advancement for my own as well as others' good. May this prayer come true.

—Taittray Upanishad, 10.32.35

Hindu sages created the mantras with the sole aim of imparting virtuous spiritual knowledge and enhancing peace and harmony among all creatures.

The Vedic sages created *Om*, to become the symbol of the Divine. Most mantras start with this sacred word *Om*, as in the following:

(O Almighty God) Om, in whom the Vedas have their origin and who pervades all the elements, my soul is Thy fuel. O Agni (lord of fire), blaze intensely with this, advance and bless us with worthy offspring, with good cattle and animals, with divine glory, plentiful food, and spiritual advancement.

—Yajur Veda, 3.1

The respectful attitude toward nature is unique in ancient Hindu thought. It differs markedly from that of the modern science, which until very recently always boasted of conquering and exploiting nature for the material benefit of mankind.

The prayer of Gayatri Mantra heralds the augmentation of the "spiritual" mind of divine virtue and peace, by drawing parallels between the awakening of the human mind and the rising sun. Transforming the human mind from conventional intellect towards "spiritual" higher awareness of good value and morality occupied the aggregate attention of Hindu Rishis; they prompted human beings to always walk on the path of goodness and integrity.

NOTE: All the above mantras have been taken from two sources:
Vedic Prayer (contact Kuldip Mangal, 11-MIU Road, Twickenham, Midda-TWZ5HA, UK).
Deepchander Bellani. Ved Prakash (Sindhi Language). India:
Akhil Bhartiya Sindhi Arya Sabha, 1979.

8 The Essence of the Vedic Philosophy

The Vedas touched every aspect of Hindu life. Sacrifice rituals formed an important part of Vedic life, so a Hindu became adept at performing many fire ceremonies (*havan yajna*). *Yajna* is essentially a ritual of self-purification. The ritual is accompanied by Sanskrit chants and prayers as *ghee* (clarified butter), and other offerings such as grains, flowers, and incense are offered into holy fire. Symbolically it represents surrender of self (ego) to God.

During the Vedic period, society was divided into four classes. The highest was the *Brahmin* class, who claimed to have been born from the mouth of God. *Brahmin* is considered one who follows the path of the Divine *Brahma. Brahmins* were well versed in the Vedas, so they were given the responsibility of performing the many rituals on different occasions. They also guided the lay people toward a worthy religious life. The *Kshatriya,* or warrior class, came next. They were in charge of defending and upholding the rule of law. After this came the *Vaishya,* who were the merchant and agriculture class. The fourth class was the *Shudras* the servant class, who would manually serve the upper three classes.

It is believed that originally this division was based on the merit and aptitude of individuals, as mentioned in the Rig Veda. The categorical recognition of the hereditary caste system in the official *Manu Shastra,* however, tilts credence toward the contrary. Even so, castes were not rigid and pernicious. There were even free marriages among persons from different groups, as well as interchanging from one caste to another. As time passed, however, the system took a rather vicious turn and caused much antagonism and hostility among the classes.

The role of *Brahmins* has occupied the Hindu mind vigorously throughout history. On one hand, they have most admirably carried on the mantle of preserving the vast heritage of Vedic scriptures in the face of many impediments and obstructions, but on the other hand, they maintained an unholy dominance and authority throughout millennia and caused the sharp divisions in the society.

In the Vedic society, a man's life was divided into four stages, or *ashrams:*

Up until age twenty-five, a man was in the **brahmachary ashrama.** He obtained a good education and training in all walks of life under the supervision of a skilled and able teacher. This teacher/student relationship (the *guru/shishya* relationship) is unique in Hinduism. During this period, a man abstained from any sexual activity. It is believed that by conscious spiritual *sadhana* (practice), the sexual energy would be sublimated into life-giving forces that lend vigor and strength to the body. During this period, man was especially coached to revere and obey his parents and the elders in his family. This stage laid the foundation for a good spiritual conduct in life afterward.

In the second stage, **grahastha ashrama,** the man married and raised his family. Hindus believe that getting married and raising children is a religious duty, and they virtually exhaust all their resources and efforts toward this divine task. Even as he is urged to take proper care of his wife and children, however, a man's duties toward his parents, brothers, sisters, community, and country always remain at the forefront. He would also enjoy all the legitimate pleasures of life and acquire property—but only by righteous means. A man and woman, as husband and wife together, take the responsibility of conducting this *ashrama.* The man is the head of the family in Hindu society. When the family atmosphere becomes polluted and unstable, it is his duty to perform spiritual meditations (*sadhana*), as well as other corporeal duties to correct the anomalies and misapprehensions. He must, however, fulfill his responsibility with love and subtle guidance. He must never hurt his wife, verbally or physically, whatever the provocation. Says Manu, *"Prosperity shuns the home, where the woman is dishonored."* It is the duty of the man to provide for the family and to procure a good house, which the woman makes into a home. He may provide not only for the necessary articles but also for fine things and jewelry. The woman, on her part, is always ready to welcome him when he returns from work and to provide a secure and joyful atmosphere to relieve him from his work stress. The woman also has the primary duty of caring for the children in the most appropriate manner, guiding and leading them to fulfill their assignments with sincerity and virtue. In the home, mother is likened to the deity *Shakti*. She wields spiritual power (*siddhi*), which she extends to her husband so that he is successful in all his manly endeavors, and withdraws the same automatically when she is hurt, depressed, or disappointed, compromising his success in the outside world. The man and woman are assigned their respective Vedic codes—*purusha dharma* and *stri dharma*, respectively. It is pertinent to note that the great lawmaker Manu laid special importance to this ashrama of human life. It is only during this period of his life that a man earns and sustains not only himself but also for his family and all members in the other three stages. The condemnation of mundane and temporal activities is not advocated. In fact, it is precisely these activities, performed in the rightful manner as spiritual duties that lead to the divine fulfillment. Also, it is important to realize that those who forsake their worldly duties prematurely, before taking care of their family and children, in search of spiritual advancement are, in fact, transgressing this Vedic law.

The third stage is the **vanaprastha ashrama.** *Vana* in Sanskrit means forest. When the man has fulfilled his family obligations, he takes retirement from his business or work. He bestows all family responsibilities on his son and then spends more time in spiritual practices and social service. He gets more involved with charitable work. The forest symbolically represents solitude and peaceful surroundings. An individual is encouraged to help and serve family and society by sharing his experiences and imparting moral teachings to youth and children.

The last stage is the **sanyasa ashrama.** Man renounces all material belongings. He lives a very austere life and spends almost all his time seeking spiritual salvation (*moksha*). A Hindu is instructed to walk the last phase of his stay in single file; he might look within, meditate, and search for the Divine. It is only in the solitude of aloneness (*sanya*) that an individual might experience *Brahman*, the immanent, transcendental God.

In every stage of life, a Hindu is prompted to follow virtuous spiritual path according to one's aptitude and position. *Pravrutti marga* (householder's path) advises individual to perform one's allotted duties in accordance with the discipline of dharma. Neglecting one's householder's duties and paying more attention instead to spiritual meditations or rituals may be regarded as contravention. *Nivrutti marga* (renunciant's path) on the other hand prescribes attainment of spiritual divine knowledge and performance of devotion or *bhakti*, without the householder's responsibilities. *Nivrutti marga* is meant only for the Sanyasins, who have relinquished the worldly life; for others the *Pravrutti marga* is prescribed.

In the words of Swami Vivekananda, "*Everyone who has tasted the fruits of this world must give up in the later part of life.*" This is the basic principle of Hindu philosophy and is quite opposite of the Western point of view. *Sanyasa ashram*, however, is not for everyone. According to the original Vedic thought, only those who have perfected themselves spiritually in the first three stages may enter the highest state of *sanyasa;* otherwise, it may become superfluous and meaningless. It was in the time of Jainism and Buddhism that monastic institutes of *sanyasins* were introduced, allowing persons with the highest spiritual aspiration to become the *sanyasin,* bypassing all the household duties. Afterward, Hinduism also accepted this new order of s*anyasins.* Even so the *sanyasa* became a valid option only for the most evolved souls.

There was thus a division of vocation in relation to the age of the person. According to the Vedic philosophy, all stages of life impart their own unique experiences, which are essential for soul growth. Interestingly, there has been some research in the modern medical science of psychiatry regarding the different stages of a person's life. Dr. Carl Jung stated in his book, *Modern Man in Search of a Soul,* that human life may be divided in three parts. Jung especially dwelled on the third part as the period of spiritual pursuit. The similarity of this concept with the Vedic philosophy cannot be merely a coincidence. When a man does not act according to his station of life, he often invites misery and shame on himself. The Hindu concept of *ashramas* is thus vindicated.

Another interesting point is that Hindu sages planned out human life based on a hundred years or more, with four divisions of twenty five years each. It seems rather strange that so early in the history of mankind, such longevity was experienced.

Along with the four stages of a man's life, Vedic teachings also discuss four goals *(purushartha)* in life: *kama, artha, dharma,* and *moksha.* Man must put his best efforts toward attaining these goals:

Kama refers to the satisfaction of sensual desires. This activity is seen in the entire animal world, but as human beings, this activity needs to be disciplined by a set of rules and regulations.

Artha refers to acquiring material possessions. This activity is of a higher nature and is seen only in human beings. Human beings need food, clothing, and shelter; at the same time a code of conduct was created to keep vigil on human beings. Athar Veda states, *"One may amass wealth with hundreds of hands, but distribute it with thousands of hands."* Charity is the watchword in Hindu philosophy. *"To live is to give, and give as long as you live."* The rhetorical condemnation of material possessions does not conform to Vedic teachings. Indulgence in sensual activities as well as having worldly possessions is considered legitimate, even necessary, as long as the spiritual laws of *dharma* are used for regulation. "*Riches in Vedic India were always despised if they were hoarded or unavailable for charitable purposes. Ungenerous men of great wealth were assigned a low rank in society.*"[27]

Dharma has been used to imply religion in Hindu code. The literary meaning of this word is duty and righteousness. *Dharma*, simply put, is a spiritual behavior of treating all with respect, love, and compassion. Self-defense and fighting for the just cause forms an important part of the righteous duty, but revenge is not sanctioned in Hindu religion.

Moksha refers to seeking salvation. Man, by performing his duties very well and conducting his life with principles of righteousness, would ascend on the ladder of virtues and finally attain freedom from repeated birth/death cycles.

Vedic society was built around these codes of conduct. Rig Veda states, "*Where there is a clash between a greater good and smaller one, the interest of the greater good prevails. In the interest of the family, one individual may be given up. In the interest of the village, one family may be disregarded. In the interest of the nation, one village's interest may be sacrificed.*" Giving (*dana*), rather than grabbing, became the Hindu ideal; the highest gift is considered the giving of spiritual knowledge.

To maintain a vigil on his performance, man is reminded of five debts: **deva rina, rishi rina, pitri rina, nri rina,** and **bhuta rina:**

Deva-rina: the debt toward God, the creator and protector. Nature gods, such as the sun (*Suraya*), moon (*Chandra*), wind (*Vaayu*), rain (*Indra*), and earth (*Dharti*), were worshipped, and special care was taken toward their protection.

Rishi-rina: the debt toward the sages—"*May he abide by their teachings.*"

Pitri-rina: the debt toward his parents—"*May he always respect and care for them.*" Vedic scriptures advise the householders to care for their parents and close relatives all through life. The elderly, especially, must be comforted, honored at auspicious times, and never left alone for extended periods.

Nri-rina: the debt toward all mankind—"*May he serve all humanity.*"

Bhuta-rina: the debt toward the subhuman creatures, the animals— "*May he never be cruel to animals.*"

One of the most impressive aphorisms of Hindu society in the Vedic period was "*No one among them shall, under any circumstances, be a slave; but that, enjoying freedom themselves, they shall respect the equal right to it that all men possess.*"[28] (Original source: Arrian). This dictum became the foundation of charity and philanthropy in the Hindu society.

Hindus had several codes and instructions outlined for them to adhere to the righteous path of truth, duty, and morality. Life was divided in four phases, with each phase comprising of its own set of duties. Class division was planned according to one's capacity and aptitude. Although there are several references that this class division was not meant to be hereditary in character, it did take the ugly turn, being betrayed by human weakness and vulnerability. Despite several attempts made in different periods of history to amend these faults, the caste system prevailed for millennia, and has not yet been fully eradicated. The present Indian constitution encompasses adequate provisions in order to safeguard the weaker sections; it even offers benefits to compensate for the past injustices. Transformation of human mind indeed takes a protracted time!

9 Vedas through the Passage of Time

Even today, more than five thousand years after the origin of the Vedas, a Hindu simply cannot visualize a good life without the observance of the Vedic principles. When a child is born, when he is later baptized with the thread ceremony, when he is married, and finally, when he dies, there always will be Vedic ceremonies. Whether it is a new business, sickness in the family, or a religious festival, Hindus always look toward their religious priests to guide them, bless them, and give them eternal support.

In the beginning, rituals were a very important part of Hindu worship. The main function of these rituals was to usher in a solemn and sacred atmosphere and prepare the devotee to receive the hymns of knowledge in the most appropriate manner. The real teaching was, of course, conveyed in the hymns of knowledge. Clarified butter (known as *ghee*), rice, and many other things were offered as sacrifice in the fire of the *Havan Yajna,* an ancient Hindu ritual of Aryan origin. Later in the Upanishad scriptures, the sages downplayed the importance of the rituals. It was felt that followers were paying too much attention to them, while ignoring the real teachings of the knowledge of the Divine.

Rituals are the symbolic deeds for sacrifice (*yajna*), which is considered to be the basis of a good life. Rituals would prepare a person to perform various duties properly; they were not meant to be the end in itself.

In the Bhagavad Gita, the actions performed by an individual are considered to be the ritual sacrifice, thus introducing the concept of *karma,* which has now become a household word in the West, too. Karma is identified as our good or bad deeds, and we may reap the effects of our actions during this life, as well as in future lives. The Gita's emphasis shifted toward the actual practice of what was preached: "*If the devotee does not practice what he learns, it would be hypocrisy.*" In more recent times, Swami Vivekananda and Mahatma Gandhi emphasized service as the *yajna* ritual.

Throughout millennia, there have been many vital and significant changes in the Hindu philosophy. The caste system of the Vedic period still prevails, but it has been modified considerably. The evil practice of "untouchability" has been abolished in the constitution. The Rig Veda states, *"In Mankind, nobody is higher or lower, nor is anybody of middle status"* (5.59–60). This gives ample evidence that the caste system was not hereditary in character in the early Vedic period. Later, it is mentioned in the Mahabharat: *"Neither birth nor sacraments nor study nor ancestry can decide whether a person is twice-born (i.e. a Brahmin); character and conduct only can decide."*[29]

In Hindu society, a woman's position and status also have undergone many changes. In the early Vedic period, women were barred from reading the Holy Scriptures. Views and attitudes, however, changed soon. Along with male gods, there appeared many female goddesses, some of them even more powerful and more revered than their male counterparts. The male dominance of the Vedic era soon met its first challenge. In the Upanishads we encounter two very fierce female scholars, Maitreyi and Gargi, who pose most arduous and demanding questions to the learned sages.

In the Hindu scripture Manu Shastra, it is recommended that a woman always remain under the protection of a man. As a child, she may be under the supervision of her father; after marriage, her husband may protect her; and if she becomes widow, she must live with her son. This has been resisted by some as a sign of weakness and inferiority of women, but such a practice may also provide much-needed security for weak and vulnerable females--this was especially so in the ancient times, when hard manual work was required for daily existence. It may be pointed out that in the same scripture, women are also idolized: *"Mother excels even a thousand fathers in glory."*[30]

The combined and extended family system in Hindu society provided abundant scope of social participation to women at all levels. Even today, Hindu society generally abhors the idea of women living on their own. Yet the tragic reality is that the injustices and humiliations of both the lower caste and the female sex did continue for thousands of years—human weakness prevailed!

The changes in the Hindu society, as perhaps in all other societies, have not come easily. There has been stiff resistance at many junctures, although there have been no quarrels and blood-shed in such matters in the Hindu society. Along the long passage, some reformist movements formed new, separate religions and sects, but the new ideas did not always prevail for long. The followers of the new faith often reverted to the rituals and customs of their own! The evolution of the human mind cannot be hastened. It moves at its own pace.

It is important to realize that there is always a human agency associated with the functioning of any religion. Many present-day leaders in the Hindu religion have underscored the need for change and modification, when the situation demands. For instance:

Sri Ramakrishna Paramhans, an apostle of Hinduism and a modern messiah, has clearly stated that in Vedas, the sand is often mixed in with dough. We should chew with care, discarding the sand.

Paramahansa Yogananda, founder of the worldwide organization Self-Realization Fellowship, has likewise asserted that the teachings of all the sages need to be modified according to time and situation, keeping the basic truth of the Vedas intact.

Swami Sachchidanand, a prominent living saint from Gujarat, India, has written in unambiguous terms that the Vedas may be God-inspired, but human beings revealed them. There will, therefore, always be an element of human error, which may be rectified as necessary.

American philosopher J. B. Pratt made the following relevant remarks: *"The reason for the immortality of the Vedic religion of Hinduism is that while retaining its spiritual identity, it has been changing its outward form in accordance with the demands of the time; and particularly it is the only religion which has been able to meet the challenges of science, which governs the thought and life of the Modern age."*

The average Hindu youth today perhaps does not have a proper concept of the Vedas. Some might even think that the Vedas are outdated and irrelevant. This is not true. In fact, the Vedas have stood the test of time most admirably. There are, at present, numerous institutes and places of worship all over the world that teach the principles and practices of the ancient Vedic philosophy of India. There is a full fledged Vedic township and university, which was started by the renowned Maharishi Mahesh Yogi in the state of Iowa in the United States, and there is the International Vedic Hindu University in Orlando, Florida. Catholic theologian Raimundo Panikkar wrote a scholarly book, *The Vedic Experience*, while living in Banares, India, from 1964 to 1976.[31] There is a phenomenally fast-growing interest in Hindu philosophies of meditation, yoga, non-violence, Ayurveda, and many other Vedic subjects likea stronomy, cosmology, health-science, philosophy, and logic etc.

Vedas have indeed come to stay, not only in Hindu society but also in the rest of the world, as part of the common spiritual heritage of mankind.

Hinduism is also called the Vedic religion, as Vedas are the very foundation of this faith. Even today, all Hindus commonly practice Vedic rites, including the ones settled outside of India. Nonetheless, changes to the same have been made time and again. The original rites have been considerably modified; the lengthy, repetitive rites have often been replaced with shortened, meaningful ones. Yet, prolonged "Havan" ceremonies lasting over several hours, with hundreds of devotees participating and scores of priests chanting together are not a rare sight! The old and the new run hand in hand. An individual may opt for any as per his/her choice. Many respected saints and sages have drawn attention to the shortcomings of some Vedic customs, but none have ever downplayed the importance of the Vedas. Over time, suggestions have been incorporated to supplant the Vedic rites with "actual deeds-karma" or "service actions", but the Vedic ceremonies and sacraments continue to survive over the millennia in one form or another.

10 Upanishads: Culmination of the Vedas

The Upanishads or Vedanta (the end of the Vedas) are the scriptures that contain the essence of the Vedic philosophy. "Upanishad" literally means "learning at the feet of"; thus pointing to "at the feet of a Master." Thus was born the ancient guru system in Hindu society. In each of the Vedas, there are two main divisions: the *Karma Kanda* deals with the rituals, and the *Jnana Kanda,* deals with knowledge or wisdom. The Upanishads are part of the *Jnana Kanda.* The guru would lead his pupil (*shishya*), step by step, to the stage whereby the pupil recognized the Self, or the Divine in himself. This is indeed the avowed final destination of a Hindu life.

Discovering the Divine, or Self, within also implies elevating oneself to the highest spiritual status. This is, in reality, the sacred stage of all virtuous conduct. The Upanishads are therefore considered a road map, complete with a "guru guide," to reach the highest peak of human development.

The Upanishads truly heralded free thought in Hindu society. In the Upanishads, we also see the identification of the sage (the *Rishi*) associated with each teaching program, a factor that was conspicuous by its absence in the Vedas. The major Upanishads, or the Primary Upanishads, were formed along with the Vedas. These were compiled before the Buddhist era, around the seventh century BCE or earlier. The learned gurus of the Upanishads brought the important teachings to the forefront and downplayed the teachings that were less relevant to mankind. The teachings were properly explained with correct interpretations.

The earlier Upanishads (*Brhadarayaka* and *Chandogya*) relied strongly on the rituals used to interpret the spiritual knowledge. The later Upanishads became more and more liberated from the rituals, however, moving toward internal processes of meditation and personal religious experiences. It is more likely that some factions at this stage totally defied the orthodox Vedic supremacy and formed a separate group that advocated the pre-historic ancient philosophy of renunciation and meditation, naming it as the *Sramana* ideology, which ultimately gave birth to Jainism and Buddhism.[32] The later Upanishads became more and more liberated from the rituals, however, moving toward internal processes of meditation and personal religious experiences. External rituals were subordinated to internal spiritual practices, called *sadhanas*. The rituals, however, did continue their influence and dominance in many different ways in the Hindu society. Even as the new religions and sects opposed and denounced the old rituals, they soon formed their own new rituals. Both the rituals and meditation have grown in Hindu system side by side ever since. An individual may prefer one over the other according to one's own aptitude and propensity. There is no serious antagonism in Hindu theology; rather there is complete freedom to pursue one's own path.

Hindu thought continued to march with the passage of time. Newer Upanishads came into being. In the post-Buddhist and post-Shankaracharya eras, a number of minor Upanishads were created to impart the spiritual teachings to posterity. Indeed, even the writings of modern holy men and women might be regarded as divine revelation, thus maintaining an evolutionary continuity of the Hindu tradition.[33]

More than two hundred Upanishads are in writing. Among the 108 Upanishads available, the most important ones are *Mundaka, Isha, Kena, Katha, Aitareya, Taittiriya, Chhandogya, Prashna, Shvetashvatara,* and *Brihadaranyaka.*

The Vedas taught worship of the gods of nature, such as the sun, sky, wind, and fire. The Upanishads emphasized that behind the façade of these many gods, there is but one Supreme God. In fact, the concept of one universal God was also originally expressed in the Rig Veda itself:

Ekam sad vipra bahudha vadanti.
(One alone exists; sages call it by various names.)

In the Upanishads, this ancient philosophical thought came to the forefront, overshadowing the idea of multiple gods, who were considered simply as the manifestation of the transcendental Supreme Divine. Modern world has adopted this concept of God more vigorously, especially in the face of the many religions and sects around the world. It is interesting to note that the Supreme Court of the United States recommended the use of the term "Supreme Being" in place of "God" in the Constitution of the United States, after hearing the plea in which the above quotation of the Rig Veda was presented.[34]

Some of the most important hymns of the spiritual knowledge are reproduced:

From the Chandogya Upanishad,

"Speech, eyes, ears, limbs, life are in union with spirit."

Thus, we see how the sages created the union between body and soul. Soul and body work together. Condemnation of the body and senses is not the right attitude. Putting the body to proper and good use is the right way.

From the Isha Upanishad,

Everything belongs to the Supreme Self. Self is the supreme. It is everywhere and all powerful. It gives us the breath-to-breath to live. We may claim nothing as our own. A wise man sees unity in all. Spiritual knowledge comes from austerity, self-control, and meditation.

The Vedic gods of nature are not disowned, but they are certainly subordinated. The subtle, formless, transcendental, spiritual God was conceived already in the Vedas, but now, in the Upanishads, this concept is highlighted and forcefully presented. God is everywhere, in all beings and so, too, within one's own self. The concept of transcendental formless God also points to the universal aspect of the Divine; same God is present everywhere and in everyone. This realization of oneness with all beings at once sows the seeds of love and adoration with each other.

In the Mundaka Upanishad, we learn that: -knowledge is of two types: lower knowledge (*Apara Vidya*), which deals with the secular knowledge of grammar, sciences, rituals, astrology, etc.; and higher knowledge (*Para Vidya*), which deals with divine or spiritual knowledge. Indeed, the Para Vidya is more concerned with the inner spiritual transformation of man than with only the book knowledge, which is also considered to be the *apara*, or the lower knowledge.

"As the flowing rivers disappear into the ocean, leaving their names and forms, so the wise man, freed from name and form, attains the highest of the high—the eternal Parampurusha." [35]

Swami Paramannanda, one of the pioneer gurus of Hindu philosophy in the West, writes:

"In the Vedas, we find a clear distinction between what man calls his own self, the Jivatman, and the Divine Over-self, the Paramatman. The search for God is man's eternal quest. Every person must do this for himself. The method of this individual search can be traced to the Upanishad teaching. It is not so much the learning of the Divine, which is important; it's living like the Divine that is essential in this pursuit."

The Upanishads heralded the true learning of the religion. The practice of Guru-Shishya (Teacher-Student) originated in Hindu

theology and has continued over millennia. Free discussion and question-answer tradition was set in motion; students were encouraged to confront their teachers with the most arduous and grueling questions, till all their doubts were answered with agreeable explanations and interpretations. This system truly laid the foundation for rational teaching.

11 Spirituality in Everyday Hindu Life

In the Upanishads lies the key to unlock the spiritual wisdom of ancient Hinduism. The *Brahman* represents the essence of all cosmos, and the soul or *atman* projects the individual being. This teaching is punctuated with the refrain *tat tvam asi*, or "You are That." In this equation, "you" means *atman*, and "That" means *Brahman*. The most intimate connection between the individual and the Divine has been pointed out.

In Prashna Upanishad: "*May our ears hear the good. May our eyes see the good. May we serve Him with whole strength.*"

The body and the senses are tools. Service is the purpose of life. We may not be able to fulfill our purpose if the tools are not in good shape.

Taittireeya Upanishad is also well known for the teacher/pupil relationship. The following is the convocation address to the student at the time of graduation:

"*Do your duty. Speak the truth. Learn and teach. Control senses. Be hospitable. Be humane. Serve the family. Procreate. Educate your children. Austerity is necessary. Do not neglect your spiritual, nor your worldly welfare. Always learn and teach. Forget neither God, nor ancestor. Treat your mother as God. Treat your father as God. Treat your guest as God. Treat your teacher as God. Look for men greater than yourself, and welcome them. Give with faith. Give in proportion to your means. Give with courtesy. Give to the deserving.*"

After five millennia, this address has not been bettered. Respect of elders, parents, guests, and teachers is noteworthy. They have been elevated to the status of God. So great has been the cultural impact of these teachings that in many homes even today, a person will not sit down in the presence of his or her parents or gurus until asked by them to do so. Noteworthy is the teaching, *Do not neglect your spiritual, nor your worldly welfare.*

Another spiritual gem of everyday life:

"*Let there be no neglect of Truth. Let there be no neglect of dharma. Let there be no neglect of welfare. Let there be no neglect of prosperity. Let there be no neglect of study and teaching. Let there be no neglect of the duties toward the Gods and the ancestors.*"

—Taittiriya Upanishad

Also in the Taittireeya Upanishad, this is written about food: *"From food are born all creatures. They live upon food and in the end they become dissolved in food. Food is all things. Food is the medicine."*

Food is highly respected in Hindu society. No one would put his foot over the food grains; it would be considered most disrespectful.

About breath: *"Gods, men, beasts, live by breath (prana)."*
As long as man lives, he breathes. Hindus devised very special techniques for correct breathing. These techniques have been referred to in the *Yoga Sutra* as *pranayama*.

About knowledge: *"Gods worship knowledge as the highest expression of spirit."*

Knowledge (spiritual knowledge-*Jnana*) is accorded the highest importance. One can gauge the advancement of civilization by this one parameter.

About hospitality: *"Never turn anyone from your door; gather enough food, and say to the stranger Sir, the dinner is served."*

Even today, Indian hospitality is famous, despite the poverty and hardship of the present times.

From the Brihadaranyaka Upanishad:

"Lead me from the unreal to the real
Lead me from darkness to light
Lead me from death to immortality."

This famous stanza of the Upanishads once again emphasizes the value of knowledge.

Swami Muktananda, a leading spiritual master of the twentieth century, who established many well-known centers in India as well as the United States, always emphasized that as human beings; we may attain the spirituality only through the body and senses. The body and senses thus need to be cared for and preserved. We need to use these in the right way to achieve union with God. If man becomes too old or too sick, his body and senses become dysfunctional, and he may no longer be able to contemplate, pray, and meditate.

These teachings of the ancient scriptures created deep impression on Hindu society. There are several stories and parables in ancient Hindu scriptures, which propagate various spiritual virtues. One such story narrates of a king, who had to cut and give away his entire body to protect a pigeon from a hawk, which was following it to secure its food. The king did so to keep his word of honor that he had given to the pigeon. Also this narration emphasizes the virtue of protecting the weak and vulnerable from the strong and finally the intervention of God to safeguard the virtuous as in this parable the gods descended to save the king in the end

Throughout the Hindu scriptures, "virtue of truth" has been hailed uppermost. In the annals of English judges and administration, during the British colonial power, one judge wrote, "*I have had before me hundreds of cases in which a man's property, liberty, or life depended on his telling a lie and he has refused to tell it.*"

The Vedas and the Upanishads strongly emphasized on virtuous behavior. These verses serve as a constant reminder to mankind to live a life of truth and morality, to perform his/her duties candidly, and to neglect neither spiritual virtues nor the worldly responsibilities.

NOTE: All quotes of the Slokas are from: Max F. Muller. *The Upanishads.* New York: Dover Publications, 1984.

Vedic Knowledge for the Modern Youth

(Contributed by Stephen Knapp (Sri Nandanandana dasa)
Author of over 20 books on Vedic culture, www.stephen-
knapp.com)

Hindu youngsters of today have adopted the American or western approach to accepting their parent's tradition, which is called "What's in it for me?" In other words, if they do not understand something, or if they cannot relate to it, or if it makes no sense or seems to have little relevancy to their lives, they will not take it. So these days they have to be able to see the purpose of it. They need to understand the meaning and usefulness behind the tradition. And there is nothing wrong with that. In fact, that is the basis for being properly educated in the culture.

The Hindu youth should be aware, however, of the possibilities that can be attained or learned from the ancient Vedic tradition as it is applied to the modern age. In essence, the youth of today needs to know that the understanding and practice of the Vedic tradition is going to improve and enhance their life and the meaning of it like no other form of education. They should know that it is going to help them reach their higher potential in today's world, both materially and spiritually. It is going to give them the fulfillment that everyone is looking for, which is to be at peace, balanced and whole within oneself. And those answers and insights need to be provided in some way or other, in more clear and rational manner. In this way, when a person combines the means of today's education and society with the understanding of the timeless Vedic tradition, the great Indian heritage, it is the means by which they can reach their fullest and highest possible development in this world.

12 The Secret of the Hereafter

In the Katha Upanishad, there is an important piece of dialogue between the seeker of knowledge, Nachiketa, and Yama, the lord of death.

Nachiketa was the young son of Vajasarva. He was barely twelve years old when, as a witness to a sacrificial ceremony of his father, a disturbing thought entered his mind. He confronted his father and challenged him about the futility of sacrifice of old, unproductive, and useless cows. Nachiketa reminded his father to sacrifice something that is more important instead. On being repeatedly questioned by his son, Vajasarva announced in disgust, *"I am sacrificing you, Nachiketa, to the lord of death, Yama!"*

Nachiketa arrived at the home of Yama, the lord of death, and waited for three days, without eating any food or even drinking water. When Yama returned, he was told about this, and he was immediately struck by the supreme effort of the young boy. He then offered three boons to Nachiketa as reward for this austerity.

As his first boon, Nachiketa requested, *"May my father be relived of all anxiety and anger in regard of losing me. May he sleep in peace."* The boon was immediately granted.

As his second boon, Nachiketa requested, *"May I know all the rituals of the fire sacrifice, which would ultimately lead an individual to be released from fear of death, and heaven."* This boon, too, was granted without any hesitation.

Nachiketa then asked as the final boon, *"What happens to man after the death? Some say he exists after the death; others say he does not exist. I wish to know from you, Yama, the lord of death, this vital secret of the hereafter!"*

Yama, on hearing this, offered Nachiketa many other temptations as alternatives to this inquiry. This he did to test the young Nachiketa about his resolve in seeking the spiritual knowledge of this nature. Finally satisfied with Nachiketa's sincerity, Yama imparted the most intricate instruction to young Nachiketa thus:

"To man come both the good (shreya) and the pleasant (priya) things in life. The wise, who discriminate, choose the good, but the foolish, who do not discriminate, choose the pleasant for the sensual satisfactions. The path of the good leads to God, to the imperishable spiritual kingdom; the path of the pleasant leads to the

perishable domain of physical birth and death cycle."

Written thousands of years ago by Hindu seers, the *"Upanishad of the Hereafter"* has become a subject of intense philosophical discussions across the world.

"Fools dwelling in ignorance, yet imagining themselves wise and learned, go round in crooked ways like the blind leading the blind." The ignorant do not think of the hereafter. They are mentally blind to what happens in the future.

Hindu seers paved the way of permanent joy in the virtue of God, rather than in the transitory pleasures of the senses. Worldly pleasures were subordinated to internal joy. Thus was sown the seed of renunciation of the material possessions in Hindu spiritual life. *"He who does not possess discrimination, whose mind is uncontrolled and impure, he does not reach that goal, but falls again and again into samsara, the realm of birth and death cycle."*

In this Upanishad is laid the foundation of the Hindu philosophy of reincarnation, according to karma. The final destination of salvation (*moksha*) would come when the individual completely surrenders the ego and unites with the Divine. Hindu sages envisaged human life as the final step on the ladder of evolution, after which the being would merge with the Supreme Divine (after many birth cycles) by performing the highest practices of sacrifices, austerities, and meditations. Such is the essential Hindu notion of birth cycle, *samsara*. A being has to undergo the process of life repeatedly, for eons of births, until all spiritual teachings are perfected.

Life after death (reincarnation) has been one of the most important philosophical concepts in Hinduism. This phenomenon has kept the minds of Sages occupied for a very long time. Human life is regarded as the most precious, not just because of the development of mind and intellect, but also because human beings have the capability to develop higher levels of superior consciousness of divine merits of virtue and morality. Ordinary intellect often strives for material benefits known to bring pleasure. Instead, the sages prompted mankind to focus on living a life of spiritual value and virtue. The final destination of salvation (moksha) is achieved only when the individual completely surrenders the ego and unites with the Divine. Hindu sages envisaged human life as the final step on the ladder of evolution, after which the being would merge with the Supreme Divine (after many birth cycles) by performing the highest practices of sacrifices, austerities, and meditations. Such is the essential Hindu notion of birth cycle, samsara.

NOTE: Quotes in this chapter are adapted from Swami Parmanand *The Upanishads.* Cohasset, Mass.: Vedanta Center Publishers, 1981.

The Current Major Sources of Hindu Review

A mega project of Sanskrit Dictionary is under way: It has been described as one of the world's biggest lexicography work, begun in 1948 and expected to be completed in another 50 years from now. The Sanskrit dictionary project undertaken by the Deccan College of Pune has already seen three generations of lexicographers at work and many more to go. The Sanskrit dictionary project is unique; with ten million words from the Rig Veda to texts written until 1800 CE studied and their etymological meanings provided.

Work on Catalogue of Sanskrit manuscripts called Catalogus Catalogorum (CC) is underway by the University of Madras. Theodore Aufrecht first started the project and compiled the first catalogue (1891-1903). An ambitious target of 40 volumes is in progress to develop a complete online database of the ancient manuscripts.

Indira Gandhi National Centre for Arts (IGNCA) and the French Institute of Pondicherry associated with the Aurbindo Ashram are in the process of microfilming and digitalizing all rare Hindu manuscripts.

An 11-volume "Encyclopedia of Hinduism" was recently launched at Hardwar, India. The ambitious project was originally conceptualized by Swami Chidanand Saraswati over two decades ago and some 10,000 people are believed to have pitched in, directly or indirectly, towards completion of this magnum.

Kailash Ashram at Rishikesh is regarded by some as the last word in the Vedanta studies. Great Saints, like Swami Vivekananda, Swami Abhedananda, Swami Ramatirtha and Swami Shivananda have studied in Kailas Ashram. Today Kailash Ashram is being directed by H.H. Swami Vidyananda Giri Ji Maharaj, who is the 10th Pecthacharya in the linage of Scholars. At present His Holiness is 84 years old. He is considered to be one of the greatest leading scholars in the field of Shankara Advaita Vedanta in India Today.

13 The Code of Conduct

This chapter is devoted to two of the minor Upanishads, which form the very root of Hindu philosophy. In Hindu scriptures, the teachings may not be prescribed as commands, nor are there punitive threats extended to those who would defy. Even so there are many virtuous teachings in all these scriptures. Without the spiritual teachings, what other role does a religion have to play? The core of these teachings is presented as "A code of conduct" in the form of *yamas* and *niyamas* in the Shandilya and Varuha Upanishads. The yamas are the don'ts, which harness and control the impulsive, lower sensual nature, with its governing impulses of fear, anger, jealousy, selfishness, greed, and lust. The niyamas are the do's—the religious observances that cultivate and bring forth the refined soul qualities, lifting awareness into higher realms of compassion, selflessness, wisdom, and bliss.

The *yamas* are those activities, which we perform from our lower animal nature, and which may cause hurt and harm to others. Generally these activities are also not sanctioned by the secular laws of our society, and may invite punishment by the court. The *niyamas* are the higher actions, also named as "spiritual" or "virtuous" deeds. There is generally no law in the secular court, to force a person to perform these actions, and no punishment is meted to anyone if the same is not performed. Even so there is widespread acceptance and appreciation of such actions in society anywhere. This vindicated the superiority and ascendancy of the religious teachings over the secular code.

The Yamas:

1. *Ahimsa* (nonviolence): Practice non-injury in thought, word, and speech; and live peacefully with all.
2. *Satya* (truth): Always be truthful. Satya has been placed as second to the yama of ahimsa or non-violence. If telling the truth would be harmful to another being, the truth may be withheld or modified. The truth also needs to be spoken in gentle and soft tones.
3. *Asteya* (nonstealing): Uphold the virtue of non-stealing and non-coveting another's property.
4. *Brahmacharya* (practice divine conduct): Control lust by remaining celibate when single and faithful in marriage.
5. *Aparigrah* (control greed): One may acquire reasonable and good

things in life, but control of desires is essential so that one may not hanker needlessly after worldly possessions beyond limits.

6. Exercise patience and restraint: Be agreeable. Don't argue, dominate conversations, or interrupt others.
7. Foster steadfastness, overcoming non-perseverance: Achieve your goals with a prayer, plan, persistence, and push.
8. Practice compassion: Conquer callous, cruel, and insensitive feelings toward all beings. Be kind to people, animals, plants, and the Earth.
9. Maintain honesty: Renounce deception and wrongdoing. Act honorably. Obey the laws of your nation and locale. Pay your taxes.
10. Neither eat too much nor consume meat, fish, shellfish, fowl, or eggs. Enjoy fresh wholesome vegetarian foods that vitalize the body. Follow a simple diet, avoiding rich or fancy fare.

Niyamas:
1. *Shaucha* (purity): Uphold the ethics of purity, avoiding impurity in mind, body, and speech. Maintain a clean, healthy body.
2. *Santosh* (contentment): Nurture contentment, seeking joy and serenity in life. Live in constant gratitude for your health, your friends, and your belongings.
3. *Tapa* (sacrifice): Be prepared to make sacrifices, and learn to be calm and patient under most difficult circumstances.
4. *Svadhya* (study of the scriptures): Learn the Holy Scriptures regularly.
5. *Ishwarapranidhan* and *puja* (devotional worship): Cultivate devotion through daily worship and meditation.
6. *Prayashchitta* (atonement): Atone for misdeeds through penance,
7. *Dashamamsha* (offering to God's cause): Be generous to a fault, giving liberally without thought of reward.
8. *Sadhana* (meditation): Cultivate an unshakable faith. Believe firmly in God, gods, guru, and your path to enlightenment.
9. Develop a spiritual will and intellect with your *sat guru's* guidance.
10. *Vrata* (sacred vow): Embrace religious vows, rules, and observances. Honor vows as spiritual contracts with your soul.
11. *Japa* (chant your holy mantra daily): Recite the sacred sound, word, or phrase given by your guru.

These *yamas* and *niyamas* constitute Hinduism's fundamental ethical codes. Good character and conduct is the foundation of spiritual life in Hinduism.

Minor Upanishads are scriptures that have been compiled after the Buddhist era. In effect, these scriptures and other teachings of the learned saints and sages have continually been added to the previous scriptures, maintaining a successful flow of spiritual traditions. These and other such teachings are never antagonistic to their predecessors; they have merely added some clarifications, supplemented few modifications, and made suitable subtle changes, as necessary. One example from above list of "yamas" will explain: "Always be truthful. Satya (truth) has been placed as second to the yama of ahimsa (non-violence). If telling the truth would be harmful to another being, the truth may be withheld or modified. The truth also needs to be spoken in gentle and soft tones."

NOTE: This chapter is adapted from: *Hinduism Today.* Kapaa, Hawaii: Himalayan Academy, April-June 2004

Other important sources of research on ancient Hindu scriptures include:

- Mysore Oriental Research Institute
- Puliyannur Tantric collections, Calicut University
- Rashtriya Sanskrit Vidyapeetha, Tirupati
- Academy of Sanskrit Research, Melkote, Karnataka
- Oriental Research Institute, Trivandrum, Kerala
- Sri Chandrasekharendra Saraswati Visva Maha Vidyalaya, Kanchipuram
- Sri Venkateswara Univ. Oriental Research Institute, Tirupati
- Dakshinannaya Sharada Pitham, Sringeri, Karnatak
- Nedumpilli Mana I - Irinjalakkuda, Kerala
- Joglekar, Koglekar and Samba Dihshita collections, Gokarna

The World Association of Vedic Studies (WAVES) holds International Conference every year in USA and other countries. In 2010, the theme of the conference was: Vedic Knowledge for Civilizational Harmony. Vedic heritage is vast, diverse and complex. These conferences are attended by Vedic scholars of the highest caliber.

Many important universities in USA and other countries are at present involved in Research and Advanced Studies of Hinduism in their respective "Religion" departments.

14 Consciousness: Cosmic Intelligence of the Divine

In Hindu scriptures, terms like "consciousness," "divine wisdom," "*Brahman,*" and many others are liberally used. These words convey nearly the same meaning in common use, but they have remained somewhat abstract for majority of the people. As Pure Consciousness, God is the manifest primal substance, as infinite intelligence and power. Hindu sages realized God or the Divine as a phenomenon either without any form (*nirguna*) or as manifesting in various forms (*saguna*). They realized that there is but one Divine for all beings, as well as for the nonbeings. It is immanent, transcendental, and universal and is present in all places in the entire cosmos. The sum total of all energy and consciousness is perceived as God. Hindus believe different names of gods are merely icons in the infinite divine spectrum.

According to Hindu philosophy, "consciousness" is primarily inactive (*purusha*). This comes in contact with the active component called the *prakruti*--the primordial materiality of nature. Human beings are born with three basic characters of nature called the *gunas*:

Sattvic, which represents purity

Rajasic, which represents activity

Tamsic, which represents dullness or inertia

These three are the basic characteristics or *gunas* of all beings and determine the nature of actions performed during the lifetime. According to Hindu theology, human beings alone have the capacity to alter these gunas or the basic attitudes by using the free will. The transformation of the gunas is indeed the main task of all human life. According to Hindu philosophy, this task may not be accomplished in one lifetime; rather, it may evolve through eons of birth cycles. The consciousness, or the divine power, although inactive by itself, is the life force behind all activity. It has been compared to the energy of electricity, which is the moving force behind all tools and gadgets. The transformation of the inner being, or *antahkaran*, has been considered as the most prized pursuit of human life. From the lowest quality of the *tamas,* the dull and evil attitude, toward the *rajasic,* the active and productive trait, and further to the *sattvic* nature of purity and benevolence are the gradual evolutionary steps for the soul of the individual, until finally it attains the highest perfection, the super-consciousness of the Divine, and merges itself into the Divine, losing its separate individuality. This is the stage of salvation, or *moksha,* of the soul from the recurring birth and death cycles, known as *samsara.*

This internal transformation is attained by meditation and spiritual practices *sadhana.* Spiritually exalted persons gradually identify themselves more with the soul, *atman,* than with the body. Intense and sustained mental concentration on higher spiritual thoughts liberates them from any physical afflictions. Indeed, in Hindu thought, over-identification with the physical body and other material possessions is considered to be the root of all human suffering.

Hindu seers often compare this communion with the spiritual consciousness to the deep leap of a diver who swims to the ocean depths in search of pearls. The pearl is the Divine wisdom. Time and again, Hindu sages have advised to look within one's own self and discover the Divine. Hindu philosophy asserts that when the mind is pure and applies concentrated attention, it may attain spiritual knowledge, or *jnana,* and one may discern what is not normally perceptible to the senses. In Hindu philosophy, this Divine consciousness, the Divine, and God are essentially one and the same thing.

Albeit the concepts of Soul, Consciousness, etc. are firmly believed and accepted in Hindu philosophy, they still remain rather unresolved by modern science. These metaphysical spiritual concepts lie beyond the current paradigms of science. Even so, several other Hindu views and philosophies like "vegetarianism", "environment protection", "meditation" etc. are being gradually embraced and respected by the world at large. There is a great possibility that further advancement in technologies may indeed uncover scientific clues to these unresolved metaphysical secrets of Hinduism.

15 Soul: The Seed of Divinity

In the Hindu pantheon, soul has been very firmly eulogized. Soul is the most powerful; body, mind, and intellect, in comparison, are fleeting and transient, even an illusion. Our body and all material objects are in a constant state of change, but the soul is regarded as eternal and imperishable.

Hindu philosophy envisages two types of bodies: the physical or gross body (called *thul sarira*) and the subtle, invisible body (called *suksma sarira*). Soul has been identified as the subtle, immortal, transcendental *suksma sarira*.

Hindu seers have often referred to a conflict between heart and brain—not the anatomical heart in our bodies but the soul heart of the suksma sarira.

As Swami Vivekananda says:
"It is the heart, which takes one to the highest plane, which intellect can never reach; it goes beyond intellect and what is called inspiration."[36]

According to Hindu philosophy, soul is the eternal constituent, which is invisible and metaphysical in nature and acts as a vehicle for reincarnation from one body to another. It also carries within it the notation of the past karmas, as well as a genealogy map of our tendencies, the *vasnas*.

It is the eternal and transcendental nature of the soul that kindles the flame of fearlessness, or *abhay*, in human beings. Lord Krishna tells Arjuna: *"Thou art the reservoir of omnipotent power. Arise, awake and manifest the Divinity within."*[37]

Knowing the true self, the higher self, is true knowledge (called *para vidya*). Hindu seers are taught to disentangle themselves from the false, superficial ego-self (*neti neti*—"I am not this") and instead, to assert, "I am that" (*tat twam asi*). Soul is the divine seed in each being.

Death, in Hindu philosophy, is part of the long, immortal life, which has been described as the great journey, or *mahaprasthana*. Death is a sacred event, punctuating intermittently in this mahaprasthana. Death is considered merely an interlude in the long passage of the soul, one that one should neither fear nor look forward to prematurely. When the karma of this life is over, one passes over to the next journey.

Even though the soul has been identified as the true representative of an individual being, the physical body and the death of it have been a subject of great consequence. A Hindu is expected to take full advantage of precious human life, which is the essential tool for the spiritual evolution of the soul through eons of birth cycles.

The soul, or *atman*, is considered to be the seed of the Divine, which has all the potential to become godlike, if nurtured and cultivated properly. As the individual human soul (the *jivatman*) becomes more pure, free from the impurities of many tendencies (*vasnas*), it becomes more divine in nature. Thus, the *jivatman*—the individual human soul—has the seed potential of the Divine but is not the Divine itself. It needs to be purified of all its egoistical nature in order to become godlike and merge into the Divine (known as *paramatman*).

Hindu seers have outlined an evolutionary path for an individual toward spiritual maturity. In the words of Satguru Sivaya Subramuniyaswami:

"Our individual soul is the immortal and spiritual body of light that animates life and reincarnates again and again until all the past karmas are resolved and its essential unity with God is fully realized." [38]

The incarnation of God (*avtar-karan*) is repeatedly observed in Hindu tradition. These divine souls guide humanity to discover spiritual truths. Acceptance of multiple God incarnations has helped Hindu philosophy to grow continuously and remain ever fresh; this has been the Hindu way. According to Sri Ramakrishna, a God incarnate is like a big ship that can carry many people, while a human saint is like a small boat.

A leading senior monk of the Vedanta Temple of New York, Swami Yogatmananda, shared the following anecdote:

"Once, many devotees met with God and asked Him how they all might meet with the Divine. God told them that they might ascend the high ladder of virtues and austerities and reach Him, ultimately. The devotees then told God how difficult this route would be for most of them, and only a rare few would ever reach this goal. God agreed. The devotees then put a proposal to God for consideration: Would it not be a good idea, if instead, God would use the same ladder and come down occasionally to meet with many devotees at one time?" [39]

The concept of eternal soul and reincarnation, although essentially a Hindu doctrine, has many supporters in other faiths, too. A cross section of people that includes industrial magnet Henry Ford, renowned author Victor Hugo, Christian Unitarian minister Rev. William R. Alger, and innumerable others have accepted this philosophy. In fact, in a 1990 Gallup poll, it was revealed that the percentage of Christians who believe in reincarnation is about the same in the general population as the percentage of those who do not believe in this concept.[40]

For Hindus, the "soul" (atman) is an eternal, transcendental, formless phenomenon, which is manifested through physical bodies repeatedly passing through eons of life cycles. According to Hindu philosophy, just as the physical body parts and intellect develop over many years of life, so the individual soul (jivatman), which is but a seed of the divine "paramatman", too develops though eons of life cycles. The soul matures and progresses by cultivating spiritual virtues; these divine merits are deemed more worthy in Hindu philosophy than any physical or material asset. The evolutionary development thus exceeds much beyond one life cycle in Hindu theology.

The Muktabodha Indological Research Institute
(Contributed by Dr David Katz)

The Muktabodha Indological Research Institute is dedicated to the preservation of ancient texts from the religious and philosophical traditions of classical India and to making such texts accessible for study and scholarship worldwide. A core project of the Institute is the Muktabodha Digital Library, an online manuscript collection containing important Sanskrit texts in multiple digital formats, including searchable electronic texts, and a sophisticated search engine. The library holds an extensive collection of Kashmiri Shaivite texts, as well as manuscripts from the Kaula-Trika, Virashaiva, Pancaratra, Shree Vidya, Shakta and Natha Yoga schools. In collaboration with the French Institute of Pondicherry and the Ecole Francaise d'Extreme Orient in Paris, Muktabodha has helped to digitally preserve a portion of the world's largest collection of endangered Shaiva Siddhanta manuscripts, recognized by the United Nations cultural organization, UNESCO, as part of its "Memory of the World" collection. The Muktabodha Digital Library can be accessed through the Institute's website at muktabodha.org.

The Muktabodha Indological Research Institute is an initiative of Gurumayi Chidvilasananda, the spiritual head of the Siddha Yoga path, and was established with the support of the SYDA Foundation, the organization that protects, preserves, and facilitates the dissemination of the Siddha Yoga teachings. As a not-for-profit educational foundation, the Institute is financed by private donations and grants.

16 The Divine Path of Virtue

By "spirituality," Hindus mean an eternal union or connectedness with the Divine and, through the Divine, with all creation. Hindus also believe in connectedness through time, spread over eons of birth cycles. Hindu philosophy recognizes spirituality in a very special way. The unique features of Hinduism are its belief in *karma* (As you sow, so shall you reap), *punarjanam* (reincarnation), *samsara* (the eternal cycle of birth and death), *moksha* (salvation), and *avtar-karan* (God incarnation).

The world, according to Hindu philosophy, is like a teaching institute, or *ashrama,* in which one learns in various phases of one's karma through eons of birth cycles.

Hindus believe that our present status and position are determined by our past actions (or *karma*). Karma, which has now become a household word in the West, is basically a form of energy. It moves in the form of thoughts, words, and actions but most potently in thoughts. Whatever good or bad we do, it will come back to us. Hindu Rishis maintain that the main purpose of life is to transform our minds toward virtue and divinity. Once we are able to transform our minds, all of our past sins and errors may be mitigated or considerably modified.

The concept of reincarnation is unique in Hinduism, as well as in religions that originated in India, such as Jainism, Buddhism, and Sikhism. Hindu philosophy also accepts that the spiritual knowledge gained in one life stays forever and does not vanish after death. Man may thus continue his journey of spiritual evolution from the stage of learning he had reached in his previous life.

After attaining the intellectual mind, the human mind has two choices: It may go downward on the path of ego, or it may go upwards on the path of divine spirituality, toward the Divine, the spiritual consciousness, or the super-consciousness, and wean itself away from the direction of personal ego. Peace (*shanti*) comes to the person of higher spiritual consciousness. Hindu sages have promoted peace above all else. In Hindu theology, the saint or sage (*sant*) is considered one who has completely annihilated his ego. Hindu theology is essentially God-centric. The spiritual masters prompt a human being to remain humble and devoted to God at all times. Continuously remembering God, while performing any actions, imparts the divine virtues to all deeds, which become free from any evil or sin. Hindu philosophy recognizes that the Divine is within all beings. The soul of an individual, the *jivatma*, is but a part of the divine soul, the *paramatma*, even though it may be in a dormant and deluded condition.

It is a common experience that when we give happiness to others, we feel happy; and when we make others unhappy, we too become unhappy. This is indeed God's gift to man. God has made the human apparatus highly cognitive in order to perceive and feel in great depth the ultimate truth.

According to Hindu philosophy, God has given each human being, a perfect life to learn and grow. Through experience we mature out of fear into fearlessness, out of anger into love, out of conflict into peace, out of darkness into light and union with God.

Gradually, religion and spirituality became the way of life in Hindu society. Swami Vivekananda said:

"Not politics nor military power, not commercial supremacy nor mechanical genius furnishes India with that backbone, but religion; and religion alone is all that we have." [41]

Hinduism encompasses beliefs in certain unique concepts like karma (As you sow, so shall you reap), punarjanam (reincarnation), samsara (the eternal cycle of birth and death), moksha (salvation), and avtah-karan (God incarnation). These concepts which remain unrecognized by modern science, present answers to many vital questions which have forever baffled mankind: Why are some born in good fortune and others in such miserable conditions? Why some do not reap the benefits of their good work when they are still alive? What is the real purpose of life etc? According to Hindu philosophy, human birth is the most precious as it grants beings with a thinking mind. Yet, evolutionary development is not void of obstacles; human mind must overcome the hurdle of "ego", with the help of discrimination and free will. Often, man falters and falls down while fronting this most arduous hurdle! Nonetheless, Hindu viewpoint reassures that ultimately, all souls will mature through eons of birth cycles, earning the coveted goal of moksha – salvation. One is prompted by the saints to always be on guard and pursue the path of divine virtue to progress on their paths.

17 The Hindu Trinity (*Trimurti*)

In the Aryan Vedic period, the deities of nature became the gods in all worship and rituals. But soon the idea of one Supreme God became established. In the Creation Hymn, the *Nasadiya Hymn* of the Rig Veda, the single primordial principle *tat* or *that* has been described. This Vedic Hymn points to the abstract, formless, transcendental, and all-pervading principle of pure consciousness.

Common man then, however, as perhaps now, was not yet ready to understand the abstract God so easily. Hindu seers came forth with the idea of the Trinity of Gods, the *Trimurti*. Three Gods, with different faces, were projected, and each was mythological in origin. The three Gods were each given a human face for easy acceptance.

The Trinity of Hindu Gods consists of Lord of Creation, Brahma; Lord of Preservation, Vishnu; and Lord of Dissolution, Shiva, who is also called Mahesh. In Hindu philosophy, however, this envisages one continuous chain of events. For example, the destruction of the morning is the creation of the evening, and the destruction of the evening is the creation of the night, and so on. Even death in Hindu thought is merely an interlude from one event to another. Destruction or death is the dissolution, which is again followed by creation.

Lord Brahma, the Lord of Creation, is also called the Lord of Progeny (*Prajapati*). He has four faces and four arms. The four faces represent the four Vedas. The four arms of Lord Brahma are symbolic of the four aspects of his inner personality: the mind (*mana*), the intellect (*buddhi*), the ego (*ahamkara*), and the divine consciousness (*chitta*). He is wedded to Saraswati, the goddess of knowledge.

Lord Vishnu is the Lord of Preservation. Literally, Vishnu means "all-pervading." Thus, the symbolic significance of the Divine as formless and transcendent is emphasized. He is portrayed as a dark-blue youth, upright in position. He, too, is a god with four arms, representing omnipresence and omnipotence. One hand holds the conch (*sankha*), signifying creation; the second hand holds the discus (*sudarshan chakra*) to signify the universal mind; the third hand carries the mace (*gada*) to signify life force; and the fourth hand carries the lotus (*padma*) to signify the universe.

Lord Vishnu's consort is *Lakshmi*, the goddess of wealth and prosperity.[42] Lord Vishnu is also identified as *Narayana,* possibly originating from the pre-Vedic culture.[43] Lord Vishnu in the Hindu pantheon is emblematic of complete evolution. He has been presented as taking ten incarnations. In each incarnation, he has acted as a savior of the world. The ten incarnations of Vishnu present an amazing account of the evolutionary phases in the Creation. The first incarnation of Vishnu is in the form of *Matsya*, a fish; he protected the sacred Vedas from being lost in the great deluge. In the second incarnation as *Kurma*, a tortoise, he held the universe in balance when the gods and demons began to churn the ocean to extract the nectar of immortality (*amruta*). In the third incarnation as *Varaha*, the boar, he killed the demon Hiranyaksha and saved the Earth from drowning in the ocean. In the fourth incarnation, Lord Vishnu came as the half-lion/half-man *Narasimha* and destroyed Hiranyakasipu to save the demon's own son Prahlada, who believed in eternal god Narayana. In the fifth incarnation as the dwarf *Vamana*, he helped the gods, who were treated unjustly by king Bali. In the sixth incarnation as Lord *Parshurama*, he fought with the kings to save the Rishis. In the seventh incarnation as Lord Rama, he destroyed wicked Ravana, as described in the epic of Ramayana. In the eighth incarnation as Lord Krishna, he killed the evil and atrocious Kamsa and also guided the truthful Pandavas against unjust Kauravas in the battle of Mahabharata. In the ninth incarnation, he appeared as gentle and non-violent human being, full of wisdom, as Lord Buddha. He taught the technique of meditation and inner transformation of the mind to overcome the sorrow and evil of life. In the tenth incarnation, which is yet to come, he would be called *Kalki* and would again become the savior of the just and the righteous. He would ride on a white horse, representative of the indestructible hidden nature of things.[44] The Kalki legend is familiar and has repeated in one form or another in most cultures, such as Persian, Jewish, Christian, Tibetan, and many Central Asian cultures. Even Native Americans had their version in the legend of Kukulkan.[45]

Lord Shiva is described in the next chapter.

After the Hindu Trinity of Brahma, Vishnu and Shiva, much of the divine power and glory were bestowed from the earlier Vedic gods of nature to these Divine entities. However in Hindu pantheon, the old was never completely discarded. Some of the Vedic gods have persisted till today; Indra, Yama. Varuna, Agni, Suray, Vayu, and Soma together are known as "world-guardians". Many other new gods apart from the

Trinity appeared on the scene; Ganesha, Skanda, goddesses who became consorts of the Primary gods of Trinity, animal gods, river gods etc came to the forefront. In the epic scriptures, God was presented in the real human form as God-incarnate. In Hindu theology, God-hood essentially is a symbolic phenomenon, signifying the highest spiritual and virtuous attainment.[46]

Such has been the universal approach of Hindus that they even called the gods of the other religions the Vishnu incarnations. Lord Buddha and Lord Christ have been considered to be Vishnu incarnates. This is really not so surprising, as Hindu philosophy teaches, *Ekam sad vipra bahudha vadant*—"One alone exists; sages call it by various names."

Hindu theology has often been labelled as one that harbors multiple gods. However, the concept of One Supreme God was clearly mentioned in the earliest of Hindu scriptures-the Rig Veda:

> *Ekam sad vipra bahudha vadanti.*
> *(One alone exists; sages call it by various names.)*

In the later scriptures, the Upanishads, this ancient philosophical thought came to the forefront, overshadowing the idea of multiple gods, who were then considered simply as the manifestations of the One transcendental Supreme Divine.

In modern times, this concept of God has been adopted more vigorously, given the existence of many religions and sects around the world. It is interesting to note that the Supreme Court of the United States recommended using the term "Supreme Being" in place of "God" in the Constitution of the United States, after hearing the plea in which the aforementioned quotation of the Rig Veda was presented.

In contemporary times, the thought of different gods for different religions and communities, competing and often quarrelling over the names of gods, is gradually being disfavored. More understanding people around the globe believe that God is but one, but names can be many!

Kashmir Shaivism, also known as the Trika

(Contributed by Swami Shankarananda, Australia.
He can be contacted at swamiji@shivayoga.org)

A number of Hindu philosophies put great emphasis on the idea of Consciousness. Among them, the philosophy of Kashmir Shaivism is outstanding. It is an ancient philosophy that had its heyday in medieval times and has returned to prominence in recent years. Its foundational text is the Shiva Sutras by Vasugupta, from the ninth century CE.

Kashmir Shaivism virtually disappeared for a number of centuries, until Swami Lakshmanjoo revived it in the 20th century. Another important figure in Kashmir Shaivism's spread was Swami Muktananda, who presented its teachings to a broad audience.

Kashmir Shaivism is a philosophical system, and also includes a wealth of yogic practices and meditations (upaya) for the practitioner to attain the state of liberation, or complete freedom (svatantrya).

The philosophy of Kashmir Shaivism says that the universe begins as pure Consciousness (Shiva). At this stage, there is only One. Then, Shiva decides to become many. He contracts and becomes individual human souls, and also the material world. After some time, these souls begin to wake up and investigate their true nature. They meditate and do spiritual practices and eventually recognise their true identity as Consciousness. So Kashmir Shaivism says that everything is Consciousness in the beginning, in the middle and in the end, and there is nothing apart from Consciousness.

Kashmir Shaivism is particularly appealing to the modern reader because it does not deny the reality of the world, but says that the world is a "play of Consciousness".

18 Shiva: The Mystic Divine of Meditation

In the Hindu Pantheon, Lord Shiva occupies one of the earliest and foremost places. His carving is found in the ancient Sindhu-Saraswati civilization. There he is seen in his famous yogic pose, meditating. He is, therefore, considered to be the originator of yoga and meditation. Siva, or Shiva, also means "auspicious one." Lord Shiva, who is considered to be the Lord of Death and Dissolution, thus gets a new look. As the auspicious one, Lord Shiva is hailed as the Lord of Compassion. Legend has it that when the gods (*devtas*) and the demons (*asuras*) churned the ocean to extract the nectar of immortality, there first appeared a most noxious poison, harmful to all beings. They all rushed to Lord Shiva, who, in his compassion, drank the dark poison to save the universe. Lord Shiva, however, did not swallow the poison but retained it in his throat. He is, therefore, also known as the god with the blue throat, the *Neelkantha*. The poison became the ornament necklace for Lord Shiva, encouraging mankind not to hesitate to help others and to mitigate their sorrows.

According to Hindu mythology, Lord Shiva was first married to Uma. She was the daughter of Rishi Daksha, who had insulted Shiva because he was not well dressed and did not have material possessions. Uma then pleaded before her father that the man's virtues were much more important than material possessions or outward appearances. Thus, it became established in Hindu society that virtuous behavior is a better asset than wealth and material objects, such as jewels or gold. But when Uma's father, Daksha, continued with his arrogant behavior, Uma threw herself in the fire of the *yagna havan*, with a vow that in her next life, she would again become the consort of Lord Shiva. She fulfilled this vow by becoming the goddess Parvati, daughter of Himalaya, in her new incarnation.

Lord Shiva is also portrayed as the Lord of Dance, *Nataraja*. Here, he is presented in a most magnificent dancing extravaganza, with four arms and hands. The upper-right hand holds the *damaru*, a small percussion tool, representing sound. In the Hindu mind, all language, music, and knowledge came from sound. The upper-left hand holds a tongue of fire. Thus, one hand indicates creation and the other points to destruction, symbolizing the unity of these two processes. The third hand (front right) is seen in the *abhaya hasta* position—that is, it is gesturing the sign of grace and protection of the Lord. The front left hand is in the *gaja hasta* position—it is formed in the shape of an elephant's trunk, which had the ability to pick up the heaviest log or the smallest needle. The left foot is raised up in the air, pointing toward the salvation of man, and the right foot is resting on the struggling dwarf, symbolic of the human ego of ignorance. We may crush our ignorance with the sword of knowledge in order to achieve salvation (*moksha*).

The matted hair of Lord Shiva holds the sacred river Ganges, signifying the power and purity of mankind. Even when the Lord dances with abandon and ferocity, his face is serene and calm in superb, deep meditation, showing the path of utmost action with complete relaxation. He is also presented as *Bhairava*, the fierce wielder of *trishula*, the trident of love, wisdom, and action. In the famous sculpture of the south-faced Lord Dakshinamoorthy, Shiva is seen as the youthful guru, teaching his pupils by his eloquent silence. His youthful face symbolizes that the man of realization has transcended time and achieved immortality. In *ardhanarisvara* form (half male, half female), Lord Shiva is projected as the *Purusha* (the male form as divine) on one half and as the *Prakruti* (the female form as nature) on the other half, to be combined by the *Purusha* to become active and enlightened. This is seen as the seed of divinity in all beings, which manifests in the course of evolution. This form of Lord Shiva recognizes the presence of both male and female components in each individual. Thus was born the concept of Shiva and Shakti to represent the Divine and all its energy. Yet another form, *Hari-Hara*, has two images, half Shiva and half Vishnu, merged together, signifying the ultimate unity of all forms of the Divine.

In the Hindu pantheon, Lord Shiva is referred to as *Mahadeva*, the absolute and the greatest god. It is also believed that Lord Shiva first spontaneously appeared as a high mountain in the form of Arunachala in South India, as the first *Jyotir Lingam*. Subsequently, he also presented himself as smaller Jyotir Lingam in the cylindrical stone shape in twelve different places. His appearance in the form of *Shiv Lingam*, where indirect human agency was involved around the *Lingam*, is also in twelve places.

In the Shiv Purana, Shiv Lingam has been referred to as *niraakar*, or the formless presentation of Lord Shiva. In the *saakar*, or formed presentation of human appearance, he is known as Mahesh or Jagdeeshwar. Most Shiva devotees recognize the Lingam as an abstract icon of the Divine. The sexual aspect of Lingam as a symbol of Creation in the form of a male phallus is subordinated to the spiritual perspective.

Lord Shiva has three eyes—the sun, moon, and fire. The third eye, *"agni"*, also is considered as the eye of inner vision; hence, it is often invoked at the time of meditation. It is said that with the third eye, he burned desire, or *kama*. He therefore is also named *Trilochan*, the lord with three eyes. He has the crescent moon on his forehead, signifying knowledge and mystical vision. His matted hair and ash-smeared body indicate austerity, and around his neck is the serpent energy, *Kundalini Shakti*, moving from the spine upwards. Lord Shiva has two sons, Ganpati and Skanda. His main consort, the goddess Parvati, assumes other forms as well, such as Durga, the bright one; Sati, the devoted wife; Bhairavi, the terror inspiring; or Kali, the black one. *Nandi*, the white bull, is the vehicle of Lord Shiva and is present at the entrance of all Shiva temples. In scriptures, Nandi represents man (*jivatman*), who is in eternal search of the Divine.

Lord Shiva is one of the Gods in the Hindu Trinity - Brahma, Vishnu, and Shiva. In the Vedas, Lord Shiva is also known as as "Rudra", the god of storm associated with destruction. It was from this narrative that He came to be known as the God of Destruction amongst the three primary mythological Gods. However, soon a significant benevolent characteristic of "Compassion" was discovered in Him, when He drank the dark poison to save the universe. Instead of swallowing the poison, Lord Shiva retained it in his throat and is therefore known as the god with the blue throat, the "Neelkantha". Gradually, many more features were discovered like His utmost austerity smearing His body with ashes, His mastery of the art of dancing as "Natraja", His stance of Yoga and Meditation which designated Him as the originator of these two pursuits etc. This established a dynamic pattern in Hindu theology to search and discover more and more attributes in all divine manifestations to become the role models for mankind, to be inspired and prompted to imbibe similar qualities and virtues in their own life.

Spiritual Gems from Tirukural: I

"Of all virtues summed by ancient sages, the foremost are to share one's food and to protect all living creatures."

"Not allowing a day to pass without doing some good work is a boulder that will block your passage on the path to re-birth."

"The highest principle is this: Never knowingly harm anyone at anytime in any way."

"If a man be his own guard, let him guard himself against rage. Left unguarded, his own wrath will annihilate him."

"Those who are free from vanity, vulgarity and venomousness will prosper in deserving dignity."

"Of what avail is an outer appearance of saintliness if the mind suffers inwardly from knowledge of its sin?"

"It is compassion that sustains the world's existence. The existence of those bereft of it is a burden to the Earth."

"Pleasant words, full of tenderness and devoid of deceit, fall from the lips of virtuous men."

"Self-control will place one among the Gods, while lack of it will lead to deepest darkness."

"It is said that all good things are natural to those who know their duty and walk the path of perfect goodness."

"Among the many precious things a man may acquire, none surpasses a nature free from envy toward all."

"Whatever you may fail to guard, guard well your tongue, for flawed speech unfailingly invokes anguish and hardship."

(Source: Spiritual Teachings-Himalayan Academy, Hawaii, USA)

19 Sri Rama: The Lord of Propriety

Epic scriptures Ramayana and Mahabharata are categorized as *Itihasa* scriptures. Conventionally, we may consider *Itihasa* to mean the historical tales, but in Hindu theological narrations, the descriptions are often mixed with mythological and spiritual input[47] to make them more forceful in their teaching value. Some have interpreted *Itihasa* as *"Thus we should live."* This rendition imparts a higher moral value to these scriptures.

Rama is believed to be the seventh incarnation of Lord Vishnu. According to Vaishnavites, He descended on earth around 10,000 years ago to eliminate evil forces. However the historical concept by R.C. Majmudar describes 1950 BCE more likely. The story of Ramayana is the story of Hinduism; it is the true classic of all times. Literally, Ramayana means *"the ways of Rama."* Rishi Valmiki first narrated it in twenty-four thousand verses, around 1000 BCE. From that time until today, this great tale of Lord Rama has been repeated in one form or another—a book, poetry, a dance drama called *Ram Lila*, movie, and a video serial. The Hindi version of Ramayana, *Ram Charith Manas,* written by Sant Tulsidas in the sixteenth century, and the earlier Tamil version, *Kamban,* have become equally popular.

Valmiki, who authored this great tale, was himself a *dacoit*—a highway robber—who reformed to become a devotee of Lord Rama (*Ram Bhagat*). The legend states that one day the great sage Narada confronted Valmiki and asked if his family, for whom he was committing the robberies, would share the burden of his sins. All the members of his family, including his wife, replied with an emphatic no. Valmiki then was immediately transformed, and he dedicated his life to the mission of writing the Ramayana. Thus, a Hindu would always be reminded that in the end, he would have to bear the consequences of his deeds alone.

In the Hindu Pantheon, Lord Rama is the "God of Propriety". He would become the role model for appropriate and proper conduct throughout millennia. In every situation, however stressful or provocative, he remained calm and gentle. He never became angry and never lost his temper. He was always most respectful and kind. Even when his stepmother, Kaikeyi, became the cause of his great troubles and trials, he revered her, as a Hindu ought to revere his mother. He touched her feet and took her blessing before going into exile for fourteen years. He bore malice toward none. To his parents, his manners always remained exemplary. Toward Sita (the wife of Rama), he was most loving and courteous. From him we learn the unique teaching of *ekapatni*, which means only one wife for one man. When his brother, Lakshman, was seriously wounded, he actually cried. The bond of the two brothers would become the inspiration of brotherly love in the history of mankind. Toward Ravana, the wicked king, he remained persuasive until the very end, to wean him from evil. Only after it became clear that Ravana would never change did Rama take the bow and kill him, to uphold the cause of righteousness. Hindu society has referred to Lord Rama in the human form as *Maryada Purshotam*, the perfect man, who has remained an inspiration to become an ideal son, brother, husband, and ruler. He epitomized the spiritual virtues of truth, humility, and caring for others. Every situation in the Ramayana has a moral touch, and every character has an ethical significance.

The story of Ramayana is told as follows: Raja Dashrath was a pious king of Ayodha, in northern India. Toward the later period of his life, he decided to relinquish his throne in favor of the eldest of his four sons, Rama, and pass the remaining period of his life in prayers and meditation. This would be a common desire of any God-loving person in Hindu society. When Dashrath announced his desire to abdicate the throne and offer the crown to Rama, one of his queens, Kaikeyi, on the prompting of an evil-minded relative, Manthra, reminded the king of two favors that he had earlier promised her—that Rama should be sent into a forest for fourteen years and that her own son, Bharat, should be crowned king. On hearing this, Dashrath was so shocked that he died, even before Bharat, who was away visiting his maternal grandfather, returned. Rama, on the other hand, insisted that he would carry out the promises made by his father a long time ago. One's word was the most precious duty, and a son was morally bound to uphold the honor of his father.

In the great tradition of the Hindu culture, Rama's wife, Sita, prepared to go into the forest with him. Another brother, Lakshmana, also joined the long journey to serve his elder brother Rama.

When Bharat retuned from his grandfather's home, he not only turned down the offer of the throne, but he also went to plead with Rama to return and become the king. Rama, however, remained firm in his decision, as he considered it a matter of uprightness (*dharma*) to abide by noble values and principles. Bharat then returned with a pair of Rama's sandals, which he placed on the throne to represent the exiled prince; Bharat would only be performing on behalf of Rama until his return. Thus, the greed and evil of the queen Kaikeyi and her relative Manthra were fully compensated by the sacrifice and unselfishness of the son Bharat.

There are many tales of Sri Rama, Sita, and Lakshman during their long sojourn in the forest. I have chosen but one, of an old, low-caste woman, Shabri:

Shabri was a poor old woman in the forest, who got the chance of her lifetime to meet Lord Rama and play host to him. She picked berries, and then decided to taste them, one by one, to see which were sweet enough to be served to the Lord. Rama relished these berries more than anything else. The scriptures, the *Veda Shastras*, prohibit anyone from serving something that is contaminated—certainly not to Lord Rama. Shabri, however, was not knowledgeable of these formalities. She was a low-caste, simple-hearted woman of sincerity and devotion. Lord Rama however accepted her service with great love and granted her the salvation (*moksha*).

Hindu religion is replete with such instances, when time and again the old conventions are broken. In the epic tales of both the Ramayana and the Mahabharata, the caste system is denounced. But this evil, however, prevailed in Hindu society for long time, emphasizing human weakness and vulnerability.

Ramayana has been the beacon of light for Hindus for millennia. Lord Rama's sense of sacrifice and dedication toward his father is an object lesson for all mankind. The love among the brothers has been depicted with touching emotion, and the portrait of Sita as the ideal wife is greatly remembered in every household.

Lord Rama would become the role model for appropriate conduct. Hindu society has referred to Lord Rama in the human form as "Maryada Purshotam", the perfect man, who has remained an inspiration to become an ideal son, brother, husband, and ruler. He epitomized the spiritual virtues of truth, humility, and caring for others. The legend of Shabri describes the major evolutionary step to cut across the caste system. To Hindus, Lord Rama has been a guiding star for every situation and circumstance in life, whenever they are in any difficult and challenging situation.

Spiritual Gems from Tirukural: II

"Benevolent man considers himself poor only
when he is unable to render his accustomed duty to humanity."

"Neglecting valuable advice, an ignorant man
becomes the cause of his own misery."

"Just as the Earth bears those who dig into her,
it is best to bear with those who despise us."

"If men fathom what it means to have virtuous and wise friends,
they will find the means to procure such friendships."

"It is disgraceful to be discourteous towards others,
even to unfriendly fellows who treat you unjustly."

"A kindness done in the hour of need may itself be small,
but in worth it exceeds the whole world."

"Nothing on Earth is imperishable,
except exalted glory, which endures forever"

"A long and joyous life rewards those who remain firmly
on the faultless path of Him who controls the five senses."

"Perfect men hold as good their own good character.
They count no other goodness so genuinely good."

"Prosperous as his life may appear, unless a man
measures well his wealth, it will disappear without a trace."

"Who is there who can conquer those
who have relinquished all hostilities?"

"Is it because they are unaware of the joys of giving
that hard-hearted men waste their wealth by hoarding it?"

(Source: Spiritual Teachings-Himalayan Academy, Hawaii, USA)

20 Victory of Righteousness Over Unrighteousness

Toward the end of their stay in the forest, Ramayana portrays a powerful climax, complete with drama, emotion, and action. The mighty, learned, but evil-minded and misguided king of Sri Lanka, Ravana, arrived on the scene to depict the havoc of lust in human life. Lured by the beauty of Sri Sita, Ravana first sent his ally Maricha in the garb of a golden deer to tempt the gullible her, who at once fell for his outward appearance. She persuaded Rama to follow the deer and try to capture it for her amusement. When Rama had not returned after a considerable time, Sita sent Lakshmana to search him. Before leaving, Lakshmana drew a line across the doorway and instructed Sita not to cross the line, for her own security. Ravana now came himself in disguise, and he approached Sita as an ascetic for alms. He then lured her with deceptive words to come out, crossing the line drawn by Lakshmana.

Many centuries later, parents, elders, and others who cared for young men and women would tell them not to cross the *Lakshman Rekha*—the limit of propriety—to safeguard against any evil in hiding. They would be warned, especially the women, to observe the rules of the discipline; otherwise, they might suffer the consequences of protracted harm and humiliation, which Sita had to suffer at the hands of the wicked Ravana. Valmiki chose the most powerful character of Sita, the mother symbol in all Hindu culture, to depict human weakness and to prove beyond any shadow of doubt that a person may be vulnerable at any time.

After Ravana abducted Sita, Rama sent his emissary, Hanuman, to search for her. Hanuman was the monkey god, and he told Ravana—directly and through other noble souls in his court, especially his brother Vibhishna—to wean himself from the path of vice and return Sita to Rama. But Ravana was too obsessed with the desire of physical indulgence with Sita. Desire makes man blind, and he loses his power of discretion. Also, Ravana was too arrogant. Even though Ravana had obtained special boons from God because of his knowledge and meditation, in the end he lost everything. Any person who follows the path of sin and arrogance is, therefore, called a Ravana. Ramayana is the story of victory of virtue over vice.

In the Ramayana, the role of Sri Hanuman is indeed most special. Hanuman has been portrayed as monkey and is thus symbolic of subhuman genesis. But his devotion, sincerity, strength, love, and sacrifice have been much more than any human capability. In this epic, once again Lord Rama cuts across the false barriers and puts the greatest honor on the head of Hanuman—he is elevated to be a god in Hindu religion and even is considered to be the *avatara* (incarnation) of Lord Shiva.

After defeating Ravana, Rama gave back the kingdom to Vibhishna, the brother of Ravana, thus establishing an eternal legacy for the Hindus that they might not usurp any possession that does not belong to them. To this day, nearly one billion Hindus across the world celebrate the returning of Rama as their most important festival, *Diwali*—the Festival of Lights.

Swami Vivekananda has described the immortal character of Rama in these words:

"Rama, the embodiment of truth, of morality, the ideal son, the ideal husband, the ideal father, and above all the ideal king, this Rama has been presented."[48]

In the earlier Vedas, it was proclaimed "Ahimsa Parmo Dharma"-Non-violence is the primary dharma. However, it was soon realized that violence cannot always be averted. When all other methods of dealing with an unjust and unrighteous situation do not yield the desired result, one may be compelled to use force and power to protect the innocent and pure from evil and sinful. Lord Rama thus vanquished Ravana to uphold morality, and destroy wickedness; non-violence was no longer unconditional and absolute in Hindu society.

After defeating Ravana however, Rama gave back the kingdom to Vibhishna, the brother of Ravana, thus establishing an eternal legacy for the Hindus that they might not usurp any possession that does not belong to them. Hindus have honored this bequest ever since.

21 Mahabharata: The War Within

The Mahabharata—literally, the story of greater India—is the other twin that has decorated Hinduism, along with the Ramayana, throughout millennia. In the Ramayana, the scene of war is across the ocean, far away from the kingdom of Rama. In the Mahabharata, the scene of war is at Hastinapur, in their kingdom. In both, the war is between the virtue and the vice, right and wrong, good and evil. Indeed, the Mahabharata is the story of the war within our own bosom. The Bhagavad Gita, which is the divine message of this grand epic, is the epitome of Hindu spiritual philosophy.

The Mahabharata is the most fascinating story of this grand legend, narrated by another great Hindu mind, Ved Vyasa, between 400 and 300 BCE. It is the world's longest epic poem, consisting of one hundred thousand verses. "Vyasa" literally means "arranger." It may, however, be possible that this is not the name of any one individual; rather, it may denote the position of a compiler. Historians and scholars have established that the Mahabharata was, in fact, written and compiled over many centuries, beginning from the first half of the first millennium BCE and reaching its completion toward the first century CE or even later. In the Ramayana, the story revolves around God, in the form of Lord Rama. In the Mahabharata, it is centered on another God, Lord Krishna.

The story of the Mahabharata begins with an ancient king of Hastinapur, who had two sons. The elder son, Dhritarastra, was blind, so he was barred from sitting on the throne after his father's death. The younger son, Pandu, ruled for some time but died prematurely when all his five sons, collectively called Pandavas, were still young. In this situation, the old blind uncle Dhritarastra was asked to become the king temporarily until the Pandavas became eligible. In ancient Hindu scriptures, the language used by the great Rishis is often symbolic. Dhritarastra's blindness, therefore, was not so much physical as it was mental. He could not discriminate between right and wrong. Once he became the ruler, his greed for power again flared up in his mind. He had one hundred sons, all called Kauravas, the eldest being Duryodhana. In the Mahabharata, the five Pandavas represent the virtues, while the hundred Kauravas represent the vices. When the

Pandavas grew up, Duryodhana played a foul trick in order to usurp the kingdom. Yudhistra, the eldest of the Pandavas, was a man of unimpeachable truth, but he had a weakness for the game of dice. His absolute commitment to the virtues of truth and righteousness earned him the legendary status of *Dharamraj,* the prince of religion. Duryodhana, with the help of his cunning maternal uncle Shakuni, defeated Yudhistra by deception. Dhritarastra, the blind father, remained silent and gave his son tacit support for his immoral acts by not intervening; rather, he hoped that his son would become the king. How often a similar drama unfolds in our own lives when we see our own kith and kin do wrong, but we turn a blind Dhritarastra eye!

When Yudhistra lost everything and his right to the kingdom was gone, he became desperate. He gambled his own five brothers, and later, to his ultimate shame, also lost the common wife of all the Pandavas, Draupadi. After this, Duryodhana became even more wicked. He ordered that Draupadi be undressed before the full court. Yudhistra and his four brothers watched the horrible scene without speaking, but they hung their heads in shame. Draupadi represents our honor; when she was put in this most difficult situation, she looked around and begged for help from all. When no one came forward, she cried for Lord Krishna, who at once saved her honor by providing unending yards of cloth to keep her covered and intact. Much later, Draupadi would confront Lord Krishna, asking why he had not helped sooner. The Lord replied that as long as she was looking for help in other places, he would not come, but whenever she remembered him in full faith, he would always be there. This is Lord's promise; our God is the spiritual power within us. When man is banking only on his own physical and material aspects, the Divine energy is subdued. Man, however, may tap into the infinite energy of the Divine whenever he wants, if he only he will turn from the material to the spiritual.

After the Pandavas lost the game, they were ordered to go to the forest to spend the next twelve years in exile. When they returned, they requested that they be given a small piece of the kingdom where they could live peacefully. The haughty and unjust Duryodhana turned down this request. Lord Krishna, who was their distant cousin, intervened but to no effect. The Pandavas, with the consent of Lord Krishna, declared war with the Kauravas. Once again, as in the case of Ramayana, it became clear that although war is not a good choice, it could not always be avoided. Both Pandavas and Kauravas approached Sri Krishna for help. The Lord declared that he himself would be available on one side, without any army or armament; on the other side would be all his men and materials, but without him. This is a clear signal for man to choose between God and Mammon. Arjuna, the most proficient warrior prince among the Pandvas, at once opted for the Lord, and, in equal haste, Duryodhana chose the army and other materials. The Pandavas won the war with the guidance and blessings of Lord Krishna.

The Mahabharata is a war within oneself—a war that we all have to fight, within our own conscience, between the right and the wrong. Arjuna, under the guidance of Lord Krishna, kept his attention totally fixed on God throughout the period of war. This helped the Pandavas to not only win the war but this spiritual instruction became a saga of sacred scripture, the Bhagavad Gita, which would transform the lives of innumerable people, across the millennia and all over the globe.

The main purpose of religion is to guide people on the just and virtuous path. The saga of Mahabharata deals with the crucial challenge of the war within one's own self. The different characters of this great epic depict internal mental attitudes and mindsets, which chiefly dictate how humans behave and act in different situations.

Hindu philosophy states that human beings go through repeated birth cycles, with the next birth being assigned to a person on the basis of his/her past actions-karmas. Only as a human being, one is bestowed with mind to discern the right from the wrong, as also free will, to strive to change the natural born tendencies toward virtue and purity.

Dhritarastra is born with the vasna of greed, which he succumbs to and gives a tactic support to his son Duryodhana, who is not only greedy, but when unrestrained became haughty and sinful.

Yudhistra, eldest of the Pandva brothers, is born with utmost truth and honesty, but had the vasna of an evil habit of gambling; he ultimately lost not only all the wealth that he had, but also all his brothers and their commton wife Draupadi, with dire consequences to face.

Pure and virtuous to the core, Draupadi initially looks for support in men and material. Only when she realizes how unreliable these sources are, she turns to the Divine, who immediately comes to her aid.

Arjuna had steadfast faith and devotion toward God, and he never faltered. With his mind utterly focused to God at all times, he was able to win, without any tribulation.

Through eons of birth cycles, one may gradually learn and grow; the saga of Mahabharata gives a clear insight of the inborn tendencies (vasna) in human beings, and how the virtuous become the ultimate winners.

22 Bhagavad Gita: The Song Celestial

Bhagavad Gita, the song of the Lord, as it literally translates, is the very backbone of Hinduism. Not only Hindus, but also many others, read this great, ancient scripture. It contains the essence of the Vedic knowledge and spiritual philosophy in seven hundred verses (*slokas*), contained in eighteen chapters. The first English translation was in 1785. Sir Edwin Arnold's version, *The Song Celestial*, later became the most popular. Innumerable commentaries have been offered on the Gita. Arguably, more people have read the Gita in English than in Sanskrit or any other Indian language.

Hinduism is truly an evolutionary religion. Each successive scripture contains the essence of many previous scriptures, with subtle changes and modifications. The Bhagavad Gita is the culmination of the Vedas and the Upanishads in the form of a dialogue between the seeker of guidance, Arjuna, and the fountain of knowledge, the Lord Himself. Before the war of Mahabharata, Arjuna, the Pandava prince in charge of leading his side, became disheartened. When he noticed the persons with whom he would have to fight, he was overcome with emotion. He declared that he would rather give up his right to the kingdom than to fight with his kith and kin. The Lord then gave the divine instruction to Arjuna in the form of Gita; it deals with the difficult issues of man's spiritual journey.

Modern science recognizes the process of the evolution of man through gradual transformations, from the lowest forms to the highest. But it leaves the most vital step—the ethical or moral development of man—completely untouched. Modern science avoids the task of the accountability of man's virtues and vices; the ancient Rishis addressed these questions in a meaningful way. Modern science has not even attempted to find what happens to man after his physical death; Hindu philosophy established the very vital link of man from one birth to another, through eons of life cycles. Modern science appears unconcerned with the very purpose of life; Hindu Rishis considered this to be the most pertinent question.

From the beginning, Lord Krishna explains to Arjuna that death is merely a change in the process of a person's eternal life. Death, according to Hindu philosophy, is not the final stage but merely an interlude in the long journey of our souls, which pass through eons of birth cycles to develop and evolve, until they attain the final destination of moral and ethical maturity.

In Gita, the Lord gave the instruction of the highest worth—"detachment". There is also a major, if subtle, departure from the philosophy of renunciation, or *sanyasa,* as had been preached earlier. After listening to the spiritual discourse of the Lord, Arjuna did not renounce the world and become a hermit; rather, he fought a fierce battle to uphold the cause of righteousness.[49] Nonviolence, or *ahimsa,* has been qualified. Gita deals with the subject of detachment in a new philosophical manner. Detachment, or *vairagya,* is not so much the relinquishing of the fruit of one's actions but rather an inner transformation, so that we may feel infinitely more happy and joyful through positive feelings in our mind by the performance of the virtuous and spiritual deeds, rather than through obtaining any material possessions. Detachment is essentially the act of giving up something lower so we can be free to grasp the higher.

According to Hindu philosophy, "desires" are the cause of all unrighteous and sinful behavior. Freedom from all sensuous and worldly desires would bring an end to all vices, such as anger, covetousness, pride, jealousy, fear, and sorrow. Material possessions only bring temporary pleasure, which is often smeared with impure, violent, and destructive means to acquire such effects. Spiritual conduct, on the other hand, brings more lasting and permanent inner happiness of joy (*ananda*).

In the Gita, the Lord mentioned very clearly that as humans we simply couldn't do without action. We are so made that even in the Himalayas; we remain active in action, both physically and mentally. Those actions that we do at the lower level of our individual self, the ego, will sooner or later boomerang with evil consequences, but spiritual and virtuous actions, which we offer at the footsteps of the Lord, will bring us the eternal peace and joy. This is the key to Karma yoga.

The Lord explained to the seeker in Arjuna that through good and righteous deeds, we may obtain the happiness of actions here, as well as the bliss of those in our afterlife.

In Gita, the Lord gave the instruction of the highest worth—"detachment". There is also a major, if subtle, departure from the philosophy of renunciation, or sanyasa, as had been preached earlier. After listening to the spiritual discourse of the Lord, Arjuna did not renounce the world and become a hermit; rather, he fought a fierce battle to uphold the cause of righteousness. Gita deals with the subject of detachment in a new philosophical manner. It is essentially the act of giving up something lower so we can be free to grasp the higher. All along, the Lord has prompted Arjuna, to be ever ready to do the righteous deed, and perform whatever duties he is allotted with courage and fearlessness. As a kshatria-soldier, he must not be afraid to fight for the right cause and uphold his honor. He may never be afraid of death, nor of any personal considerations. Only by performing his duties in a proper manner, would he earn the benefit of good merit-karma, which would fetch him spiritual rewards in this life as well as after his death. Gita has laid down clear distinctions between material benefits and the spiritual rewards of eternal joy-ananda, which one feels after performing the righteous deed. The Holy Scripture of Gita has also re-emphasized boldly that there would be good rewards in the here-after; that death in Hindu philosophy is merely an interlude in the long journey of the soul, and not an end by itself.

Spiritual Gems from Tirukural: III

"Food, clothing and such do not differ much among people;
what distinguishes good men from others is modesty."

"Their families decrease and their vices increase when men,
ensnared in sloth, do not put forth earnest effort."

"As a man's shadow follows his footsteps wherever he goes,
even so will destruction pursue those who commit sinful deeds."

"All that you learn, learn perfectly, and
thereafter keep your conduct worthy of that learning."

"Words from the lips of upright men
are like a steadying staff in a slippery place."

"Give to the poor and become praiseworthy.
Life offers no greater reward than this."

"They say love's greatness is this: it yields to good families
worldly happiness here and heavenly bliss hereafter."

"Disparaging words are painful even when uttered in jest.
Hence, knowers of human nature are courteous even to enemies"

"A married woman is one who vigilantly guards herself,
cares for her husband and protects their unblemished
reputation."

"Touch, taste, sight, smell and hearing are the senses--
he who controls these five magically controls the world."

"There is nothing too difficult for the man who
consciously conceives and carefully executes his work."

"A fortune amassed by fraud may appear to prosper
but will all too soon perish altogether."

(Source: Spiritual Teachings-Himalayan Academy, Hawaii, USA)

23 The Spiritual Teachings of Gita

Some of the most important *slokas* (verses) are reproduced below:

"Whence has this dejection come upon thee at this critical hour, for this is unworthy of noble people, bringing neither heaven nor fame."
    —Chapter 2, verse 2

Thus, in the very beginning of this greatest of Hindu scriptures, the Lord utters a clear and unambiguous message: to be firm, to be courageous, and to fight for right action at all costs. Personal and family considerations are not of much importance for noble people when the question of righteousness is at stake.

"Just as the soul in this body passes through childhood, youth, and old age, so does it pass into another body; the steadfast is not deluded."
    —Chapter 2, verse 13

Hindu spirituality believes in the eternal nature of the soul. The physical body is considered but a tool with which the soul can perform, through eons of births.

"Your right is to work only, but never to be attached to the fruits thereof. Let the fruit of action be not your object, nor let your attachment be to inaction."
    —Chapter 2, verse 47

The Supreme Lord exhorts man that he should let go of attachment to the lower self and material gains, and instead, unite with the Divine. Working vigorously for a spiritual duty, without any selfish motive, is regarded as the most worthy achievement in life. In Gita, detachment is not in renouncing the work, but rather it is essentially the act of giving up something of lower value so we can be free to grasp the higher.

"But a man of disciplined mind, though moving about amongst the objects of the senses but with his senses under control, is free from likes and dislikes, and thereby attains tranquility."
    —Chapter 2, verse 64

In this important verse, there is a clear directive of how a person may attain peace of mind by controlling the sensual desires, and then how to move further toward surrendering oneself to the Divine.

"The virtuous that partake of what is left after sacrifice are absolved of all sins. Those who eat for the sake of nourishing their bodies alone eat only sin."
    —Chapter 3, verse 13

Work has been assigned as duty in Hindu scriptures. Our daily work is also to be taken as a form of worship—the *yagna*. This philosophy is based on the spiritual principle that we all are but one family. As in the home, the householder first takes care of the needs of other family members before paying attention to his own needs.

"For whatever a great man does, the same is done by others as well. Whatever standard he sets, people follow."
—Chapter 3, verse 21

Those who are the elders in the family and community, those who are teachers, and those who are leaders have an additional responsibility to set a good example for others. They need to perform good and noble acts so that they may inspire others to do likewise.

"Let a man lift himself by himself; let him not degrade himself, for the self alone is the friend of the self and self alone is the enemy of the self."
—Chapter 6, verse 5

In the Bhagavad Gita, more than in any other religious scripture, taking full responsibility for one's actions is explained. Man alone must meditate and exercise his free will to free himself from the lower, sensual world to reach the higher, spiritual life.

"Having set in a place his firm seat ..."

"Concentrating the mind and controlling the functions of mind and senses, he should practice yoga for self-purification."

"Let him firmly hold his body, head, and neck erect and still..." *"Serene in mind and fearless ... his mind brought under control and fixed in Me."*

"Ever contended, the yogi of subdued mind attains lasting peace consisting of Supreme Bliss."
—Chapter 6, verses 11–15

In these verses are given the complete instructions for performing meditation and yoga. It is through the meditation (*dhyana* and *sadhana*) that one reaches the Divine, abandoning the worldly thoughts. It is to the immense recognition of the ancient Hindu sages that millions of people around the world sit and meditate precisely according to these directions.

"But the yogi, who strives with diligence, cleansed of all sins, perfecting himself through many lives, and then attains to the highest goal."
—Chapter 6, verse 45

Hindu philosophy believes in the continuity of the soul journey through eons of birth and death cycles until it becomes perfected after becoming free from all sins and evils. The body is used as a working place to purify the soul, to make it fit for the final ascent into the

Divine.

"At the time of death, with mind full of faith and devotion, meditating on me, he reaches the Supreme Divine."

—Chapter 8, verse 10

The Lord emphasized the importance of meditating on God at the time of death, thus starting the great tradition among Hindus to become more religious and spiritual in the later part of their lives.

"He who has no ill will to any being who is friendly and compassionate, free from egoism and attachment, even minded in pain and in pleasure, and forgiving."

—Chapter 12, verse 13

If we love God with all our heart, see Him in all beings, and do not worry about the rewards thereof, we shall usher peace and joy in our life.

"Fearlessness, purity of heart, steadfast in the divine knowledge, charity, self-restraint, sacrifice, study of the scriptures, austerity, honesty, and integrity—these are the divine virtues of the spiritual person."

—Chapter 16, verse 1

"Nonviolence, harmlessness, absence of anger, renunciation, equanimity, abstinence of malicious talk, compassion, freedom from greed, gentleness, modesty, absence of fickleness."

—Chapter 16, verse 2

"Splendor, forgiveness, courage, cleanliness, purity, absence of animosity, freedom from vanity—these are all some more qualities of the person endowed with divinity."

—Chapter 16, verse 3

Thus, Hindu philosophy has offered a long list of moral and spiritual values for mankind in these most precious verses of the Bhagavad Gita. The Bhagavad Gita has been hailed all around the world as the torchbearer of spiritual virtues.

"The happiness, which may be like poison in the beginning and like nectar in the end, born of blissful knowledge of the Self, that happiness is sattvic."

—Chapter 18, verse 37

The Lord again narrates the ancient Upanishad teaching. We may not be tempted by what appears sweet in the beginning, nor may we reject that which is bitter. The material and sensual rewards often appear tempting and attractive in the beginning. The joy and bliss of the spiritual and virtuous deeds are more important.

In Bhagavad Gita, a person is directly held responsible for his behavior and action. In Gita, more than in any other religious scripture, taking full responsibility for one's actions is explained. Man alone must meditate and exercise his free will to liberate himself from the lower, sensual world towards the higher, spiritual life. Some have the tendency to think that by just completely surrendering to God, all their problems would be solved and wishes fulfilled. Gita teaches the great lesson of work in the spiritual and virtuous manner and to perform all the duties most sincerely and diligently.

Bhagavad Gita also puts a very pointing finger on the elders and leaders of the community. The elders need to be more careful and responsible in all their behavior.

Gita lays down detailed instructions for performing meditation and yoga. It is through meditation (dhyana and sadhana) that one reaches the Divine, after successfully abandoning worldly thoughts. The Lord emphasized the importance of meditating on God at the time of death, thus starting the great tradition among Hindus to become more religious and spiritual in the latter part of their lives.

Bhagavad Gita thus culminates the spiritual teachings of Vedas and Upanishads, by expending a more direct approach, presenting God in human form (Lord Krishna) to deliver the message in its most authoritative and convincing manner. Even so, God has also been presented in a new manner as a very close friend and well-wisher. God even drives the vehicle, the chariot of Arjuna in the war-front to demonstrate the most intimate and informal relationship between the being and the Creator! Arjuna remains most humble and obedient before Lord Krishna, recognizing the Lord as the Supreme power above anything. These innovative modifications and variations in Gita conform to the dynamic character of Hindu philosophy.

24 Idol Worship: The Plethora of Gods

Without a doubt, Hinduism has the unique distinction of worshipping the most gods of any religion. The credit for this goes to our ancient sages, the *Rishis*, who adored and glorified these gods in an ingenious manner. Not only is each god grand and divine, but he also has his own unique personality and attributes. In the Hindu pantheon, the gods are like the icons with which the ordinary devotee may identify the Divine more easily. Ancient scriptures portray the gods by using a story telling method, making the theme more important than the event.[50]

In the epic scriptures, with the historical tales of Lord Rama and Lord Krishna, the concept of God incarnate became established in Hinduism. Both Lord Rama and Lord Krishna are considered as Vishnu incarnates in the Hindu pantheon. Lord Rama is known for his sense of propriety, or *maryada*. He would never do anything that was inappropriate. Lord Krishna is complete in all respects—the *puran avtara*—but he is also the god of love, or *Prema*. He has a bewitching smile and a handsome face, and he holds a melodious flute to his lips. He would never utter words of anger or hatred. Every Hindu has a choice to choose his own God. He may also choose many gods, instead of just one. By thinking of a god and meditating on him, a person would imbibe the divine virtues and attributes within his or her own self. This was indeed the grand plan of our learned sages, which has worked wonderfully well throughout millennia.

God is an evolutionary concept in Hinduism. As a person ascends gradually on the path of spirituality, through eons of birth cycles, his/her divinity shines more and more. Some of the most important ones, apart from the primary trinity of gods, are presented:
Lord Ganpati, who is also called Lord Ganesh, has always been one of the most favorite gods. In the Hindu mythology, he is the son of Lord Shiva and the goddess Parvati. He has an elephant head, signifying great wisdom. Lord Ganpati is adored as the god who can remove any obstruction. He is, therefore, also called *Vighna-harta* (one who removes obstacle) Whenever a Hindu embarks on any auspicious or major venture, such as a wedding or a new home or business, the first invocation is to Lord Ganpati. Lord Ganpati is also regarded as the

embodiment of *Shabda Brahman;* guiding and blessing all our spiritual knowledge.

Lord Subramanya is the other son of Lord Shiva. He is the six-faced god, signifying his multifaceted personality. He is much venerated, especially in South India, as the god of valor. He is regarded as the master guru of Kundalini yoga, born of Lord Shiva's mind, to awaken and propel the soul onward in its spiritual journey. He is also known by many other names, such as *Muruga, Murkan, Kartikeya, Skanda, Shanmuga,* and *Kumara.*

Hanuman Bhagwan is a revered god of the Ramayana epic. He is the leader of the monkey army, who helped Lord Rama in searching for and finally rescuing the goddess Sri Sita. He was the epitome of service and sincerity. He remained celibate throughout his life and, in accordance with Hindu philosophy, conserved all his energy. Many sing the popular *"Hanuman Chalisa"*, the long prayer in verse, in honor of Lord Hanuman. He is even considered as the incarnation of Lord Shiva and the son of the god of winds, Vayu, thus establishing a pattern in the Hindu pantheon of creating relationships between the different gods.

Satya-Narayan Bhagwan is the god of boons. Hindus worship this god frequently to express their gratitude for favors received and for a good life. Many worship *Shri Satya Narayan* as the combined form of three gods: Lord Brahma, Lord Vishnu, and Lord Maheshwara.

Lord Dattatreya is the god in whom all three forms of the primary gods, Brahma, Vishnu, and Shiva—also manifest together.

Narad Bhagwan is the popular mythological god who works as a messenger between the sages and the Supreme Divine and is hence named as *Deva Rishi* (God's sage). In ancient scriptures there are many tales of this deity, who skillfully and with a great sense of humor, navigates complicated and difficult situations.

There are innumerable other gods, such as *Kubera,* god of wealth; *Garuda,* god of birds; *Himavan,* god of mountains; *Anathan,* god of snakes; and many more.

Of the three primary Hindu gods, Lord Vishnu took repeated incarnations in different times. Even as Lord Krishna, he manifested again and again, subsequently as Lord Tirupati in South India, Lord Shree Nath in Rajasthan, Jagan Nath in Puri Orissa, and Lord Swaminarayan in Gujarat.

Along with the male gods, the female goddesses also proliferated in Hindu religion, either alone or as the consorts of the male gods. Thus, innumerable goddesses appeared on the Hindu stage. Some of the most important goddesses, apart from those mentioned earlier, are Sri Sita as the consort of Lord Rama and also as the earth goddess; Sri Radha as the consort of Lord Krishna; Sri Ganga as goddess of the River Ganges; Cow as the earth goddess; and Kali, Uma, and Sati as the consorts of Shiva.

Hindu philosophy recognizes that spirituality is manifested more prominently in certain individuals and is then called *vibhuti*. **Satyavadi Raja Harishchandra, Shravan Kumar, Bhagat Prahalada, Bhagat Dhruva, Ahilya Devi, Jatayu, Raja Janak, Rishi Visvamitra, Savitri and Satyavan, Gargi and Maitreyi, Maharathi Karana, Sri Radha, Sri Yashoda** and many others are mentioned in the Hindu tradition. Parents often read these stories to their small children to instill good behavior.

There has been much speculation regarding the phenomenon of so many gods in Hinduism, but this need not be disturbing. According to Hindu philosophy, behind the façade of so many manifestations, there is but one, universal, eternal, omnipotent, formless, and transcendental Divine.

There has been some criticism regarding idol worship, known as *murti puja*, in Hinduism. Originally, in the Vedic period, there was no idol worship. This practice may have been adapted from the Dravidian culture of temple worship. The description of God in the Upanishads as *Neti-Neti* (Not This-Not This) points to the transcendental and formless aspect of the Divine. The idol worship or *Murti Puja*, however, has been securely accepted as an icon or symbol to represent the Divine.

Robert Arnett, the internationally known author of *India Unveiled*, has very aptly said:

"Hinduism is greatly misunderstood in the West. Most Occidentals do not realize that Hinduism is a monotheistic belief only in one God, who, as creator, is beyond time, space, and physical form. The entire pantheon of Hindu gods and goddesses are merely symbolic representations of different attributes of the One Un-manifested Spirit."

The concept of many gods evolved from the very beginning. First, it was the "nature gods" like the sun-suray, moon-chandrama, fire-agni etc. As and when the early people observed different manifestations of the superior nature elements, they considered them as different gods-the powers beyond their

imaginations. As Hinduism was not founded by one single person, various interpretations and opinions were assimilated without protest and dispute. In fact, this also laid the foundation of absorbing the concept of many in place of one in almost all philosophical perceptions and beliefs. As time passed, different ethnic communities presented their own viewpoints about the forms of gods as they perceived. God was projected with different attributes and potentials. He was conceived as an infinite power of knowledge, and virtue. Soon it was realized that behind so many, there is but one formless, transcendental, and eternal God, as described in the Upanishads. On the other hand, this model of many gods also has persisted in Hindu theology, with even more new gods being presented periodically. Occasionally living persons with highest spiritual virtues too have been deemed and worshipped as gods.

25 Goddesses in Hinduism: The Icons of Female Power

The concept of goddess has been present since the prehistoric period of the Sindhu-Saraswati civilization. Around the same time, a similar female goddess phenomenon also became noticeable in other world cultures. There are carvings of exuberant feminine deities in the Saraswati-Sindhu excavations, and there are similar figures in the Greek and Egyptian culture.

In the early Vedic period, the female aspect of the Divine was pushed to the background by the prominently masculine *Brahminic* tradition. Even though there appeared to be serious discrimination against women in the Vedic laws and rituals, this soon was more than compensated by assigning high status to female goddesses. The Vedas asserted man as the head of the family. Soon, however, the female goddesses projected women in an equal, occasionally superior position, thus making adequate counterchecks for a power struggle between the two genders!

Goddesses in human form also appeared later as consorts of their male gods: Parvati, the goddess of power, with Lord Shiva; Saraswati, the goddess of learning, with Lord Brahma; and Lakshmi, the goddess of wealth, with Lord Vishnu. Hindus recognized women as the creative power, or *Shakti*. In all Hindu rituals, the female consort became an essential and equal participant. The Puranic scripture *Devi Mahatmya*, which was most likely compiled between the fifth and seventh centuries, describes at length the concept and phenomenon of the supreme goddess in all her glory. Scriptures mention that Lord Rama prayed before goddess Durga, before embarking on war with Ravana. Thus woman became the symbol of power and energy in Hindu philosophy. Also when the man wants prosperity, he worships goddess Lakshmi; when he wants knowledge, he worships goddess Saraswati. Thus woman occupies the highest status, complimentary with man.

Unlike most other religions, Hinduism recognizes both the father and the mother aspect of God, the mother aspect being even more appealing to many devotees. When in distress, one is apt to approach mother more likely than father!

Introduction of such a high status to womanhood in Hinduism heralded a great revolution in human society. The downgrading of women was perhaps the legacy of the olden times, when men wielded the power by hunting and other physical activities, and women served as humble submissive partners. In many other cultures, women would have to wait until almost the twentieth century to gain equal rights. Even so, human nature betrayed its weakness time and again, and women did suffer many hardships and humiliations over the centuries in Hindu society.

Hailing the Ganges and a few other rivers as goddesses is rather unique in Hindu culture. The river, especially the Ganges, has been accorded the highest status because of its enormous contribution toward man's life and prosperity. According to the scriptures, a few drops of water from the Holy Ganges would attain salvation for a dying man. So too the cow has been accorded the divine status. In the ancient verses of the Rig Veda, the cow is referred as goddess and is identified as the mother of the gods, Aditi. In Hindu mythology, *Kamadhenu*, a cow able to fulfill all desires, was the chief possession of Indra, lord of gods.

In her book *Hindu Goddesses*, Chitralekha Singh mentions:

"Durga worship occupies a prominent place. Her name implies that she is 'invincible', 'inaccessible', or a terrific goddess. She also appears as Uma, Parvati, Gauri, Kali, Sati, Tara, and other 1008 names. (Each name would have her special attributes.) In all these forms, the goddess conquered the demons and upheld the reign of virtue over vice."

"The mother aspect of the Hindu goddess has been eulogized repeatedly. Alongside the energy (Shakti) component, the abundant motherly love of the female goddesses of the Hindu religion has been the subject of much study and propagation. In the recent times especially, the erotic nature of the female goddess has been severely curtailed. The mother phenomenon has been instead promoted."

"The most popular images of Vaishnodevi, Maa Ambaji, and Santoshi Maa, may be seen as a religious movement in this direction." [51]

This shift in the attribute of the *Shakti* goddess from the fierce expression of the destroyer to the loving expression of a mother has become more prominent in recent times. This, in fact, is in accordance with the basic pattern of the Hindu dynamic philosophy, which opts for change with times and situations.

One of the most popular versions of the Hindu goddess is of *Kali*. She is portrayed as black female with a protruding tongue, wearing a necklace of human skulls and standing over the body of her consort, Lord Shiva. Goddess Kali originally hails from prehistoric times. Her fierce looks are meant to challenge and frighten the wrongdoer. Sri Ramakrishna however adopted the recent shift in the attributes of Kali, to demonstrate the compassionate and loving motherhood.

There also has been an unmistakable spurt of activity in the female religious leadership in modern Hindu society. Sri Sarda Devi, who held the highest position of authority after her husband, Sri Ramakrishna Paramhansa, passed away, is a shining example of divinity in the human form in our own times. She adopted the ancient dictum of the Mahabharata: *tasmat tikshnataram mridu*, which translates to "*by gentleness one can overcome the greatest difficulty in the world.*" Repeatedly, she emphasized, "*Do not look at the faults of others, lest your eyes should become impure.*"

The energy, or the *Shakti*, phenomenon has often been associated with animal sacrifices. This is especially noticeable in the Kali temples, but many other Shakti goddesses, such as Vaishnodevi, Ambaji, and Santoshi Maa, as well as the present Hindu female spiritual leaders, dispensed with animal sacrifices and meat eating.

There is a growing feeling in the world that the female power of spiritual energy, *Shakti*, in the form of love, compassion, and the strong arm of protection will become the savior of the mankind in future.

Although there is evidence of ancient feminine deities in the prehistoric Saraswati-Sindhu civilization, the female aspect was pushed to the background in the Vedic Era due to the dominance of the masculine Brahminic tradition. Women were not even allowed to study the scriptures! Soon however this misstep was rectified. In the Upanishads we encounter two very fierce female scholars, Maitreyi and Gargi, who pose most arduous and demanding questions to the learned sages. Later, in Puranic scriptures, feminine deities assumed their full stature, in the form of female consorts to their male counterparts. As is the custom in Hindu theology, the gods often bow down to and worship each other; scriptures mention that Lord Rama prayed before Goddess Durga before embarking on his war with Ravana. Thus woman became the symbol of power and energy in Hindu philosophy. When man wants prosperity, he worships Goddess Lakshmi; when he wants knowledge, he worships Goddess Saraswati. It is rather exceptional that even rivers like Ganga (Ganges) and animals like cow were allotted the 'Goddess' status in Hindu culture. In more recent times, the soft loving mother aspect of Goddess has been more eulogized in preference to the fierce energy (Shakti) identity. Sri Ramakrishna worshipped Goddess Kali Maa, more in the soft motherly form. His consort Sri Sarda Devi, who held the highest position after his passing away, remains a shining example of divinity in the human form in our own times. She adopted the ancient dictum of the Mahabharata: tasmat tikshnataram mridu, which translates to "by gentleness one can overcome the greatest difficulty in the world." Repeatedly, she emphasized, "Do not look at the faults of others, lest your eyes should become impure." The dynamic pattern is noticeable.

26 Jainism: Renunciation and Non-violence

Jainism started with Mahavira (599–527 BCE), who was an elder contemporary of Buddha. Jains, however, believe that he was the last of the twenty-four *Tirthankaras* (liberated souls). His immediate predecessor, Parsvanatha, is also a historical figure who lived in the eighth century BCE. It is said that the first *Tirthankara* was Rushabhadeva, who probably lived around 8500 years ago. The naked standing figures (*kayotsarga*) of the Sindhu-Saraswati civilization are considered to be the representations of Rushabhadeva.[52] He had a son Bharata, after whom the name *Bharat* was expediently adopted for ancient India.[53]

The roots of the Jain philosophy thus go toward the distant past to the prehistoric era of the Indian subcontinent, when meditation, an ascetic way of living, and vegetarianism seemingly first found their place in human history. These philosophical concepts became established as the ancient Indian ideology of the oral tradition, which in course of time would feed all the emerging spiritual philosophies, including Hinduism, Jainism, and Buddhism. Later, it became known in part as *Sramana* ideology. *Sraman* in Sanskrit means monk.[54]

The possibility of the common origin of all these religions is thus very strong. The teachings are similar in many respects. The basic concepts of Hinduism—namely *karma*, *punar-janam* (reincarnation), and *moksha* (salvation)—are also seen in Jainism, Buddhism, and later in Sikhism. These concepts are unique to the religions of Indian origin and are therefore a strong binding factor for this group of religions.

It was in the period of Mahavira and Buddha, however, that certain castes in Hindu society started to protest against the dominance and authority of the *Brahmin* upper classes of Aryan origin—the *Brahmins* set themselves apart as exclusive intermediaries between mortals and the Divine Supreme. There was also protest against animal sacrifices in the rituals (*karma kanda*).

Jainism owes its origin to the philosophy of *Jina*, the conqueror. Jina was coined when Mahavira returned after twelve years of rigorous ascetic practices to win complete control over the erring and destructive mind; he started to preach the *Jaina* path of purification of the soul.

Many centuries before the modern concepts of democracy and individual freedom, Jainism gave the world the philosophy of *anekta*, the concept of different points of view. The philosophy of non-absolutism was a tool against dogmatism, which perhaps is the root cause of many human conflicts.[55]

The ancient Indian philosophy of *ahimsa* went beyond ordinary non-violence. It is the true gentleness in preventing the subtlest harm to anyone. *Ahimsa* has occupied special attention in Indian culture through different periods of time: There is clear call for *ahimsa* in the earliest scriptures, the Vedas. In the epic of the Mahabharata, there is mention of *"ahimsa parmo dharma"*—non-injury is the prime religion. The teaching of one universal all-pervasive divinity as propagated in the Upanishads creates an attitude of reverence, benevolence, and compassion for all animate and inanimate beings. Belief in the philosophy of karma envisages that all that we send out to others in thought, word, or deed will return to us, in this life or in future reincarnations by some cosmic process. Even so, in both the epic scriptures of Ramayana and Mahabharata, violence could not be totally avoided and the war was resorted as a last resort to uphold the righteousness and protect the innocent.

Patanjali (200 BCE) regards *ahimsa* as a precondition (*yama*) and a vow before embarking in the training of yoga. Two thousand years ago, saint Tiruvalluvar said it so simply: *"All suffering recoils on the wrongdoer himself. Thus, those desiring not to suffer should refrain from causing others pain"* (Tirukural, 320). Jain believers not only are vegetarian, but they also take special precautions to avoid hurting even the smallest of the creatures, such as insects and worms. No wonder, then, many felt these teachings were too difficult to be practical in everyday life. Only monks were to lead a life of extreme simplicity. Jain monks cover long distances, walking barefoot lest they may hurt any creatures underneath their feet by wearing shoes. They wear a cloth mask in front of their mouths to prevent the inadvertent swallowing of any organisms in the air. They eat the simplest food, avoiding eating any root vegetables, for example, which may contain living germs. The Jain monks and even the laity hold extended fasts for many days in order to purify their souls. Even though Buddha shifted his stance in favor of a moderate middle path, the position taken by Mahavira was un-compromising in this regard. When Mahavira started this religion, he also introduced the order of female priests, which in itself was a revolutionary action in its time. Strict adherence to the principle of renunciation, however, divided the Jain society into two divisions: the *Digambaras*—the sky-clad—in which the monks would be totally naked, and the *Svetambaras*, in which the monks wore white robes. These extreme attitudes would soon become socially unpractical. Even as the male monks in the *Digambara* sect were naked, the Jain nuns were not required to be without clothes. Over the course of time, all the harsh restrictions were confined to only the monks and nuns, but the laity was relieved from many constraints. Indeed, most of the lay devotees preferred becoming well placed financially, well fed, and well dressed. They were, of course, expected to observe the principle of the three jewels of Jain teaching: right knowledge, right faith, and right conduct.

There are, at present, about ten million Jains residing mainly in India. Earlier, Jainism did not spread beyond India, as there were severe travel restrictions for the Jain monks; there also was disinterest in the Jain community for propagating their faith to others. Today, Jains have invested their assets in more productive and philanthropic fields. Jain temples are world famous for their artwork, especially in marble. They avoid any activity that would involve violence, and they do not engage in trades engaged in leatherwork or any commerce involving the use of animals for profit. Many ancient concepts of Jainism compare favorably with modern ideas, such as the rights of animals, the preservation of wild life, and ecological issues.

Mahavira preached thus:

He who knows what is bad for himself knows what is bad for others, and he who knows what is bad for others knows what is bad for himself. One whose mind is at peace and who is free from passion does not desire to live at the expense of others. He who understands the nature of sin against earth, water, air, fire, plants, and animals is a true sage and understands karma.[56]

Albeit Jainism started with Mahavira in 5th century BCE, its roots were probably established much earlier. It is believed that in the distant ancient period, the estimated period of which remains unknown, a new tradition of human life became founded in the puniya bhoomi (pure land) of Bharat (Indian subcontinent). This became known later as the Sramana ideology. Sraman in Sanskrit means 'monk'.

This new system was based on the concepts of meditation, an ascetic way of living, and vegetarianism- these philosophies seemingly first found their place in human history. The Sramana ideology would later feed, in different ways, all the religions- Hinduism, Jainism, Buddhism, and Sikhism-that were founded in India. Jainism also introduced the concept of 'anekta'-different points of view. In today's world, which is full of conflicts arising out of dogmatic attitudes, such open-arm views of the Dharma philosophies of the Indian origin may serve as a great antidote. Inspired by ancient Sramana ideology, Jainism adopted "renunciation" rather extremely. The Jain monks and even the laity hold extended fasts for many days in order to purify their souls. Even though Buddha shifted his stance in favor of a moderate middle path, the position taken by Mahavira was uncompromising in this regard. Strict adherence to the principle of renunciation, however, divided the Jain society into two divisions: the Digambaras—the sky-clad—in which the monks would be totally naked, and the Svetambaras, in which the monks wore white robes. These extreme attitudes would soon become socially unpractical; only the monks observed the codes fully.

NOTE: Jainism used the local dialect Prakrit (Ardha-magdi)

27 Spiritual Teachings of the Mahavira

The most important attribute of both Jainism and Buddhism is in the adoption of a simple and logical attitude of virtuous behavior for salvation of the soul. Good, ethical conduct takes the place of the mystical power of the Divine. This has been described as rational understanding, or *samyak dristi*. Jainism does not believe in God as an individual identity but rather as an ideal.[57]

To their credit, Jain monks roamed across the country, carrying the message of religion and spirituality to the masses, rather than expecting the seekers to come to them in the Himalayas or other distant places. The main teachings of Jainism are presented below:

The *Namaskar Mantra* (the Fivefold Obeisance):

Salutations to the prophets (*arhats*).
Salutations to the liberated souls (*siddhas*).
Salutations to the preceptors (*acharyas*).
Salutations to the religious instructors (*upadhyas*).
Salutations to all the saints (*sadhus*).

- Supreme forgiveness, supreme humility, supreme straightforwardness, supreme truthfulness, supreme purity, supreme self-restraint, supreme austerity, supreme renunciation, supreme detachment, and supreme continence are the ten characteristics of (Jain) *Dharma*
- His forbearance is perfect who does not get excited with anger.
- A monk who does not boast even slightly of his family lineage, caste, learning, austerity, scriptural knowledge, and character practices humility.
- He who is always cautious not to insult others truly commands respect.
- We call him a *Brahmin* who remains unaffected by objects of sensual pleasures, even while surrounded by them.
- He who observes the most difficult virtue of celibacy is neither infatuated nor attracted, even on observing feminine charms.

- Fight your own self. What will you gain by fighting with external foes? One who conquers one's self, he experiences supreme bliss.
- One should not be complacent with a small debt, a slight wound, a spark of fire, and insignificant passion.
- Service to the preceptor, avoiding the company of ignorant people, scriptural study, solitude, contemplation on the meaning of holy texts—these constitute the pathway to emancipation.
- Those who take wholesome and healthy food in less quantity never fall sick and do not need the services of a physician.
- As long as the body remains strong, he should use it to practice self-restraint. When the body is devoid of its strength completely, he should renounce it without any attachment, like a lump of clay.
- After listening to scriptures, a person knows what good and evil deeds are, and having known both, he should practice that which is conducive to reaching the highest goal.
- The seven vices (from which a householder should abstain) are: (1) sexual conduct with a woman other than one's own wife, (2) gambling, (3) taking intoxicants, (4) hunting, (5) uttering harsh words, (6) giving disproportionate punishment, and (7) misappropriation of others' property.
- One should desist from buying stolen goods, inciting another to commit theft, and avoiding the laws of the State.
- One should refrain from accumulation of unlimited property due to insatiable greed, as it becomes a pathway to hell and results in numerous faults.
- Carefulness in speech consists of avoiding slanderous, ridiculous, harsh, critical, boastful, and meaningless talk as such carelessness brings good neither to oneself nor to others.
- To get up at the arrival of an elder, to welcome him with folded hands, to offer him (an honored) seat, to serve him with a feeling of reverence—these constitute humility.

Both Jainism and Buddhism have adopted simple ethical behavior as a model for religious teaching in place of the mystical power of God. Both also introduced the arrangement of sending monks around to preach instead of the laity traveling long distances to hear and talk to learned sages. This practice too was soon picked up by the Hindu society and has continued to grow till present day. Jain spiritual preachers vow to live a celibate life, and live in most simple and austere manner. They may never get angry, nor be boastful in any manner. Jain priests may not insult anyone, and may not succumb to sensual pleasures anytime.

There is a general appreciation of such conduct in religious persons; as such, setting up and pursuing such lofty standards of moral behavior would always be regarded as most worthy and commendable.

NOTE: All quotes are adapted from *Thus Spake Lord Mahavira*

Spiritual Gems from Tirukural: IV

It is the principle of the pure in heart never to injure others,
even when they themselves have been hatefully injured.

"There is nothing too difficult for a man who, before he acts,
deliberates with chosen friends and reflects privately."

"Let a man conquer by forbearance
those who in their arrogance have wronged him."

"As the intense fire of the furnace refines gold to brilliance, so does
the burning suffering of austerity purify the soul to resplendence."

"Beware of leaving any work undone, remembering that the world
abandons those who abandon their work unfinished."

"Perseverance generates prosperity,
and the lack of it engenders poverty."

"Procrastination, forgetfulness, sloth and sleep--
these four shape the ship bearing those destined for ruin."

"The world has no use for those who have no use for resolute
action, whatever other strengths they may possess."

"Respect is not just in words and behavior.
We must respect others' viewpoints and wishes."

"Forbidden deeds, however well accomplished, inflict sorrow
on those who seek after rather than shun them."

"Never indulge in admiring yourself.
Never be drawn toward deeds that do not benefit others."

"Four traits define the true gentleman: a smiling face,
a generous hand, a courteous demeanor and kindly words"

(Source: Spiritual Teachings-Himalayan Academy, Hawaii, USA)

28 Buddhism Emerges

Around the same period of history (500 BCE), another major religion of India, Buddhism, was born. This is the only religion that originated in India but spread and flourished more outside its borders. Buddhism took strong roots in China, Tibet, Cambodia, Thailand, Japan, Indonesia, Laos, Malaysia, Myanmar, Korea, and Sri Lanka, and it is still very popular in many of these countries. Buddhist monks also went to the West, to far places such as Egypt, Syria, and Greece. It is believed that as many as eighty-four thousand monks were sent out of the country to propagate the spiritual message of the Buddha. According to historian Professor Mahaffy, Buddhist monks preached in Palestine and Syria a couple of centuries before the birth of Christ.[58]
Socrates, the famous Greek philosopher (469 – 399 BC), and teacher of Plato, in his writing has quoted, "*The soul being immortal, having been born again and again, and having seen all things that exist; ...all learning is but a recollection...*". (Hinduism Today July-Sept '17, p 14) This gives a strong indication that he may have come in contact with Hindu/Buddhist Rishis in some way.
In the opinion of the learned Anglican priest C. F. Andrews, the ideal of *ahimsa* (non-violence) was planted in a holy manner from the Hindu origin. In India, however, after the initial period of its rapid rise, there was a sharp decline in the influence of Buddhism, mainly due to the heavy destruction of the Buddhist monasteries at Nalanda and other places by the Muslim invaders. The renaissance of Hinduism brought about by Sri Shankaracharya was another important reason.

Gautama was the prince born in northeast India. His original name was Siddhartha. After his birth, an astrologer predicted that he would be an ascetic. His father, the king, did not want this to happen, so he prevented the young prince from coming into contact with any sorrowful events, which might turn his mind toward a more spiritual search. The king's plan failed, however, as the prince did come face to face with the realities of old age, disease, and death. The phenomenon of *kaal chakra*, or the cycle of time, was impressed deeply upon his mind. Later, this concept of inevitable suffering would become the pivotal point of his teachings to the entire world.

Prince Siddhartha, who was by now married and had a son, left the palace in search of enlightenment. He performed penance for twelve years by going through extreme degrees of physical austerity and discomfort. Toward the end of this period of penance, he once nearly fainted from hunger and exhaustion. He then realized that by physical torture alone man would not attain the spiritual goal. He therefore gave up extreme degrees of penance, just as he had given up the extreme degrees of indulgence twelve years previously. He adopted the new middle path of moderation. This would be the cornerstone of his spiritual practices in the future. But it was ultimately the process of deep meditation, while sitting under the famous banyan tree at Sarnath that brought him the enlightenment he had been seeking for so long. Later, when asked whether he was a god or an angel, he simply acknowledged, *"I am awake, and I know."* [59] He came to be known as Buddha—the wise one!

The middle path of Buddha is, in fact, the path of using one's own superior mind intelligently and with spiritual compassion and love. Buddha's avowed declaration not to fall before the worldly temptations (*mara*) and, at the same time, not to succumb blindly to the demands of the extreme renunciation (*sanyasin*) is truly a major transformation in religious philosophy. The Buddha also asserted the role of free will in human development. Although Buddhism became separated as a new faith, Hinduism adapted the spiritual thinking of Buddha in a positive and effective manner. There appears to be a misconception that Buddha did not believe in the Vedas. In fact, he rejected only the ritualistic nature of the Vedic teachings. His teachings are otherwise mainly based on the Vedic concepts.

When anyone insulted Lord Buddha, he simply ignored him, saying, *"I do not accept what you offered me. Your gift (of abuses) therefore stays with you!"* He introduced a policy of tact in place of arguments and quarrels. Later, his famous disciple Emperor Ashoka laid down his arms after a successful though bloody war, in quest of peace and accord. His reign of forty years is considered unparalleled in history, as he may have been the first ruler to condemn war without qualification. He sent religious peace missions to many lands, such as Burma, Ceylon, Egypt, Syria, and Macedonia. He called for a conference of all faiths to promote dialogue and discussion in place of war and quarrel. He however laid a strict condition that no one would be allowed to talk derogatory about anyone else. This may be regarded as the beginning of the interfaith movement in the world. Among his many inscriptions of Buddhist teachings on the pillars, one is most notable: *"For he who does reverence to his own sect while disparaging the sects of others with intent to enhance the splendor of his own sect, in reality by such conduct inflicts severest injury on his own sect."* [60] Buddha taught compassion for all, including those who have caused harm to us. To return good for evil, benevolence for injury, love for hate, and compassion for harm are some of the characteristics of the qualities of the *bodhi mind.*[61] Buddha also pointed out that human happiness is completely interdependent; helping others helps us. The message of the Buddha conquered many lands, without sending a single fighting soldier anywhere.

Buddha also rejected the caste system outright and preached religion without the rituals. After the great enlightenment, Buddha immediately saw the need to propagate this vital knowledge to all humanity. He also met his wife, Yashoda, and son, Rahul, whom he had left earlier. He explained that regardless of any material possessions that a son may inherit from his father, the legacy of spiritual teachings is much more worthy and important in life. He then continued to teach for forty-five years before passing away at the age of eighty, on the auspicious day of the full moon. Unlike most other gurus and teachers, he stressed that others should adopt his teachings only when they were convinced about the efficacy of his message in their personal lives.

Modern scientists have discovered that we use only a small fraction of the vast supply of the neurons in the brain. In meditation, we awaken and excite more of these dormant neurons into activity. Some of these neuron centers are activated to think and contemplate in more wise and useful ways than the hitherto used lower centers. We then may see the happenings of the world in an entirely different way, realizing the sacredness of life more vividly, as well as perceiving the spiritual purpose in our universe.

There is great amount of overlapping in the teachings and practices of all the religions that originated on Indian subcontinent. Buddhism and Jainism were essentially reform movements in the Hindu spiritual philosophy. The caste-weary people from all classes jumped onto their bandwagon with great enthusiasm. The priests, who had commanded the highest status, were dispensed with. Human weakness, however, prevailed, with all its faults and foibles. New rituals replaced the old ones. The monks and other holy men came to the forefront in new garb— alas along with all their shortcomings and vulnerabilities!

Changing the practices that make up the religion may not be so difficult, but changing the hearts of the followers is not as easy. Very often, the followers are not able to keep pace with the high ideals of the founders.

According to historian Professor Mahaffy, Buddhist monks preached in Palestine and Syria a couple of centuries before the birth of Christ.

Even though Jainism, Buddhism, and Sikhism later became separate religions, Hindu society accepted them with open arms, and regarded them as "reform" movements. Many of their new and modified changes in course of time would heavily influence Hindu culture. Buddha adopted the new middle path of moderation. This would be the cornerstone of his spiritual practices in the future. This "middle path" of Lord Buddha has also been generally welcomed in Hindu theology. In fact, this philosophy has become the cornerstone of spiritual practices for many persons in the world, regardless of their religion.

It was finally the process of deep meditation, while sitting under the famous banyan tree at Sarnath that brought him the enlightenment he had been seeking for so long. Later, when asked whether he was a god or an angel, he simply acknowledged, "I am awake, and I know." He came to be known as Buddha—the wise one! Meditation has been a watch-word in Hindu religion from ancient times, but Buddha propagated it to a whole new level; the whole world has adopted "meditation" with great enthusiasm and keenness. There are now meditation centers in all places, even in prisons!

The caste system was rejected by Buddha in an outright manner, as he preached a religion without rituals. In the same way, excessive rituals associated with the Hindu religion too have been scorned periodically, right from the Upanishad times. They however continue to remain accepted in Hindu society, although changes and modifications have been adopted continually. Buddha also opted heavily for rational, ethical conduct backed by common sense and free will, in place of rigid scriptural commands. This teaching too has found great favor, especially in the modern generation across the globe. Hinduism has approached all of the emerging religions with a soft, welcoming attitude. Lord Buddha has even been regarded by some Hindus as the ninth avatar (incarnation) of Vishnu.

29 The Spiritual Teachings of Buddha

Buddhism has attracted a large following from all walks of people because of its basic tenet: *Dharma stands for the greatest good of the greatest number of people.* This simple philosophy appeals to many people, regardless of the faith they may be following.

Swami Vivekananda said, *"Buddha, the great one... never thought of a thought and never performed a deed, except for the good of others."*

The ancient method of meditation and change of the inner heart, or *antah-karan*, became more strongly pronounced in Buddha's doctrine. At the same time, he also stressed right association (*satsanga*) as the preliminary step. Both Jainism and Buddhism discarded the classical language of Sanskrit in favor of the local common languages of the masses. The language used in the ancient Buddhist scriptures is *Pali*, which is a modified form of *Prakrit*.

Buddha taught four Noble Truths:
1. The Existence of Sorrow. Sorrow is part of life. We cannot totally avoid it. We must learn to accept it.
2. The Cause of Sorrow. Whatever happens has a cause. The cause may be in the immediate past, or it may be the result of earlier births.
3. The Cessation of Sorrow. Not all but most sorrow can be overcome.
4. There is a way, which leads to the cessation of sorrow.

Buddha also taught the Eightfold Path:
1. Right Understanding (Free from superstition and delusion)
2. Right Thought (Worthy and intelligent thoughts determine our acts.)
3. Right Speech (Be kind and truthful. Avoid idle talk.)
4. Right Actions (Be peaceful and pure.)
5. Right Livelihood (Do not hurt any living beings. Avoid hunting, selling of weapons, liquor, and livestock for slaughtering.)
6. Right Effort (Practice self-training and self-control.)
7. Right Mindfulness (Develop an active, watchful mind)
8. Right Concentration (Practice deep meditation—*dhyana*.)

In the Buddhist scripture, the *Bhante Henepola Gunaratana*, there is special instruction regarding speech:

Skillful speech not only means that we pay attention to the words we speak and to their tone but also requires that our words reflect compassion and concern for others.

Even as Buddhism spread in many countries, its influence in India, on the other hand, lessened over centuries. This is partly attributed to the renaissance efforts of Hinduism by a series of highly spiritual seers, such as Sri Sankara. But it is also believed that there was a genuine accommodation, by both the Hindus and the Buddhists, to live in harmony and accept the viewpoints of one another. Indeed, the relationship of Hinduism to other faiths and sects, which sprang as its offshoots, has always remained conciliatory to a very large extent.

Buddhist teachings are not in variance with the Vedic teachings, but are modified. In this religion, the practice of meditation (already mentioned in ancient Hindu scriptures) has been given the highest importance. The congregation of spiritual worshippers together-"satsang"-too, became an essential tool in spreading the spiritual teachings, thereby replacing the mystical high power of the priest. Even the language used was changed from classical Sanskrit, which had become nearly a monopoly of the Brahminic class, to the common, mass-spoken language, Pali. In Hindu rituals and religious ceremonies, on the other hand, Sanskrit has continued to remain the apex language. These rites and religious formalities are yet performed by hereditary Brahmins to a very large extent, even in foreign countries, where many Hindus are now settling. Some changes have undoubtedly taken place in recent times; appointing a priest is no longer strictly based on the hereditary caste system. In some Hindu temples of USA, one may see a Caucasian priest, chanting the Sanskrit slokas in brief, and later explaining the meaning elaborately in English! Similar changes are taking place all over, including in India. The practice of women priests, which was unknown earlier, is becoming a common sight! Hindu society has largely adopted a soft non-resistant attitude toward such changes.

NOTE: All quotes are adapted from "Thus Spake Lord Buddha," Sri Ramakrishna Math, Mylapore, Chennai India, 1998.

30 Srimad Bhagavatam: A New Trend in Hinduism

Between the eighth to the sixth centuries BCE, the idea of theism was established in Hindu society. Theism recognizes that there is a supreme distinct god (Bhagavan) or goddess (Bhagavati), who generates the cosmos, maintains it, and finally destroys it, and who has the power to save beings through his grace.[62]

Around 200 BCE, Vishnu or Bhagvata worship became more prominent in India. The ancient god *Narayana* merged with the historical tribal gods Vishnu and Krishna, forming the most formidable Vishnu sect (*Panth*). The followers of this sect believed in non-violence and offered prayers to the idol (*murti*) of Lord Vishnu in different forms. They also offered various types of vegetarian food items to God; these were later distributed among the devotees.[63] Srimad Bhagavatam heralds this era of devotion.

Srimad Bhagavatam is the grand tapestry of Puranic tales that are woven around the Lord. Srimad Bhagavatam is one of the authoritative Hindu criptures, and is regarded by some as the fifth Veda. The date of composition is probably between the eighth and the tenth century CE, but may be as early as the 6th century CE.

The story goes that after composing the great Mahabharata, Rishi Ved Vyasa was not yet fully satisfied. Sage Narada then told him to write a scripture on devotion, as the vast majority of people might not be able to attain salvation through the long and arduous process of *jnana* or *karma* (knowledge or action). This is especially true during *Kali Yuga*—the age of darkness—when vices are dominant in society. It is believed that in the Kali Yuga, utterance of God's name with sincerity and devotion is sufficient to attain the *moksha*, or salvation. The Srimad Bhagavatam was thus composed, collecting many tales from the ancient Puranas.

The Srimad Bhagavatam contains the Puranic tales of the ten incarnations of Lord Vishnu, the most prominent being Lord Krishna. God-incarnation is the main theme of this scripture; the incarnation in human form is born to human parents and lives and dies like any human being, but during the course of his or her life he or she performs actions that can be possible by God alone.

The fabric of the Srimad Bhagavatam, however, has been woven in such a way that all the other gods and sages have been included in one-way or another. The mythological connection of one god to another was established, thus creating a sense of harmonious relationship among the various factions, which threatened divisive tendencies. Behind the façade of these legends and stories of the Lord are, of course, the spiritual and moral teachings for the mankind.

The *Krishna Bhav*, which also has come to be known as the *Prem Bhav*, is essentially a perspective and disposition of love and goodwill. Literally, Krishna means *"one who attracts."* Even when weapons are used in war out of necessity, there may be no feelings of hatred or animosity. Man is prompted to perform *Bhagavad Karma*, the divine deeds, which have the sanction of the Lord. These deeds would be of purity and virtue; these deeds would be away from sin and wickedness. A Hindu is therefore asked to keep God in his mind all the time, not only on selected occasions.

According to an ancient legend, a virtuous Puranic king, Parikshit, was doomed to die from snakebite in seven days. He was then led to listen to the Bhagavatam Katha by sage Suka, son of Veda Vyasa, which described the whole story of all ten incarnations of Lord Vishnu—this would bring him immortality, not just of the physical body but rather the salvation of his soul—*moksha*. Thus, a philosophical idea was proclaimed that a man on earth has but a limited span of life, and in this period he may strive to attain the salvation. An individual is inspired to sit in meditation and surrender oneself to the Divine.

One of the most important sections of this scripture deals with the divine love play of Lord Krishna with the maids in Gokul. The maids, or *gopis*, of this town are completely enthralled by the Lord. When they hear his flute, they are mesmerized; they leave everything and rush to him. The rich display of the Lord's rhythmic dance-sports, or *raas leela*, has endured in Hindu social life. Rich as well as poor, young and old, men and women, all dance to the lilting musical notes and celebrate the Lord's joy. Once again the Hindu sages created an extravaganza of artistic pageantry with fabulous colors and designs. The sages used symbolic language in their narrations—the maids are the men and women of this earth. When they are able to listen to the flute of the Lord, and when they tune themselves to receive his call, they then are ready to abandon everything else and follow him with all their heart. These *gopis* have their household responsibilities, too, but they do not care. There is nothing higher than the Lord. The Divine represents the ultimate in truth and virtue. The message to mankind is symbolic, yet quite loud and clear. *Raas leela*, the Lord's dance-sport, is not the display of sensual passion, as some might think. It is, rather, the sublimation of the physical desire to divine worship. Hindu sages discovered many spiritual techniques or *sadhanas*, to quench and exhaust sensual tendencies (*vasnas*).

There is also a symbolic explanation of these various legends of Srimad Bhagavatam; the good and the bad co-exist in our own mind. There is a constant war going on between these two forces. We are prompted to be governed by the divine forces and with the help of God, we are assured to succeed.

The Bhagavatam contains hundreds of tales; I have chosen two favorites. The first is as follows:

Lord Krishna had a childhood friend called Sudhama, with whom he had studied in the same ashram. Later, Lord Krishna became the king of Dwarka, but Sudhama remained a poor *Brahmin*. When Sudhama's financial condition became unbearable, his wife, Sushila, persuaded him to meet with Krishna to ask for help, if possible. Sushila gave Sudhama a small packet of boiled rice to present before the Lord as a gift. After he arrived at the palace, the Lord treated him with great love, respect, and attention. Lord Krishna then humorously asked if any gift had been brought for him. On seeing the precious objects around in the grand palace, Sudhama was rather hesitant to open his modest packet. Krishna, true to his style, pulled out the packet and ate the rice with great relish.

There is also a spiritual version of this incident, in which the Lord ate a first and second handful of the cooked rice, but as he was about to gulp the third handful, his queen wife, Rukmini, held his hand, and said, "*You have already granted him the two worlds! If you grant him the third one, what will happen to us?*" The story ends on a happy note. Upon his return home, Sudhama is pleasantly surprised that an imposing palace has replaced his poor hut. Whenever people encounter any problems of friendship, they remember the story of Sudhama. The Lord left them a yardstick; whenever they might be mean, arrogant, or unhelpful; they would remember the story and feel self-conscious about their own behavior.

The other favorite story from the Bhagavatam tells of the star hero of the Mahabharata, Sri Bhishma Pitamaha. He was a man of utmost truth and integrity. He was courageous, skilled beyond contest, and saturated with a sense of sacrifice and duty. In the war of righteousness, however, he fought on the wrong side—Bhishma Pitamaha fought for the wicked Duryodhana, to fulfill a previous vow. He fought bravely in the war until he was mortally wounded. As he was lying on the bed of arrows, especially prepared at his own instructions in order to do penance for the mistake of joining with the unrighteous side, he received an unusual farewell. There never would be another war hero who was visited by all the leaders from both sides while lying on his deathbed.

Hindu culture has exhibited an unmatched scenario of grace and dignity in this most dramatic scene from the Mahabharata. Yudhishtra, the eldest of the Pandavas, came, along with Arjuna, Draupadi, and the other brothers. They all touched Bhishma's feet, and with tears in their eyes they bid farewell, with utmost respect, to this grand old man. The Lord also came, as he promised that when a person completes all of his missions with truth and integrity, he would grant the divine vision, *darshan*, at the time of death. Bhishma's only mistake—his taking the wrong vow—was mitigated by his penance. Then at this rare moment in life, Bhishma Pitamaha was asked to teach the code of conduct for all humanity to remember in posterity. True to his honor, he spoke of all the duties for which a person is called in life. When he mentioned women and talked about upholding their respect and honor, Draupadi burst into uncontrollable laughter. When questioned, she retorted, "*Why were you silent when my honor was being looted in the court of Duryodhana?*" The anguished Bhishma replied, "*I did not resist, because I had eaten the food of the wicked Duryodhana.*" Thus was laid the guiding code for all—that a man may not eat at just any place, at the place of the corrupt and the wicked, or with those who earn their livelihood in the wrong manner.

Srimad Bhagvatam again heralds significant changes in Hindu theology. In response to the emerging new religions of Jainism and Buddhism, Srimad Bhagvatam presents a different facet- promoting generally a non-violent conduct by the people (although God may save the innocent by killing and destroying the wicked). God as an incarnation in the human form of Lord Krishna is presented in all His glory and magnificence, thus repudiating the non-theist contention of these two religions. God's infinite power and grace are highlighted, and so are the worship of God and the mutis (images) as icons of the Lord. The mystic, formless, transcendental impression of the Divine in the Upanishad Era has been replaced by the robust, direct, easy-to-recognize human face and human incarnation!

Srimad Bhagvatam is also named as the fifth Veda of the common man; as such the worship practices are rather simple and straight-forward. A new concept, that by just uttering the name of God, one may attain the moksha-salvation, has been forcefully introduced. This perception is ofcourse symbolic in nature, the idea being to pull the people toward God in whatever way possible. Gradually and with the grace of the Divine, one may become more and more pious and spiritual.

Although Lord Krishna has been presented in very simple and earthly manner, the real message of the Lord is much deeper and more symbolic. Literally, Krishna translates as "one who attracts", thus the Lord has been acclaimed as the personification of Krishna Bhav-of love and goodwill.

Srimad Bhagvatam reminds all that a person has but a limited time in mortal life to fulfill the spiritual mission. One may never forget to follow and remember God.

Spiritual Gems from Tirukural: V

"Humility is the strength of the strong and the instrument the wise use to reform their foes."

"Elephants stand firm even when wounded by a barrage of arrows. Strong-willed men are not discouraged when they meet disaster."

"Weigh a man's merits and weigh his faults,
then judge him according to the greater."

"As water changes according to the soil through which it flows,
so a man assimilates the character of his associates."

"Virtue yields Heaven's honor and Earth's wealth.
What is there then that is more fruitful for a man?"

"Among those who stand outside virtue, there is no greater fool
than he who stands with a lustful heart outside another's gate."

"What is truthfulness? It is speaking words
which are totally free from harmful effects."

"Though his every word is full of kindly virtue,
a man's mean backbiting will betray an empty heart."

"Riches acquired by proper and judicious means, in a manner
that harms no one, will bring both piety and pleasure."

"In the hands of a benevolent man,
Wealth is like a medicinal tree whose healing gifts help all."

"The whole purpose of earning wealth and maintaining a home
is to provide hospitality to guests."

(Source: Spiritual Teachings-Himalayan Academy, Hawaii, US)

31 Spiritual Teachings
Of Srimad Bhagavatam

Ved Vyasa is considered the compiler of the four Vedas. But as there were many restrictions on common people, women, and the low-caste *Shudras*, Ved Vyasa later wrote the Mahabharata and the Bhagavatam. In this way, the dominant influence of the high-caste *Brahmins* of the Aryan period was contained in these subsequent Hindu scriptures. The Srimad Bhagavatam was written for common man, who is not well versed in complex philosophies and academic deliberations. The teachings are therefore quite simple and straightforward:

- Only as much as is needed by the stomach, you may take and eat. If one takes more than that, it is sinful.

- One who sees eternal soul in all beings and sees all beings in the soul is the man of spirituality.

- For one who attains excellence in his trade or profession, it is not for any personal ego satisfaction or selfish gain; rather, it is for the service and well-being of all.

- One who uses his knowledge or strength for his own selfish ends may be destroyed, as Ravana was destroyed, even though he was a *Brahmin* of very high knowledge and a king with great power.

- According to the teachings of the Bhagavatam, the loftiest Vedantic thought is *vasudhaiva kutumbakam*—the whole world is but a family. In all beings there pervades the same cosmic spirit. There is none alien, so we need have no enmity toward anyone.

Only in the human form is one in a position to offer devotional prayers to God. Human birth is, therefore, considered as the most precious birth. By remembering God, one remembers the divine virtues of God. Man then gradually attains these virtues, such as truth, purity, compassion, forgiveness, renunciation, contentment, equanimity, austerity, peace, reading the scriptures, brilliance, courage, power, enthusiasm, pride, humility, and many more.

- The king (or the politician) in whose reign the people are unhappy and sorrowful loses his name, fame, life, and prosperity. It is the primary duty of the king (or the politician) to keep his people happy and satisfied.

- Beyond the formed God is the subtle, formless, transcendental soul, *Paramatma*, which is the root source of everything.
- Those who have overcome their ego and have surrendered everything at the feet of the Lord, they may not be disturbed by the happenings of the world.
- True saints are above arguments and controversies. They must clean the slate of their mind and look at things without uttering a word to anyone.
- Those who would dishonor others and then pray before the idol of God are not true worshippers. Those who harbor enmity toward anyone are also not the real seekers of the Lord. God is present in all beings.
- If anyone slanders others, it is an unholy practice. With such acts, we may lose the merit of spirituality.
- When man becomes old and is not able to earn money, his wife and children, for whom he worked hard all his life, often disrespect him. Yet he does not take the path of renunciation and spirituality.
- Man must always tell the truth. He should never be envious. He must be respectful to others, especially so to his parents and all elders.
- A spiritual man would feel shy and embarrassed to hear his praise, but the wicked often become swollen with arrogance after hearing their praise and flattery. We should therefore praise only God.
- Many are the sinful and wicked persons who wear the robes of saints but who are cheats and hypocrites.
- Prayer ceremony (*havan, yagna,* etc.) must not be done with any selfish motive or for any ulterior motive to harm others.
- It is the sacred task of the soul to gradually transform the mind over many birth cycles. By engaging the mind in contemplation, meditation, and getting deeply engrossed in the thought of the Lord, finally this transformation takes place.
- Man often gets trapped in the infatuation of women, children, and even animal pets that he forgets all other duties and also turns his attention away from God.
- During the fast, we must always give charity to the poor. Whenever we keep a fast, it is for the sake of self-purification. On fast days, we must not become angry, we must not be greedy, and we must not slander and hurt others.

- We must do charity but with some control. We must divide our wealth in five parts. One part is for charity. The second is for our name. The third is for increasing our wealth and prosperity. The fourth is for our own comfort and security. The fifth is for helping our near and dear ones. Thus, we must be discreet and organized in matters of our wealth and material assets. Many persons give so much charity that nothing is left for their own survival or for their family and close relatives.

It is said that there is no joy greater than the joy of giving. Coveting merely brings us fleeting pleasure. The senses are dependent upon an external supply of commodities. When the supply is stopped, the senses cannot send the feelings of pleasure anymore. Sensuality is thus a matter of dependence. The worst example of this sensual affection is drug addiction. A person may often do harm to himself and to others in procuring the substance, which gives but a fleeting pleasure. Helping others brings us the joy of fulfillment. When we are asked for help, we often retract and dry up. We are so conditioned to receive the pleasurable feelings through acts of taking and receiving that we do not realize that giving and helping can be a source of much greater and more lasting joy. We therefore should redefine our mental attitudes and welcome the calls for help as opportunities for our self-fulfillment and lasting joy.

- Forgiveness is a divine virtue. By forgiveness, we may attain God.
- Greed and lust may never be fully satisfied. However much we may get and enjoy, we remain unfulfilled and unsatisfied. Our true joy is in God and in performing the spiritual or divine actions.
- When Lord Krishna plays the sweet and melodious tunes on his flute, all become intoxicated. May they be the birds of the forest, cows, shepherds, or village maids (*gopis*). They forget everything and listen to his divine music. Such is the magic of God. Once the Divine entraps the man, he does not like to be separated. This is the eternal peace; this is the permanent bliss; and this is the everlasting joy. Whatever the entire world may say, the man of divinity forsakes all other relationships and cares not for shame or honor; he simply wants to drink in the nectar of divinity.
- Man may ever be like a forest tree. It suffers the extreme degrees of the heat of the sun but gives cool shade to others; it gives leaves, fruits, flowers, wood, coal, and so much more. Only those who serve others and lay down their lives for the benefit of others know

the true value of life. Only their lives are worthy lives.

- Spend your life in the world, but keep your mind and soul in the meditation of the Lord. When the day is over, rejoice that you will return to God. Make God your constant companion.

- All beings have the seed of God within. Even wicked persons have this divine seed within them. This seed may germinate and grow with one's own effort or by the grace of the Lord. It's man's duty to remain in tune with the Lord all the time.

- Like the honeybee gathers trickles of honey from different flowers, so, too, the men of wisdom assimilate the essence of all scriptures and choose only the good in all religions.

The Srimad Bhagavatam has become the immortal scripture of Hindus. Said the famous Srimad Bhagavatam guru Sri Mridul Shastri:

"You must always go before God with humility and simplicity. Only then will you attain the divine grace and blessings. If you will attend the full narration (katha) of the Bhagavatam for all seven days with faith and sincerity, you will have enough spiritual vibrations to get all the answers to your queries from within

The main purpose of a religion is to impart spiritual and moral teachings. Srimad Bhagavatam has simply excelled in this great mission. The teachings are presented in a very simple and earthly manner. The earlier scriptures of Vedas and Upanishads were inaccessible to women and persons belonging to lower castes; the subsequent scriptures, especially the Srimad Bhagavatam corrected this anomaly right away. Its teachings often dwell on most ordinary, daily activities like eating habits, personal behavior, and relationship with other beings etc., guiding individuals to improve the quality of their lives and adding value to the tasks they undertake, regardless of big or small. Even though Srimad Bhagavatam is most theistic and underlines God incarnation, it also recognises the basic Hindu concept of the transcendental, formless Divine behind all these manifestations, thus maintaining a sense of harmony between different philosophical ideas and opinions.
Srimad Bhagavatam also introduced the concept of

"grace". When one surrenders completely and sincerely at the lotus feet of the Lord, one may obtain the grace of God. With His grace, all previous harmful effects of the bad karmas may be mitigated. This is in contrast with the Jainism and Buddhism philosophy, where there is no room for such mercy and benevolence. All karmas must be fully accounted for. With the phenomenon of grace, Hindu philosophy moved toward mental reform and transformation as the goal, replacing proper justice and punishment.

We also often forget our vows and pledges, repeatedly committing iniquities and sins; Srimad Bhagavatam warns of such wrongful behavior. Even the most powerful persons have succumbed under the spell of lust. One may therefore avoid becoming intimate with anyone but their lawful spouse. The institute of marriage has been vindicated fully.

NOTE: All quotes are adapted from: Lokram P. Dodeja. Srimad Bhagavad (Sindhi Language). Pune, India, 1950.

Spiritual Gems from Tirukural: VI

"The mere sight of men who lust after wealth,
caring nothing for renown, is a burden to the Earth."

"Those who possess wisdom possess everything.
Whatever others possess, without wisdom they have nothing."

"Wisdom will harness the mind, diverting it from wrong and
directing it toward right."

"No fool is more foolish than one who eagerly expounds his
learning to others while failing to follow it himself."

"Neglecting valuable advice, an ignorant man becomes the cause
of his own misery."

"Doing what should not be done will bring ruin,
and not doing what should be done will also bring ruin."

"Those who eat food harvested with their own hands
will never beg and never refuse a beggar's outstretched palm."

"An incomparable state is one never devastated;
yet if devastated, it would not diminish, but prosper."

(Source: Spiritual Teachings-Himalayan Academy, Hawaii, USA)

32 Hindu Renaissance: An Era of Sri Adi Shankar Acharya

Hinduism has been a vibrant religion throughout millennia. Every religion has phases of peaks and ebbs. After a glorious epoch of the Vedic period, there came a temporary decline. The prolonged ritual ceremonies of the Aryan system, together with undue dominance of the *Brahmin* class, had a negative effect on the growth and sustenance of Hinduism. Excessive religious formalities and the over-exploitation of the lower castes caused severe damage to the cause of the religion. Time was thus ripe for alternative options to sprout. Jainism and Buddhism were born as alternative spiritual paths and in due course became very well established religions. From this big jolt, many attempts were made to revive and rejuvenate the decadent Hindu religion.

The Gupta Empire (320–500 CE) has been described, as an era of Hindu revival. There was Hindu activity in the form of construction of many magnificent temples, although this dynasty supported the Buddhist and Jain religions as well. This period has been hailed as the golden period of Indian culture, but it was not until the eighth century, that an ascetic of the highest caliber came forward to uphold the dwindling flame of Hinduism.

He was Adi Shankar Acharya (788–820). His name will be always remembered for playing a major role in reorganizing and reforming the system. In Hindu theology, it is believed that whenever there is a steep downfall of the religion, God reincarnates as the savior. Adi Shankar's arrival is considered to be the God's intervention. Not only was he a child prodigy who mastered all the major scriptures at the tender age of seven years, but he also went by foot to all four corners of the country. He then established four major religious monastic centers, or *maths*, in India: the Sringeri Math on the Sringeri hills near Mysore in the South; the Sarda Math at Dwarka in the West; the Jyotir Math at Badrinath in the North; and the Govardhan Math at Puri in the East.

Shankara also organized hundreds of monasteries into a ten order, *dashanami* system, which were assigned to these four pontifical centers, the head of which was known as *Shankaracharya*. The hierarch of the monastery at Puri is regarded as the teacher of the universe, the *Jagadguru Shankaracharya*.

Shankara brought all the warring sects under one roof and wrote voluminous commentaries on the Upanishads, the Bhagavad Gita, and the Braham Sutra. These scriptures remain classic authorities even today. Anyone who is interested in the philosophy of Hinduism cannot afford to bypass this genius of the Hindu mind. Among the many reforms that he affirmed was the toning down of oppressive formalities. Adi Shankar was a strong proponent of *Advaitya*—God is all, and everything is but his manifestation. He, however, was very accommodating to the dualistic *Dvaitya* philosophy as well. Adi Shankar's devotional poetic work *Bhaj Govindam*, mentioned in the later part of this chapter, is a testimony of his universal approach.

Indeed, it was his broad vision of integrating different divisions of Hindu society that will be forever gratefully remembered. Even as the evils of the caste system and other problems were nibbling at the roots of Hinduism, the three factions—Shaivites, Vaishnavites, and Shaktas—started to pull in opposing directions.

Shaivite Hindus worship Lord Shiva as the Supreme God. This sect is mainly based on temple worship, and Siddha yoga. Renunciation (*sanyasa*), austerities (*tapas*), meditation, and mysticism form an integral part of it. It has close links with both the ancient Sindhu-Saraswati civilization as well as the Dravidian culture.

Vaishnavite Hindus worship Lord Vishnu as the Supreme God, who has incarnated multiple times but mainly as Lord Rama and Lord Krishna. They often address God as *Purushottoma*, the noblest amongst persons. They are dualistic, considering God separate and higher than all beings.

Shakta Hindus worship *Shakti* or *Devi* as the supreme goddess in the form of the Divine Mother. The origin of this sect also may have a link with the ancient Sindhu-Saraswati culture. The Shakti goddess has many forms, too. Shaktas practice Kundalini yoga, with many rituals of Tantra. Apart from these three main sects, there are innumerable smaller divisions and sub-sects among the Hindu religious organization. All Hindu sects, however, have more unifying elements than those of division. The diversity of Hinduism is based on the ethnic origins of different groups of society as well as the distinct aspirations of the individuals. Violence among each other is conspicuous by its absence. All sects uphold the supremacy of the

Vedas and also accept the basic philosophies of *karma* (as you sow, so shall you reap), reincarnation (*punarjanam*), the eternal cycle of birth and death (*samsara*), salvation (*moksha*), and God incarnation (*Avtar Karan*). The differences among the various sects are minor and add diversity in place of uniformity.

Adi Shankar then also popularized the ancient unified sect *Smartas*—those who believed in all deities and classical Hindu scriptures. He re-established the worship of the five deities: Shiva, Vishnu, Shakti, Surya, and Ganesh (*Panch Deva Sthapana*). Later he also added the sixth Kumara, and came to be known as *Shanmata Sthapanacharya*. In the dwindling phase of Hindu society, his organizing a major unity program among the different sects caused him to be seen as a great savior. In fact, this opened later the worship of unlimited number of deities in Hindu theology, according to one's choice, without any restraint whatsoever.

The concept of adopting a preferential personal deity (*ishta devta*) became more accepted. This notion was in conformity with the essential Vedic teaching: *Ekam sad vipra bahudha vadanti* (One alone exists; sages call it by various names.) More recent Hindu temples, especially those in foreign countries, are generally multi-deity temples. The Hindu pantheon has the unique distinction of housing many different gods under one roof, adding even new gods periodically.

Soon after Adi Shankar came yet another jewel of Hinduism, also from the South: Ramanuja (1017–1137). He also largely contributed to the renaissance of Hinduism. His philosophy was based on qualified non-dualism (*Vishishta dvaita*—God is above all). God is superior to everything else. Ramanuja advocated devotion or surrender to the Supreme Lord for realization of divine knowledge. There was yet a third school of monism (*Dvaia Vedanta*), propounded by Sri Madhvacharya (1119–1278).

Sri Shankaracharya also wrote the immortal classic Bhaj Govindam, a devotional scripture in which his main spiritual teachings have become the beacon of light for millions of Hindus.
Worship Govinda, Worship Govinda, Worship Govinda, O foolish one!
Rules of grammar will profit nothing, once the hour of death draws near!
Thus, he emphasized true worship above the formalities of rituals and ceremonies.

"Many are with matted locks, with closely shaven heads, and many who pluck out all their hair and wear robes of ochre or are clad in other colors, but all this is for

the sake of their stomachs. The deluded ones, even seeing the Truth revealed before them, see it not."

He painted the picture, very boldly and bluntly, of all the pseudo saints, whether they belonged to the Hindu, Buddha, or Jain religions.

One of the most prominent authorities on Hindu philosophy in modern times, Swami Chinmayananda, has aptly noted:

"These three schools of thought are not so much competing and contradicting theories, as explanations of necessary stages we must pass through in our pilgrimage to the peak of our perfection. Only the intellectual pundits quarrel and seek to establish as the one or the other declaration as superior."

Paramhansa Yogananda said:

"A combination of personal theism and the philosophy of the Absolute is an ancient achievement of Hindu thought, expounded in the Vedas and the Bhagavad Gita. This reconciliation…satisfies heart and head." [64]

The Era of Adi Shankar Acharya has been hailed as a major reform movement within Hinduism, after its dwindling image caused by the onset of new religions of Jainism and Buddhism. He was the one responsible for curbing divisive tendencies; he roamed on foot all over India from East to West and from North to South to establish 4 main Hindu Maths in the four corners of the country, thus bringing together hundreds of small monasteries into a one unified system. This may be regarded as the first organizational effort in Hindu religion. Albeit Hinduism doesn't yet have a very strict and formal structural arrangement, this initiative of Adi Shankar Acharya did help significantly in consolidating the religion.

He wrote voluminous commentaries on the Upanishads, the Bhagavad Gita, and the Braham Sutra, and established himself as the Hindu scholar par excellence. Apart from bringing together the three different sects, he also reintroduced the prehistoric, ancient, unified sect Smartas—those who believed in all deities and classical Hindu scriptures. This major step created a great sense of harmony and agreement in Hindu society. Floodgates were opened for adopting a preferential personal deity (ishta devta). Most Hindu temples now, especially those in foreign countries, are generally multi-deity temples, although there may be one presiding deity. The Hindu pantheon has the unique

distinction of housing many different Gods under one roof and even adding new Gods periodically.

Adi Shankar Acharya also advocated soft approach in regard to rituals and customs; he attended the funeral ceremony of his own mother. Hindu sanyasins are generally restrained from participating in such duties. Even though he was a strong proponent of Advaitya, he was very accommodating to the dualistic Dvaitya philosophy. Adi Shankar's devotional poetic work "Bhaj Govindam" is a testimony of his universal approach. He thus re-emphasized the open-door comprehensive approach of ancient Hinduism in place of a hard-core and uncompromising attitude.

NOTE: All quotes are adapted from "Thus Spake Sri Sankara," Sri Ramakrishna Math, Mylapore, Chennai, India, 1998

Spiritual Gems from Sri Ramakrishna Paramahansa

Do your different duties in the world, fixing your mind on God. But practice is necessary, and one should also be alert. Only in this way one can safeguard both – God and the world. (The Gospel, p.428-29)

There are certain signs by which you can know a true devotee of God. His mind becomes quiet as he listens to the teacher's instructions; just as the poisonous snake is quieted by the music of the charmer (The Gospel, p.244)

So long as a man has not realized God, he will have to come back to the Potters hand, that is, he will have to born again and again. (The Gospel, p.416)

A householder has his duties to discharge, his debts to pay: his debt to pay to the gods, his debt to his ancestors, his debt to the rishis, and his debt to wife and children...Only a monk must not save; the bird and the monk do not provide for the morrow. But even a bird provides when it has young ones. It brings food in its bill for its chicks. (The Gospel, p.156)

Man may be likened to grain. He has fallen between the millstones and is about to be crushed. Only the few grains that stay near the peg may escape. Therefore men should take refuge at the peg, that is to say, in God. Call on Him. Sing His name. Then you will be free. Otherwise you will be crushed by the King of Death (The Gospel, p.155)

(From the Gospel of Sri Ramakrishna, Published by Sri Ramakrishna Math Madras, Mylapore, India)

33 Era of Bhakti Yoga: The Golden Period of Devotional Faith

This chapter has been named as 'The Golden Period', because it was in this period that a serious attempt was made by number of saints, sages, poets, and other reformists to do away with the harmful caste system, without sacrificing the essential good teachings of Hinduism. They basically propagated the Hindu teachings but kept the caste division out of the religion. They emphasized humility and surrender as the most important divine virtues. They also prompted the cultivation of moral virtues like truthfulness, compassion, patience, tolerance, contentment, self-control, service, sincerity etc. They usually sang in their popular vernacular languages, instead of in Sanskrit, which was out of reach for most commoners. In the Hindu culture, devotion to God became a way of life.

The *Bhakti*, or Devotional era started first in South India, with the *Alvar* and *Nayanar* saints, in the sixth century CE. The *Alvar* saints sang about Lord Vishnu, while the *Nayanars* were devotees of Lord Shiva. The *Alvar* saints developed an emotional and personal relationship with God. They would describe Vishnu as the incarnate Lord Krishna in the form of a beloved and charming cow herder, and themselves were the maids, the *gopis*, who would be love-torn in separation. Female saint Antal (725–755) became most famous with her passionate devotional songs. It is believed that the impact on Hindu society of these saint/poets was so enormous that the personal God became more accepted than the abstract, formless Divine. The poetry of these Dravidian saints later influenced the devotional traditions in various regions of India.

The second wave of the Bhakti movement, which started in the northern and western parts of India, began in the thirteenth century. The saints of this era belonged mainly to the Vishnu sect of Lord Krishna and Lord Rama. They would often compose songs of personal experiences with the Lord, in form of a *saguna* god (god with form), or they would describe the Lord as formless—a *nirguna* god. The devotees of the *saguna* worship would treat the idols of God, the *murtis*, in a most intimate manner. The physical body, the emotions, and the embodied forms of the Lord, which could be seen and worshipped, subtly replaced the soul's abstract world of the Vedic *Rishis*.[65] The *bhakti*, or surrender, relationship is described in six different forms:

1. *Madhura Bhav*—sexual love
2. *Kanta Bhav*—love of wife for husband
3. *Shanta Bhav*—love of child for parent
4. *Vatsalya Bhav*—love of parent for child
5. *Sakhya Bhav*—love of friendship
6. *Dasya Bhav*—affection of servant for his master

Thus, a man is extolled to see the Divine in all situations and relationships. It was the endowment of Hindu seers to guide mankind to spirituality in all walks of life. The *bhakti*, or surrender, should be total and unconditional, without any personal or selfish motives.

Three steps of the *bhakti* have been described:

Samarpan or surrender—this often begins with the worship of the idol, the murti.

Sambhandh or relationship with the Divine—there is a bond of love for God.

Chintan or thinking and meditating on the Divine—when a person mentally visualizes God in all beings and in all situations.

The Bhakti movement in Hinduism owes its later development to various schools:

Ramanuja (1017–1137) was the first to propagate the worship and surrender to Lord Vishnu *Vaishnav Bhakti*, which was started earlier by Alvar saints. **Madhava (1197–1280)** taught that God is the supreme, independent and omniscient. All beings are dependent and subordinated to God. **Nimbarka** paved the way for the concept of Radha and Krishna around the fourteenth century. **Vallabha (1479–1531)** taught "God with form," or *saguna Brahman*. This God is worshipped as the baby Krishna *Bankey Bihari*. **Chaitanya (1485–1534)** emphasized the importance of glorifying the name of Lord and chanting it in congregation. The present Hare Krishna movement (ISKCON) is based on this philosophy. These devotional saints, in turn, created their own traditions and sects (*sampradayas*) in Hindu society, with a great variety of attitudes and disciplines.[66]

A number of devotional saints—a few of which are noted below—entranced the followers during this period, with their spiritual songs, or *bhajans*, which have become extant in Hindu society. Even today people render these devotional songs with great passion and feeling. It is rather interesting to note that throughout India's long history, a large percentage of Hindu saints have come from non-Brahmin castes.

Bhagat Namdev (b. 1269) was born in a low-caste family of tailors. His devotional songs (*abhangs*) became most popular. He adored Lord Krishna as Vithal. His poems also appear in Guru Granth Sahib, the Holy Scripture of the Sikh religion.

Sant Gyaneshwar (b. 1332) was born near Pune, Maharashtra. He wrote a commentary on the Bhagavad Gita, "Gyaneshwari," which became very popular, especially in Maharashtra.

Sant Kabir (b. 1398) was born in Kashi into a *Brahmin* family and was later brought up by a low-caste weaver. He went to Guru Ramanand for initiation but was not accepted. One day, he purposely slept on the path taken by Guru Ramanand as he was returning from his bath at the Ganges. Guru Ramanand's feet accidentally touched Kabir's body, and the guru uttered, "*Ram, Ram*." Kabir thus got his *mantra*. He wrote large volumes of poetry with many spiritual teachings. So truthful and touching were his poems that they found a most honored place in the Sikh sacred book, Shri Guru Granth Saheb.

Sri Guru Nanak Dev (b. 1469) hailed from Punjab. From his early childhood it was recognized that he was different from other children; he was deeply involved in acts of charity. He roamed on foot all over the country and even went outside the country to propagate the name of God. His lifestyle was extremely simple and pure. He preached Hindu-Muslim unity. He had a large following that later started the separate religion of Sikhism.

Bhagat Narsi Mehta (b. 1470) was born in Saurashtra, Gujarat. He wrote many religious poems, which still are popular today. His song "*Vaishnav Jan to Taine Kahiye*" was a favorite of Mahatma Gandhi and was sung in his prayer meetings regularly.

Vallabhacharya (b 1479), a *Brahmin*, originally hailed from the South and later moved to Gujarat. He founded the sect popularly known as Vallabh Sampradaya, also called the *Pusti Marg* or "Path of Prosperity." The merchant class largely joined this sect, which believed in both the grace of God and one's personal efforts toward material gains. He was a firm devotee of Lord Krishna, particularly in the form of the infant *Bankey Bihari* and as the youth *Bal Govin*da.[67]

Chaitnaya Mahaprabhu (b. 1486) was born in Bengal. He was a devotee of Lord Krishna and spent a large part of his life in the vicinity of the Jagannath temple at Puri, Orissa. He would dance and sing, and tears would flow from his eyes. Many devotees would follow him wherever he went. It was he who introduced the chant *"Hare Krishna, Hare, Hare."*

Sant Ravidas (b. 15th century) was a poet-saint of exceptional qualities. He was born in Varanasi, North India, into a low caste family. He ridiculed the idea of a hereditary caste system. There are as many as forty-one poems written by him that are included into the Sikh Holy Scripture, Guru Granth Saheb.

Goswami Sant Tulsidas (b. 1532) was born in Rajpur, Uttar Pradesh, India. He wrote the immortal classic *Shri Ramcharitra Manas*. This Ramayana was written in the true spirit of complete surrender. It is said that in youth, Tulsidas was extremely fond of his wife. One day, when she went to stay at her father's place, he could not bear the pangs of separation. That night, there was a torrential rain. Tulsidas had to cross the river to reach his beloved wife. So deeply was he enamored that he mistook a floating dead body for a raft and, later, a snake for a rope, but he ultimately arrived on the other side with his wife. When she realized Tulsidas' blind passion, she rebuked him by saying, *"If you had shown so much love for God, you would have attained salvation."* Tulsidas was instantly transformed. For the rest of his life he was the devotee of Lord Rama. His scripture, *Shri Ramcharitra Manas*, has touched the lives of millions of people.

Bhagat Surdas (b. 1535) was blind, but his inner vision was very strong. He saw Lord Krishna in all beings. He had a melodious voice. He sang songs that he composed himself, which became very popular.

Sant Haridas (b. 1537) hailed from Brindavan. From early childhood, he was fond of the *Krishna Leela*. He was a master of classical music and became the guru of the famous singer Tansen. When Emperor Akbar asked Tansen the secret of the melody in Haridas' voice, Tansen replied, *"We mortals sing to please other men, but Haridas sings only for God."*

Sant Mirabai (b. 1560) hailed from Mewar in Rajasthan. From early childhood she was devoted to Lord Krishna. When she was just ten years old, she was given an idol of Krishna. She would not be separated from it, even for a short time. At age eighteen she was married against her will to a royal prince, Bhojraj. She took the idol of Lord Krishna along with her to her husband's home and would constantly worship and meditate on it. This annoyed her in-laws. Several attempts were made to kill her, but each time, the Lord protected her life. She spent the rest of her life singing the songs of her love for Krishna, which have become legendary: *Mere toh Giridhar Gopal, dusero ne koyi.i*

Swami Ramdas (b. 1665) hailed from Maharashtra. He brought a new awakening in the socio-political structure of his time with a spiritual transformation in the political system. He was a devotee of Lord Rama and Hanuman, and with his teachings he uplifted the lives of many. In 1706, the famous warrior King Shivaji Maharaj adopted Swami Ramdas as his guru. Swami Ramdas asked King Shivaji to conduct his rule with utmost spirituality.

Sant Tukaram (b. 1665) was born in Maharashtra. He was most compassionate to the poor and needy. He was from a low-caste family and was often humiliated for singing songs of God, because he did not belong to the higher Brahmin caste. When he sang, he often cried profusely, with words such as, *"I am not a learned person; but like a small child, I come before you, Lord!"* Ultimately, Lord Vithal appeared before him at the Pandharpur temple, and he attained salvation.

The Golden Era of the Bhakti Yoga was also a key resistance movement against the stern caste system prevalent at the time. However, these saints adopted the most humble, non-violent approach in their task. They resorted to positive methods, eulogizing the spiritual qualities of the religion, and especially highlighted and emphasized the grand virtues and merits of God. They composed hundreds of songs and bhajans in praise of the Divine, and sang them in enchanting tunes in temples, homes, and streets with utmost passion and intimacy. They preached to the common people to live simply with moral values and charity. They sang in popular vernacular languages instead of Sanskrit, which was beyond the comprehension of most. They taught people to become devotional, and to develop complete and full faith in God.

NOTE: This chapter is adapted from Asha Dayal, Bharat jaa Bhagat (Sindhi Language), Veena Devidas Mirpuri, Madras, India, 1981.

34 Sikhism: The Youngest Religion in India

It has been observed that India has produced more spiritual persons than any other place. When the quality of their spiritual and divine life becomes highest, they are considered to be God's special messengers. In the fifteenth century, India had the good fortune to produce yet one more saint of sterling spiritual qualities. Guru Nanak, the founder of the new faith of Sikhism, was born in Punjab in 1469. He was a man of rare virtues. He taught truthfulness and unity amongst the Hindus and the Muslims. Once again, in his own unique style, he reminded the people of the ancient Upanishad teaching—that God is but one. He also advised them to shun complex rituals, avoid controversies, live a simple life of manual labor, contribute earnings to the needy and poor, and pray to the Supreme Lord in complete surrender. Guru Nanak roamed from place to place with the sole purpose of spreading the holy message of God. He spoke in melodious verse, imparting the divine knowledge in soothing musical tones. He demonstrated the values of faith and integrity to his many followers by his true examples in the way in which he lived his own life. Apart from bringing a union between the Hindus and the Muslims, he also asked people to discard the old, rather vicious caste system, which had plagued the Hindu society.

The followers of Guru Nanak, who was himself born as Hindu, adopted his teachings and established the new faith of Sikhism. There were ten gurus in line to propagate these teachings with great discipline and devotion. The tenth and the last guru was Sri Guru Gobind Singh, who had to fight many wars with the Mogul emperor. Gurus always taught peace from the time of Guru Nanak, but submitting to injustice and unrighteousness is not peace; it's cowardice. It's not virtue; it's vice. Guru Gobind Singh inspired the small community of the Sikhs, both with courage and spirituality, to fight for justice and righteousness. He created the Khalsa cadre—the pure—and suffixed each Sikh name with *Singh*—the lion. The sacrifices of the Sikhs in these wars have been legendary.

After the tenth guru, Gobind Singh, the mantle of leadership, and as ordained by him, rested with the most sacred scripture of the gurus' teachings, *Shri Guru Granth Saheb*. Such was the unique attitude of the Sikh gurus that in spite of so many atrocities committed on them by the Muslim rulers, this living scripture, the Guru Granth Saheb, contains the writings of three Muslim authors. This holy book has the collective writings of as many as thirty-six contributors from all different sections of Indian society, and only six among them are the Sikhs. This, indeed, would be unparalleled in the annals of any religion in the world. All the teachings in the Guru Granth Saheb are presented as poetry, which are then rendered in classical tunes (*ragaas*) to make them most inspirational. The gurus' eternal message, *ik oankar* (God is One), reverberates throughout the Holy Scripture. Sikhs all over the globe, who now number twenty-three million and constitute the fifth largest religious group, worship this Holy Scripture with a reverence and honor that no other scripture or a living person could ever command.

The association of the Sikhs and the Hindus is like that of the blood brothers. Shri Guru Gobind Singh fought all his life to save the Hindu religion. Many Hindu and Sikh families are closely intertwined. Despite periodic discord and disunity, the gurus cemented their relationship with the blood of sacrifice.

Sikhism literally means "learning." Gurus taught their disciples to always be willing to learn. Compassion is given a very high place by the gurus. Without compassion, the religion itself would be meaningless. Some people become moralists, but without compassion, without love and tenderness, they gradually would become more and more strict, authoritative, dry, and dictatorial. Compassion, or *daya*, is pivotal in religion, or *dharma*. Sikhism is but the propagation of these principles of the *dharma* in the form of virtuous behavior. Virtue is given the uppermost position in the gurus' teachings. Without virtuous behavior, all the wealth, power, and technology would lead us on the wrong path of terror and destruction.

We are often advised to accept both the success and the failure in equal manner. This, in practice, is very difficult. *Gurbani,* the sacred teachings of the Sikh gurus, teaches us a simpler and easier method: We must pray to the Lord for redemption in time of difficulty and distress; and we must express gratefulness to the Lord when we receive a bounty or favor. In both the profit and the loss, we must learn to remember and communicate with God. Gurbani even sanctions prayer to the Lord for ordinary material commodities, even trifles, such as daily groceries and clothes to wear. We are prompted to approach the Lord as our loving parent. God is not just for high-sounding metaphysical spirituality. God is for everything that we do and desire.

Among the many teachings is a clear direction to shed our superstitions and illusions. Gurbani, however, does not advocate the renunciation of family life, the *grahstha*. Sikh gurus advised their devotees to carry on the responsibilities of the household and gradually evolve themselves spiritually through meditation and the spiritual experience of *Naam Simran*. All the gurus themselves had a married family life and fulfilled all the obligations of society.

Sikhism lays heavy emphasis on *Naam Simran*—meditation on the name of God. The famous Sant Kabir offered an interesting anecdote in this regard: A devotee came to the saint and requested the *Naam* in rather a hurry. The saint asked him to fetch a little quantity of milk. When the devotee brought the milk, the saint asked him to pour the same into an unclean utensil. The devotee was taken aback. Sant Kabir then told him that if he were so concerned about pouring a small quantity of milk of little value into an unclean vessel, how it would be proper to pour the priceless article of *Naam* into a person who had collected the dirt and rubbish of so many births. One must first cleanse oneself of all impurities before taking the *Naam*, the name of the Lord

It was in the wake of the Muslim rule that Sikhism was born. The Hindu religion was under great stress. Sri Guru Nanak, the founder of Sikhism taught people to live a simple truthful life, with complete faith and devotion in God. He lived a most spiritual and virtuous life and roamed all over to propagate his universal message to the masses, one of his chief aides being a Muslim. It was after him that many of his devotees established the new faith Sikhism; 10 gurus in succession preached the teachings with great discipline and sincerity. All the sacred teachings of the 10 gurus and many other saints of the period were collected and preserved very meticulously and accurately. These were then compiled into their Holy Book Sri Guru Granth Saheb. After the 10th guru Sri Guru Gobind Singh, and as ordained by him, the complete authority was rested in this Holy Scripture; no living guru would be commissioned in the future. Many Hindus visit gurudwaras (place of worship for the Sikhs) on regular basis. Toward the later gurus, the atrocity and cruelty of the Muslim rulers grew rather sharply. The 10th guru Sri Guru Gobind Singh finally decided that submitting to injustice and unrighteousness is not peace; it's cowardice. It's not virtue; it's vice. Sri Guru Gobind Singh inspired the small community of the Sikhs, both with courage and spirituality, to fight for justice and righteousness. He created the Khalsa cadre—the pure—and suffixed each Sikh name with Singh—the lion. The sacrifices of the Sikhs in these wars have been legendary. After the epic wars of Ramayana and Mahabharata, the Hindu community leaned more toward non-violence. Jainism and Buddhism had significantly influenced the community to maintain peace at all cost. The teachings of Hindu scriptures-Srimad Bhagwatam etc. also impelled not to fight and battle, but rather continue to do good, and let God take care of any injustice and wrong actions of others. Sri Guru Gobind Singh instead taught that confronting and challenging the evil is a God given duty; after all the efforts to maintain peace are exhausted, a war may be fought as an inevitable last choice. Even though Sikh gurus fought under the banner of their own guru and as Sikh warriors, it did have the most momentous and significant effect on the Hindu psyche. Later, another stalwart Maratha king Chhatrapati Shivaji dared and challenged the Muslim ruler; the mighty Moghul Empire soon disintegrated and collapsed. Hindus, who had become more submissive and docile, learnt their lesson. Confronting and opposing the evil became a divine responsibility. In many instances, Sikh warriors had helped and saved Hindu families from dishonor and shame, from cruelty and brutality. In return, Hindu families often bestowed one or more of their sons to become Sikhs. Hindus and Sikhs grew intertwined, even marrying into each other. Undoubtedly there have been occasional clashes too, but the gurus have cemented the two with their sacred blood; these clashes are more like family feuds.

35 Sikhism: The Spiritual Teachings

The spiritual teachings of Sikhism are universal in nature. Emphasis is on putting these teachings into practice in everyday life. Humility and service are the watchwords in these teachings. The caste system was severely rejected; Sikh gurus taught their followers to share food with others as a mark of spiritual devotion. This precious teaching has stayed in the Sikh religion in the form of the community dinner, *langar*.

The Sikh gurus have also made it very clear that we simply cannot fully comprehend the infinite nature of God:

"Each one according to his understanding gives expression about Thee in his own different way. The vastness of Thy creation is beyond our comprehension. It is not known how in primal time the world was created by Thee."

—Rahras

"Not by purifications is the Purity attained, if even I were to purify a hundred thousand times over;

Not by silence is the Silence attained, if even I were to sit in meditation deep and long;

Not by fasting doeth the hunger subsides, if even I were to obtain the treasure-load of the worlds;

A thousand, a hundred thousand acts of wisdom if I had, not one would avail;

How then may I become true? How then may the veil of falsehood be rent asunder?

Through Voluntary surrender unto His will, O Nanak, the Will that is pre-ordained."

—Japji Saheb

Sikh gurus preached the virtue of devotion and surrender most stoutly, much as we indulge in meditations, worships, and rituals; these are, however, of no avail. By the unconditional surrender may we reach God. Whatever is happening in our lives, we may accept that as His will and accept the same with utmost humility.

"Who can sing His Power? Who can sing His Bounties? Who can sing His Virtues, His great Deeds Par excellence?

Who can sing His Knowledge, the very conception whereof is so difficult?

Who can sing His molding bodies so fascinating out of dust?

Who can sing His taking out life, and restoring it?

135

Who can sing His Power to know and perceive from far away?
And yet who can sing His Power to see as nearest of the near?
To assessing Him, there will be no end even though millions over millions may
speak on Him, over and over again;
The Giver giveth, the recipients get tired;
For ages and ages, have they lived on His bounties:
The Ordainer by His will hath set out the path for all to follow;
While He O Nanak, depending on none, remained Supremely Happy in his Ever-
Blossoming Beauty."
—Japji Saheb

A breathtaking view of the infinite powers of the Supreme God has been presented here. Guru sings of God's infinite powers and glories and reminds man to understand that God is not only omnipotent, but he also is much beyond our comprehension. In our everyday lives, many things happen that we may not be able to explain.

"While on their wings, the cranes fly thousands of miles away,
Leaving their young ones behind them;
Who feeds them there? Who puts food in their tiny beaks?
These birds remember the Lord in the heart of their heart, and He
Himself goes, and fondly looks after their young ones."
—Rahras

Man often worries about his posterity. Little do we realize how mortal and vulnerable we are and how powerful and infinite is the Lord! Man often considers himself the doer; Guru reminds him gently about this fallacy and arrogance. The Lord provides even the smallest birds. We must never lose or shake our faith.

"The whole world is involved with the eighteen Puranas, the sixty eight pilgrimages
and four sources of creation. Bhagat Ravidas says that Thy Name is only I am
offering unto Thee, O God!"
—Aarti, 4.3

We study one scripture after another and wander from one pilgrimage to another. The saint says all that is not necessary; we only need to remember the Lord in our heart! Guru repeatedly emphasizes repeating and remembering the holy name of the Lord.

"I shall beg of him Thine devotion, Bhakti; Thine worship of love.
My mind and body blossom forth, through the Guru's word;

As I contemplate Thee, I find myself afloat on countless waves of bliss.
Nanak, in union with the saintly souls art Thou realized;
Through the company of the Holy"
—Asa ki, var 2
Guru's role in man's salvation has been clearly defined and stressed. The company of the holy, the *Satsang*, also has been glorified. By the grace and support of the guru, we may learn to surrender to the Divine; in the holy company, we may discover God's bliss.

"Greed is the king, Sin the chief advisor and Falsehood the mind master;
Sex passion is the next in authority.
The fire of unrighteous grabbing rageth all round;
Gianees, the spiritual heads, dance, play music, and make up themselves in different characters.
Shouting and shrieking, they sing doubtful stories of the warriors;
Foolish pundits, the scholars, engage in tricks and devices for the love of amassing wealth.
The dharmee, the religious perform religious duties, but in self praise;
And they ask for salvation!
Some calling themselves jatees-the continent, know not the way;
They discard their homes and children.
Each one believes he is perfect;
None says he is less than perfect
But when the man is weighed with weights of honor;
Then alone may he be deemed as properly weighed"
—Asa ki, var M: 1
Guru has charted the path of the Divine; the vices of greed and sex are often loaded in the minds of the false savants and pundits. They may discard their own homes and claim to be perfect, but none is good if he is impure and sinful in his heart. The real nature of these deceitful spiritual guides is fully exposed. Only through purity and virtuous behavior may we attain divine grace.

Sikh teachings strongly point out certain weak points in Hindu society as were prevalent in that period. Sikh Gurus taught that we simply cannot fathom the depth of the Divine. Even though this thought has been mentioned in the ancient Hindu scriptures, there were many Hindu scholars who were freely professing their individual views about God, Cosmos, and Creation etc. These views were often conflicted and confused with each other. Sikh

Gurus considered the ultimate knowledge of God beyond human understanding. They clearly and unambiguously put an end to such futile discussions.

They also communicated their views regarding the evil of the caste system in a very practical manner. Every Sikh gurdwara across the world serves food as community "langar", where all the participants partake of food, sitting together, from the highest to the lowest, without any discrimination whatsoever. The same food is served to all, in similar utensils, and even the preceptors join without any peculiarity.

Sikh Gurus also rejected outright the outward rituals of austerities in different forms like fasting, maun-vrat (speech abstinence) etc. They emphasized instead on the inner cleaning, sincere devotion, and accepting the will of God candidly. They pointed out and exposed corrupt and avaricious persons, who often wore religious capes and mantles, but whose practices were immoral and cruel.

NOTE: Adapted from Chellaram Lachman, Navrattan, Dada Chellaram Publications, New Delhi, 2002.

36 Hinduism in the Modern Era: Spiritual Masters of the Recent Period

The modern era maybe considered, for purposes of this book, to be from the period of English rule in India. Even though there were many indignities and exploitations associated with British foreign rule, there was also a wave of fresh air. The long period of religious repression was over, and a new age of science and democracy spanned the globe. This led to a spurt of activity in Hindu society.

The contribution of many Western scholars of Hindu theology and ancient Sanskrit scriptures has been enormous. Although partly backed by the Christian missionary movement and zeal for conversion, there was also a genuine academic interest, combined with a spiritual inclination for Hindu philosophy. Toward the end of the eighteenth century, British Orientalists, who were interested in making a serious study of Sanskrit literature, centered themselves in Bengal. Among these were Sir William Jones (1746–1794), C. Wilkins (1749–1836), and Thomas Colebrook (1765–1837)[68], who together steered what came to be known as the field of Indology. Later, the formation of a seven-volume Sanskrit dictionary—in German by R. Roth and Otto Bothlingk, and in English by Monier Monier gave further embellishment to such efforts. The arduous work of Friedrich Max Muller (1823–1900) in translating and editing the Upanishads and other sacred books was of pioneer nature. Indeed, his prodigious, scholarly, dedicated, and inspired life may be regarded as the heroic consummation of the pioneering work of all Western thinkers who came before him.[69]

The wave of Hindu philosophy spread to many countries of Europe, including England, France, Germany, and Russia. In the United States, too, a similar phenomenon took place. William Dwight Whitney (1827–1894), C. R. Lanman (1850–1941), and Maurice Bloomfield (1885–1925) developed Indology at many centers; for example, at New York, Yale, and Harvard universities. Major figures like Henry David Thoreau (1817–1862) and Ralph Waldo Emerson (1803–1882) were also influenced by it. It was mainly because of these scholarly toils that Hinduism came to the center stage in the world.

Hindu spiritual teachings, which had remained hidden for millennia, became available to anyone, including the Hindus themselves! Earlier Hindu scriptures written in Sanskrit had remained the monopoly of the *Brahmin* community, who regarded themselves as the sole guardians of the religion.

Apart from the better known scholars, there were number of unsung heroes who toiled hard to study and present the Hindu scriptures in the eighteenth and nineteenth centuries, which may be regarded as the golden period of Hindu philosophy with regard to world impact. Jewish Frenchman Anquetil Duperron (1731–1805)[70] and Greek national Demetrius Galanos (1760–1833)[71] both worked with unparalleled passion under most difficult circumstances in this field. No less is the contribution of Swami Tathagatananda of the Vedanta Society, New York, in unearthing all these gems of Indology, and publishing their enormous contribution in his masterly book, *Journey of the Upanishads to the West.*

Spiritual philosophy in the world, like science, has evolved over millennia as the combined effort of seers and thinkers; their broad vision transgressed the geographical borders time and again. Sanskrit scholar Friedrich Max Muller's comments in this regard are noteworthy: *"How imperfect our knowledge of universal history, our insights into the development of human intellect, must always remain, if we narrow our horizon to the history of Greeks and Romans, Saxons and Celts, with a dim background of Palestine, Egypt, and Babylon, and leave sight of our nearest relatives, the Aryans of India, the framers of the most wonderful language, the Sanskrit, the fellow workers in the construction of our fundamental concepts, the fathers of our natural religions, the makers of the most transparent of mythologies, the inventors of the most subtle philosophy, and givers of the most elaborate laws."* [72]

There has been harsh criticism of Muller and other Westerners for inaccurately depicting ancient Indian history. It is more likely that these were errors of human limitations and not deliberate attempts at misguidance.

What follows is a description of some of the important Hindu spiritual leaders from the modern era. Each contributed significantly to the re-emergence of Hinduism in modern times and its spread to more distant lands:

Trailanga Swami (–1887) was a Hindu yogi and mystic famed for his spiritual powers who lived in Varanasi, India. He performed number of miracles, which were properly documented by many eye witnesses.

In the beginning of the nineteenth century, Bengal was the epicenter of education and culture. **Raja Rammohan Roy (1772–1833)** was one of the earliest social and religious reformers of this time. Inspired by the Western scientific education system, he propagated a modern approach to the old Hindu system. He advocated the basic Upanishadic teachings but discarded many of the Puranic and especially the Tantric methods of worship. He also discredited the idol, or *murti* puja. He believed in giving higher education to women. He founded a religious organization, *Brahmo Samaj,* which propagated many liberal reforms for Hindu women, who had long suffered from suffocating customs. One of the most horrendous customs prevalent in Hindu society in some parts of India, particularly amongst certain Rajput tribes, was the *Sati* ritual—the burning alive of a wife along with her dead husband. A wave of awakening was brought to Hindu society with the Brahmo Samaj movement, and many such harmful practices were stopped.

Sahajanand Swami (1781–1830), a saint of highest spiritual caliber, who later was known as *Bhagwan Swaminarayan,* developed a large following in Gujarat. His devotees established the *Swaminarayan* sect in 1907. Swaminarayan temples are famous for their grandeur and elegance. It also opened its gates to the lower castes that had been barred from such places. **Mahant Swami Maharaj (1933-)** is the present head. **Pramukh Swami Maharaj (1921–2016)**, the earlier head, with his tireless efforts, was instrumental in erecting over 1100 Hindu temple around the world--some of them most stupendous and gorgeous. He also rendered greatest service in organizing massive aid projects in times of natural calamities as well as teaching and training innumerable devotees to get rid of their vices and addictions.

Akkalkot Niwasi Shri Swami Samartha (-1878) is a household name in Maharashtra, Karnataka and Andhra Pradesh. He came to Akkalkot in 1856 where he continued his physical existence for 22 years. He died in 1878.

Swami Shiv Dayal Singh Ji (1818–1878) started a new type of religious organization, *Radha Swami Satsang,* at Agra, North India, around 1850. In 1891, Jaimal Singh Ji Mahraj established a separate division, *Radha Soami Satsang Beas,* at Beas in Punjab, which now has many branches in India and abroad. This congregation stressed the teaching of true spirituality to devotees, in place of many hollow rituals. The main importance was on having a living master who initiated the devotee to the Divine. **Shri Gurinder Singh Dhillon-Babaji (1954–)** is the current head of this sect.

Swami Dayananda Sarswati (1824–1883) was born in Gujarat and later moved to North India. He was a giant social reformer and started *Arya Samaj,* which worked vigorously for uplifting the condition of women. He heavily stressed the original Vedic teachings but advocated many simple rituals in place of lengthy and complicated customs, which had plagued the Hindu society.

Sri Ramakrishna Paramhans (1836–1886) and his celebrated disciple, **Swami Vivekananda**, brought about new perceptions in Hindu philosophy. Sri Ramakrishna Paramhans taught the oneness of God for all mankind, as the ancient Upanishads had pronounced. He has been recognized as God incarnate. After he passed away, his consort **Sri Sarda Devi (1853–1920)** successfully took on the mantle of leadership of the spiritual denomination for thirty-four years until her own death. Only five days before she passed away, she gave a message, the substance of which she had lived all her life: *"If you want peace, do not find fault with others. See your own faults. Learn to make the whole world your own. Nobody is a stranger, my dear. The entire world belongs to you."*

Swami Vivekananda (1863–1902), who was the chief disciple of Sri Ramakrishna Paramhans, had the great honor of introducing the East to the West. At the World Conference of Religions in Chicago in 1893, he entranced his audience with his very first speech. The essence of Vedanta, he taught, lies in the unity of entire cosmos! His spirituality was rather dynamic, as he said, *"First build your muscles, and then work on your soul!"* He did not believe in empty rhetoric—when he led his *Sanyasin* disciples to take up brooms and clean the streets of dirt and squalor, he joined them in their work. It was Swami Vivekananda who promoted Hinduism as a pluralistic and scientific religion and who projected the idea of neo-Vedanta as a philosophy of religion beyond borders.

Shirdi Sai Baba (-1918) was a spiritual person of very high caliber. His origin is not clear, but he preached love and humility. Many miracles are woven around him. He was a man of utter simplicity.

Maharishi Aurbindo (1872–1950) abandoned politics to enter the spiritual field, and he established a well-known meditation center at Pondicherry, South India. His deep knowledge of the Upanishads, the Bhagavad Gita, and yoga attracted many seekers to come to him for guidance from all over the world. After his death, his chief disciple, a French woman affectionately called Mother, became the head of the center. She remained at the helm until her death in 1973.

Swami Rama Tirtha (1873–1906) was born in Punjab. He started his career as a professor of mathematics but was later pulled into the spiritual life. He toured Japan and America, where he vigorously spread the message of the Hindu philosophy. Later, he established his center in the Himalayas and remained there until his death.

Swami Sivananda (1877–1963) was born in the state of Tamilnadu. He studied medicine and practiced as doctor in Malaysia for few years before joining the spiritual quest. He settled in the Himalayas and founded the Divine Life Society in 1936 at Rishikesh, North India. **Swami Vimalananda (1932-)** is the current head of the society.

Raman Maharishi (1879–1950) was a true sage of deep spirituality. He renounced everything to lead the life of an ascetic in Arunachala Hill, South India. His quest in which he asked "*Who am I?*" encouraged many devotees from far and wide to come to him. He was a man of few words and guided others by mystical communications.

Sadhu T. L. Vaswani (1879–1966) was a saint of sterling spiritual height. He founded his humble cottage in Pune, India, after the partition of India. He propagated simple and truthful living and taught his devotees to render service to the poor and needy. He even cared for animals and birds. **Dada Jashan Vaswani (1918–),** who has been hailed as spiritual master par excellence, is the current head of this mission. He has traveled extensively to all parts of the world, meeting devotees, conducting spiritual retreats, giving public discourses, and offering programs on TV. He is the author of many popular religious books.

With the advent of successive Western Colonial Powers like the Portuguese, Dutch, and British, the precious jewel of Hinduism that was laying subdued and hidden as an embedded spore for a long time under the Muslim rule, was suddenly transformed into a bright shining diamond! These Western Powers had probably planned and hoped to convert the whole country of India into Christianity as they had done in other places, but instead got themselves largely influenced and swayed by the richness of ancient Hindu scriptures. These Sanskrit sacred classics, though meticulously preserved by the small valiant Brahmin community under most adverse circumstances, had remained largely veiled, even from mainstream Hindus themselves. All this became possible because of the new fresh air of democracy and individual liberty expanding in many European countries. There was an unmatched interest in the Hindu religion and philosophy by scholars from across Europe and USA. Innumerable translations and commentaries on these Hindu scriptures were published. University professors were interested enough to do their own research and presented numerous papers highlighting essential descriptions about India and the Hindu culture. Hinduism has continued to arouse interest and curiosity ever since. A number of European and American followers became very seriously involved, donating large estates and resources to help establish great spiritual centers promoting teachings based on Hinduism. Inevitably, some also became skeptic and started negative propaganda, especially about the religion's customs and rituals etc., occasionally leading to conflicts and tensions. For Hindus, it may be worthwhile to remain patient with utmost goodwill and to follow the lead given by celebrated groundbreakers like Swami Vivekananda and Paramhansa Yogananda, who worked under much harder conditions and established prodigious places of worship, which have been growing and mounting until today!

Essentially the British rule, despite the harmful and detrimental effects that it brought, also generated the fresh air of social reform in Hindu society. As the colonial rule was first established in Bengal, the maximum impact of the new wave also became more visible there. The literacy spread by leaps and bounds; old, sick customs like the ill treatment of women, especially widows, were squarely challenged. The Murti Puja (idol worship), which had become an integral part of Hindu religion, after the Puranic times, too came under serious opposition in this reform movement. In another corner of the country during the same period, the Swaminarayan Sanstha was born, professing many reforms aimed at eradicating the evils of the caste system, uplifting the poor etc., but highly promoting the temple culture, including Murti Puja. Thus, Hinduism has simultaneously accepted different, rather even opposite viewpoints, without any bloodshed and violence. It would not be uncommon for members of one family living under one roof to profess different sects without any tension or conflict. Soon, another organization Radha Swami Satsang came on the scene; it stressed on prayers, devotion to God, service of the needy and weaning from the use of meat and alcohol. This Sanstha also downplayed the rituals and Murti Puja.

After the initial reform drive, which mainly aimed at social changes, Sri Ramakrishna Paramhansa founded the core of sanyasins in Bengal, what would later become a major religious group, the Vedanta Society. He taught the ancient Vedic teaching of oneness of God, and equality of all religions-Ekam Sat, Viprah Bahuti. His chief disciple Swami Vivekananda became the pioneer who carried the message from the East to the West. He laid more stress on service activities, and promoted pluralism in religion. It will not be incorrect to state that Sri Ramakrishna Paramhansa and Swami Vivekananda sowed the seeds of Inter-faith movement in their unique humble way, without much fanfare and formal proclamations.

During this period, Maharishi Aurbindo also joined the scene; many English educated scholars got interested in Hindu philosophy, freely inter-mingling with their Western counterparts, thereby creating a new type of Hindu spiritual group. They propagated and exchanged their spiritual views and comments in a more modern style, pulling more educated and sophisticated followers both from India and abroad, into ancient Hindu philosophies.

Such was the highly charged interest that many Westerners came all the way to meet and get blessings from spiritual persons like Raman Maharishi who hardly talked and did not communicate with them easily. In fact these holy centers started by the spiritual giants are still very popular and continue to attract crowds, both local and foreigners, by their spiritual vibrations.

Yet another university professor Sadhu T.L. Vaswani from Sindh (now Pakistan), who later moved to Pune after the partition of India, joined the spiritual caravan of literary spiritualists, teaching a universal approach to religion, away from fanatic narrow-minded rigid thoughts and opinions. His main disciple Dada Jashan Vaswani has continued to carry on his mantle of spirituality and service projects zealously till today.

This period of time has truly been most dynamic and productive for Hindu thought and philosophy. There was a huge exchange of ideas and mindsets between the East and the West. Although there may have been some degree of exploitation and abuse, more genuine cooperation and mutual respect was observed in most places. For Hindus who still had fresh memories of the more harsh and severe Muslim rule, such a democratic and autonomous atmosphere was naturally a matter of great joy and elation. For the first time, many university educated persons became interested in religion. There was a power-shift from the hereditary Brahmin class to more learned and genuinely spiritual masters. In religious arena, the role of Brahmins became subdued and limited to performing temple duties and rites.

37 Hinduism in Modern Era: Spiritual Masters of the Recent Period (Continued)

In 1875, Russian mystic Madam Blavatsky founded a new movement, the Theosophical Society, in New York. Within two years, the society had moved to Chennai (Madras) in India, where it flourished under the patronage of social reformer and theosophist Annie Besant (1847–1933). It was through the Theosophical Society that many Hindu philosophical ideas became popular in the West, influencing such literary figures as Aldous Huxley and Christopher Isherwood. The society is still active today in India and many Western countries, projecting the ancient philosophy of India along with other mystical and spiritual teachings, although in a non-religious manner. The interest of Westerners in Hindu philosophy also stemmed from their genuine hunger to seek the truth beyond the narrow limits of an organized religion.[73] The propagation of neo Vedanta philosophy in a vibrant manner, without any suggestion of conversion into Hinduism, by Swami Vivekananda opened floodgates for this inclination. There has been an unabated wave of interest in Hindu spiritual philosophy since then. It has taken many forms and directions, which is completely consistent with the diversity and freedom of Hindu thought.

Westerners have taken many of the top positions in various sects. Jean Klein and Andrew Cohen, who were disciples of Sri Ramana Maharishi, have become spiritual gurus and draw large crowds when they speak. Dr. Julian Johnson, a Protestant preacher, took Sawan Singh as his guru and later was instrumental in the development of *Radhasoami Satsang* in the West. After the death of Sri Bhaktivedanta Prabhupada, multiple Western disciples became heads of the Hare Krishna sect. The Self-Realization Fellowship, likewise, has a Westerner, Brother Chidananda, as its chief. So, too, is the case with the Saiva Siddhanta sect at the Hawaii Hindu monastery. Some of Westerners have adopted Hinduism formally, while others have not changed their original faith. This type of voluntary interest in faith other than one's own is simply unprecedented in human history. Only time will reveal the final impact of this unusual phenomenon.

Baba Buta Singh Ji Mahraj (1873–1943) established the spiritual organization, Nirankari Sant Samagam in 1929, along with Baba Avtar Singh Ji Mahraj. Their teachings are based on Hindu and Sikh spiritual teachings and stress the practical application of teachings in everyday life. **Satguru Mata Savinder Hardev Ji Maharaj** is the current head of this rapidly growing fraternity, which now has branches all over the world.

Dada Lekhraj (1876–1969) started the Brahma Kumari organization as a socio-religious movement in Sind, now in Pakistan, in 1937. Following the independence and partition of India, the organization moved to Mount Abu, in Rajasthan, India. They believe in meditation, ethical conduct, and social service. The institute is involved in many spiritual activities and philanthropic projects. This organization has now adopted the new name, World Spiritual University. **Dadi Janki Kriplani** is currently the head of this Spiritual Organization.

Swami Gangeshwar Anandji Maharaj (1881–1992) became blind in his early childhood, but his inner vision opened floodgates of religious teachings. He mastered all the ancient scriptures, especially the Vedas, and propagated spiritual knowledge far and wide among his innumerable devotees.

Sant Teooram (1887–1942) was born in Sind (now in Pakistan) and rendered noble service both in spiritual and social spheres by establishing the *Prem Prakash Mandli*. His writings are preserved in an invaluable volume, *Prem Prakash Granth*. Shanti Prakash Maharaj (1907–1992) succeeded him. At present, **Dev Prakashji Maharaj** is the head at the Ulhasnagar branch near Mumbai, India.

Sri Swami Tapovan Mahraj (1889–1957) was a seer of rare spiritual dimensions. He spent a large part of his life in Uttarkashi and Gangotri in the Himalayas. He led a life of true renunciation and austerity. He roamed about in the Himalayas with great passion. All by himself, on foot, he set off on many pilgrimages. He wrote lucid account of these wanderings in many books, which have become extremely popular. Among his many devotees was the most celebrated Swami Chinmayananda, who carried his banner and Vedantic message to the far corners of the globe.

Paramahansa Yogananda (1893–1952) was a Hindu spiritual leader of exceptional attributes who came to America in 1920. He founded the Self-Realization Centers at various places in the United States and other countries. His teachings, which were based mainly on the special meditation techniques of *Kriya yoga,* attracted a large following. He adopted many Western practices in places of worship and brought about a good synthesis of teachings of the East and West. His own life story, *Autobiography of a Yogi*, has remained a masterpiece of spiritual literature and has been read by millions of non-Hindus all over the world. **Brother Chidananda (1953-)** is the current president of the Self-Realization Fellowship, with headquarters in Los Angeles, California. This organization, as well as its counterpart in India, *Yogoda Satsanga Society of India,* is a not a Hindu establishment, but most of the teachings are based on the Bhagavad Gita and other ancient Hindu scriptures.

Sant Kirpal Singh (1894–1974) was originally a disciple of Sant Jaimal Singh and Sant Sawan Singh of Radha Soami Satsang. He later started a spiritual organization, Ruhani Satsang, which became popular. He taught the unity of all religions and incorporated teachings from different masters. **Sant Rajinder Singh Ji Mahaaj** is, at present, the head of the organization, which has branches all over the world.

Swami Prabhupada (1896–1977) was a monk of rare quality, who first came to America at the age of seventy. He adopted the technique of chanting and worshiping, as did Chaitanaya Mahaprabhu in the sixteenth century. He soon created a movement of Krishna consciousness, which spread all over the world and established number of imposing Hare Krishna temples.

Ananda Moyi Ma (1896–1982) was a holy woman from Bengal who entranced her large following with her spiritual personality. She taught a devotional path with simplicity and sincerity.

Sri Nisargadatta Maharaj (1897–1981), was spiritual teacher and philosopher, who taught the complex subject of *Advaita* in most simple language in vernacular language Martahi in Mumbai. In 1973, the publication of his most famous and widely translated book--*I am That* and the English translation of his talks brought him worldwide recognition and followers.

Baba Muktananda (1908–1982), Siddha master and disciple of Bhagawan Nityananda, established his world-renowned ashrams, first in Bombay, India; and later in many cities in America and other countries. He taught the ancient Hindu tradition of *Kundalini,* based on Kashmir Shaivism, an awakening meditation technique, which has drawn many followers all over the globe. **Gurumayi Cidvilasananda (1956–)** is the current head of this religious organization, with headquarters at South Falls burg, New York.

Swami Satchidananda (1914–2002) gained fame as master of Integral

Yoga--harmonising karma, jnana, and bhakti yoga. He was the author of many philosophical and spiritual books.

Swami Chinmayananda (1916–1993) established his main ashram at Powai, Bombay. He conducted Gita *yagnas*, where he gave very inspiring discourses on the teachings of the Gita He was a master orator who gave instruction in his own inimitable style. Later, his devotees formed Chinmaya Mission. He visited America and many other foreign countries regularly and established Chinmaya Centers and temples all over the world. *Bal Vihars*, children's classes at these centers, have become extremely popular, both in India and abroad..

Swami Swaroopananda is the current head of the Chinmaya Mission worldwide.

Maharishi Mahesh Yogi (1917–2008) become world famous for introducing his own version of meditation called Transcendental Meditation, or TM. After doing austerities in the Himalayas for many years, he settled in the United States and started a full-fledged university in Iowa that is dedicated to the study of Hindu scriptures, Ayurveda, yoga, and meditation.

Pandurang Shastri Athavale (1920–2004), popularly known as *Dadaji* by millions of followers all over the world, has created a niche for himself by adopting more than eighty thousand villages for his now-famous *Swadhya* movement. Multitudes of poor communities of farmers and fishermen have benefited enormously from these socio-religious awakening centers, especially in western India. *Dadaji* called it "Gita in action." He was awarded the prestigious Magsaysay Award in 1997 for excellence in community leadership.

Baba Hari Dass (1923–) may be best known as a *mauni sadhu,* a monk who practices continual silence. Born in Almora, India, he moved to the United States in 1971. He has established a vast ashram at Mt. Madonna near Santa Cruz, California, where thousands of devotees come to learn Ashtanga yoga and obtain answers to many everyday problems. He writes his answers on a chalkboard and enlightens his followers with spiritual wisdom. Baba writes, *"There is an inner silence. It cannot be heard by the ears, only by the heart."*

Mata Nirmla Devi (1923–2011) became a famous Kundalini yoga guru, teaching this art at mass meetings that drew thousands of devotees at a time. Mata Nirmla had been busy conducting the meditation courses, called *Sahaj yoga,* both in India and abroad.

Swami Rama (1925–1996) was brought up in the Himalayas. He came to America in 1969 and immediately caught the attention of many with his deep knowledge of yogic exercises and mystic practices. He wrote many books and later established the Himalayan Institute in the United States. **Pandit Rajmani Tigunait** is, at present, the head of the Himalayan Institute at Honesdale, Pennsylvania.

Satya Sai Baba (1926–2011) became a legendary figure and is considered to be God incarnate by his many followers. The religious organization associated with his name has performed great service to humanity by providing excellent hospitals, schools, colleges, and drinking-water facilities, as well as undertaking many other social activities. His ashram, known as *Prasanthi Nilayam* (Abode of the Highest Peace) at Puttaparthi in Andhra Pradesh, is always buzzing with religious and philanthropic activities. He promoted a virtuous life, vegetarianism, abstinence from alcohol, and charitable deeds.

Satguru Sivaya Subramuniya Swami (1927–2001) began his teaching mission in Hawaii in 1957. He was an ardent Shiva devotee and did a great service in spreading the message of Saivism around the world. In 1979, he founded the magazine *Hinduism Today* to promote the cause of the Hindu religion through various activities. A large Hindu monastery has been established on 450 spacious acres at Kauai, Hawaii. **Satguru Bodhinatha Velyanswami (1942–),** the current head of the organization, has continued the great tradition of his master, as well as carrying on the spiritual lineage of the Kailasa Parampara of the Nandinatha Sampradaya and Guru Mahasannidhanam.

Swami Omkarananda Saraswati (1929–2000) was born in Hyderabad, Andhra Pradesh, and was initiated into the spiritual *sanyas* at the tender age of 17 by the renowned guru Swami Sivananda. Later, he became seriously involved in the study of Vedas and meditation and yoga practices, and he established a spiritual training center at Switzerland in 1966. He later conducts his religious activities mainly from his Himalayan ashram in India.

Mata Amritanadamayi "Amma" (1953–) was born into a poor family in a fishing village in Kerala, India. She showed her extreme compassion even when she was a small child. Soon, she attracted people to her, and she gives a loving embrace to all those who seek her blessings. She has built number of educational institutes, orphanages, hospitals, and homes for the homeless, and has undertaken many other projects for the poor and downtrodden. Recently, after receiving the prestigious Peace Award at the UN General Assembly, Amma stressed the essential spiritual power of women. This, she emphasized, is far stronger than any masculine power.

Sri Sri Ravi Shankar (1956–) has become a world figure for his unique organization called the Art of Living, which has been recognized by the United Nations for its great efforts in uniting people and cutting across the barriers of religion, gender, and class. The organization has spread to more than one hundred countries, and Sri Sri Ravi Shankar always emphasizes unconditional love as his main theme.

Amma Sri Karunamayi (1958–) has been the embodiment of a spiritual mother to her innumerable devotees all over the world. She is involved with a free hospital and many other charitable projects in India, apart from offering personal guidance. She visits America and other countries regularly and conducts spiritual retreats for the benefit of her followers.

Swami Shankarananda (1942-) is the head of the Shiva Ashram, based near Melbourne, Australia. Originally from New York, he travelled to India in 1970 where he became the disciple of Swami Muktananda. Muktananda initiated him as a swami in 1977 and instructed him to write on spiritual subjects, especially the philosophy of Kashmir Shaivism, and to awaken the Kundalini energy of seekers. In 2010, Swami Shankarananda received the title of Mahamandaleshwar ('great leader') in recognition of his work in the service of the Sanatana Dharma.

There is vast number of living saints in India, who propagate the spiritual teachings of Hinduism through their talks and TV media all across the globe. Individual description is not given for want of space; most are also covered on web sites. Inadvertently some important names may have been left out:

Pujay Morari Bapu, Pujay Sudhenshu Mahraj, Pujay Satyanarayan Goenkaji, Jagat Guru Kirpal Ji Mahraj, Sringeri Shankaracharya Sri Bharati Tirtha Swami, Shankaracharya of Jyotir Math Swami Swaroopananda, Swami Avadeshanand Giri, Mata Amritanadamayi "Amma", Swami Chidananda Saraswati (Muniji), Swami Baba Ramdevji Mahraj, Goswami Mridul Shastri, Pujay Rameshbhai Oza, Pujay Satpal Mahraj, Sadhvi Didi Ritambharaji, Ananadmurti Guru Maa, Pujya Sri Ganapathy Sachchidananda Swamiji, Satchidananda Swami (Gujarat), Paramahamsa Nithyananada, Narayan Sai Baba, Swami Agnesh, Swami Parmananda, Pujay Deepakbhai Desai, Bhagwan Lakshmi Narayan, Swami Mukundananda, Pujay Devkinandan Thakur Ji, Acharya Ishan Shivanandan, Shri Pulak sagar Ji, Shri

Kirtibhai Ji, Swami Sukhbodhananda, Pujay Shrirya Bharti, Pujay Gopal Mani Ji Mahraj, Sadhu Kailash Manu, Shri Giri Bapu, Sri valingendra Swamiji, Sri Chidananda Swamiji of Mysore, Sri Rudramuni Swamiji, of Tiptur, Dr. Sri Balagangadharanatha Mahaswamiji, Sri Shivarathri Mahaswmi of Suttur Math, Vrunda Sakhi and many others.

Hindu philosophy has continued to attract and influence many in the Western world in different ways. Some have formally adopted and converted into Hinduism while others have taken Hindu teachings as a way of life, but remained in their original faith. In fact, Hindu Gurus have never insisted on conversion as a precondition for teaching anyone. Some leading spiritual organizations now have Westerners as their heads. Some of these organizations identify themselves as completely Hindu whereas others offer philosophical teachings based on Hinduism combined with the traditions of other faiths, without any official affiliation to Hindu religion. These religious establishments which are not aligned solely to Hinduism or any other faith appear to be getting quite popular, enlisting followers of diverse religions. They concentrate and focus on spiritual teachings, freely quoting various Hindu gods and saints along with those of other creeds. These organizations do not regard themselves as non-religious either; they uphold religion as most important, but opt to remain free from any strict allegiance. This is a new development in religious development across the world, and more so in countries like US with varied population. Only time will reveal the full impact of this arrangement in the future. It may probably have a significant effect on Hinduism in different ways. These organizations have their own codes of administration and management; their worship modalities may also be quite different from the conventional Hindu temples. Many Hindus who regularly attend these new religious centers suggest and request for changes in the conventional Hindu places of worship accordingly. This process of evolution involves acceptance and adoption of what is useful and beneficial, and dropping what may be undesirable and harmful.

The present age has brought many challenges too. Many are moving liberally toward the Western style, and yet others are keen to stay conservative and orthodox. Although physical violence remains absent, there is undoubtedly a significant inter-play of words, arguments, and discussions going on, with each side advocating and glorifying their own system and practice. By and large, the situation is peaceful and calm. In Hindu society, an individual may choose very freely his or her method of worship, and pray at any place of one's choice; to a large extent this arrangement is working quite amicably.

In recent times, there has been an influx of Hindu Gurus, both in India, and in many foreign countries. These Gurus usually draw huge crowds, and are seriously involved both in their spiritual pursuits as well as often in social and charitable undertakings. Their influence and inspiration play a big part in shaping the lifestyles of many. Undoubtedly, most Swamis and Gurus are rendering yeoman service by their selfless dedication to the noble cause. But like in any other sphere of public service, there are few, who get swayed into wrong direction. By their very nature of "spiritual status", they become even more infamous and ill-reputed.

38 Hinduism and Science

There is a general feeling that religion and science are two very different—even opposite—things. This notion is not true; in fact, they may go hand-in-hand to help and improve the life of mankind. In pursuit of spiritual knowledge and wisdom, ancient sages of India made many heroic efforts. Several offshoots of these explorations resulted in the establishment of different fields of secular sciences, which have remained bonded with religion over the millennia.

The ancient Hindu scriptures of the Vedas clearly indicated this trend. Each major Veda has a secondary Veda, which deals with science or another subject of humanity. Rig Veda has the Upaveda 'ayurveda', which deals with the sciences of medicine and health. Yajurveda has the Upaveda 'dhanuveda', which deals with archery and the military. Samaveda has the Upaveda 'gandharvaveda', which deals with music. And Atharveda has the Upaveda 'sthapathyaveda', which deals with astronomy, astrology, engineering, and mathematics.

Within these Upavedas is perhaps the beginning of many scientific theories. It is believed that Hindu mathematics was one of the earliest and most advanced sciences. The concept of zero and the decimal system were both discovered in India first and later passed on to the world through Arab conquerors. Ramanujan's name was associated with the concept of infinity. Aryabhatta, who lived from 476 to 520, was considered to be the first Hindu mathematician known to the world. His treatise on pure mathematics and the eclipse system is hailed in the world of science, even today, with great respect.[74]

Science in the ancient Hindu system had the full support of the religious authorities. Modern science, on the other hand, had a severe clash and resistance from the Catholic Church. Hinduism like other religions too had to suffer the onslaught. It was finally left to the heroic efforts of great minds like Swami Vivekananda and others, who presented a true picture of Hinduism before the world and restored its lost glory to a considerable extent. There was renewed interest in the ancient teachings of the Vedanta and other Hindu philosophies. Soon, recognition came from many unexpected quarters; among them, the great scientist Albert Einstein and an equally giant literary figure Bertrand Russell. Their interest in Hindu philosophies paved the way for discovering many scientific truths hidden in the Hindu ancient scriptures.

Science undoubtedly plays a vital role in our lives. It is the mind of the man that steers science and directs it toward many achievements. Religion, on the other hand, steers the mind and transforms it toward spiritual realization. Einstein aptly described the synergistic union between the two: "*Science without religion is lame, and religion without science is blind.*"

It was to the credit and genius of the Hindu mind that it discovered the phenomenon of eternity. In the Rig Veda, there is clear mention of Earth coming from the sun. The Vedas recognized the sun as the primary source of all energy. In the Yajur Veda, it is stated that the sun moves about its own axis, and the earth rotates around the sun, while the moon rotates around the earth.[75] The Rig Veda also explains that the earth is held by the sun's attraction. The position of nine celestial bodies, *Navgraha*, mentioned in the Vedas is in line with modern astronomy. Hindu sages also described in detail the phenomenon of acceleration (*ksanika*), momentum (*vega*), and vibration (*spandana*). Modern science has nearly accepted all these accounts and recognized the worthiness of the ancient Hindu *Rishis*, who worked through their superior, spiritual minds without any of the modern technologies. Hindu philosophy also believes that if the mind becomes absolutely pure, it may have powers that are beyond the domain of the secular sciences. The extraordinary feats of many yogis have been verified and acclaimed by experts.

The ancient Hindu *Rishis* also presented the concept of manifestation and dissolution, and this too is now widely accepted by modern science. These sages of yore gave the world the first terminology for this phenomenon in Sanskrit: *sankocha* and *vikasha*. *Sankocha* means "shrinking," and *vikasha* means "expanding." Coincidentally, modern cosmologists have hailed this concept.[76]

Since its conception, the Hindu religion has enjoyed great harmony and agreement with "Science". In fact, spiritual pursuits often went hand-in-hand with secular interests. The fall out after the excessive struggle between Religion and Science in Christianity did not spare Hinduism either. Even so in Hindu society, the two are not totally antagonist now, nor of course is there any direct and deep association. The two seem to be quite independent of each other.

The world has now shown much interest in India's ancient philosophies. A number of studies have pointed attention to subjects like Yoga, Meditation, Ayurveda, and Astronomy etc. to show how these disciplines have stood the critical test of modern science very ably.

Spiritual Gems from Swami Vivekananda

Each soul is a star, and all stars are set in that infinite azure, that eternal sky, the Lord. There is the root, the reality, the real individuality of each and all. Religion began with the search after some of these stars that had passed beyond our horizon, and ended in finding them all in God, and ourselves in the same place (Vol 5, p. 69)

There is no chance for the welfare of the world unless the condition of women is improved. It is not possible for a bird to fly on only one wing. Hence in the Ramakrishna Incarnation, the acceptance of a woman as the Guru, hence His practicing in the woman's garb and frame of mind, hence too His preaching the Motherhood of women as representatives of the Divine Mother. (Vol 6, p. 328)

Awake, awake, great ones! The world is burning with misery. Can you sleep? Let us call and call till the sleeping Gods awake, till the god within answers to the call. What more is in life? What greater work? (Vol 7, p. 498)

(From the Complete Works of Swami Vivekananda, Centenary Edition, Published by Advaita Ashrama, Mayavati, Almora Himalays)

39 Meditation

"When all the senses are stilled, when the mind is at rest but alert, when the intellect wavers not, then is known the highest state of Divinity."
—Katha Upanishad [77]

Meditation—*Dhyana*---in Hindu theology, is the art and technique of experiencing the "divine" within. Many a sage sat on mountaintops, in caves, in forests, and on riverbanks and meditated deeply, for long periods of time. Even so, meditation is essentially an esoteric practice. An inert mountain or forest cannot be a substitute for an awakened and spiritual mind. In the sages' vast sojourns, varied ingenious techniques were discovered, which were then passed on to the disciples, thus creating a chain of *guru/shishya*, or the teacher/disciple relationship.

Yoga and meditation are first mentioned in the earlier Upanishads, such as *Brhadarayaka*, *Katha*, and *Svetavatara*. So, too, these are described in the ancient epic scripture of the Mahabharata and the Bhagavad Gita.[78] It was Patanjali (240–180 BCE), however, who compiled the famous *Yoga Sutra*, which outlines the eight-point program of *Ashtanga yoga*:

1. **Yama** (the don'ts): This deals with ethical restraint. The instinctive and impulsive behavior of the individual enrolling in meditation and yoga needs to be ethical and full of consideration for others. Nonviolence in thought, word, and action becomes the code of conduct. Truthfulness, non-stealing, continence (*brahmacharya*), patience, firmness, compassion, honesty, moderate diet, and purity are other necessary requirements.

2. **Niyama** (the do's): This deals with the cultivation of virtuous and spiritual qualities. Observance of remorse, contentment, chastity, faith, worship, study of scriptures, spiritual intellect, *japa* (uttering God's name), and austerity are all prerequisites in this category.

3. **Asanas**: the practice of body postures, exercising with relaxation.

4. **Pranayama**: control of breathing techniques, to concentrate thoughts and usher vitality to all parts. *Pranayama*, or breath control, has earned much attention. *Pranayama* is essentially directed toward purifying and quieting the mind, which is the seat of all emotions. Watching the breath by itself, in inhalation and exhalation, is considered an effective antidote to stress. In the opinion of Sri Sri Ravi Shankar, "*The mind is ever wandering; breathing control may be an effective whip to guide it on the right path.*"[79]

5. *Pratyahara*: to internalize attention without any distraction. Search of the Divine within one's own self has always occupied the attention of Hindu seers. The mind needs to be pure and spiritual, in the *turiya* state. *Turiya,* which literally means "fourth," represents the higher mind, beyond the waking, sleeping, and dreaming states.

6. *Dharna*: to focus on a chosen object Spiritual Divine, disregarding any other interruption.

7. *Dhyana*: to meditate on the field of inquiry, with laser beam attention. Often, the answers to many difficult questions sprout from within. Gradually, one may learn to tap knowledge from the cosmic consciousness of the Divine.

8. *Samadhi*: to ultimately unite and merge with the source; the state of self-realization. The final step, s*amadhi,* literally means "union with God" (*Sam*: with; *adhi*: Lord). There are two stages of Samadhi. One is *savikalpa samadhi*—*savikalpa* means separateness; in this Samadhi, the devotee feels himself at a separate and lower level than God. The second is *nirvikalpa samadhi*—*nirvikalpa* means having no separateness. In this higher stage of *samadhi,* the devotee completely merges with the Divine.

The role of the awakening of chakras through mind concentration and subtle visualization has been the subject of intense study and has occupied the attention of both spiritual and scientific scholars in recent times. The art and science of *Raja yoga*, or the meditation yoga, is closely associated with the awakening of the chakras in tune with various breathing exercises (*pranayamas*). There have been many different techniques, such as *Kundalini yoga, Kriya yoga, Siddha yoga, Nirvana-Sahasrara,* and *Sudarshan yoga* etc. with some variations. The seven chakras—the *Muldhara chakra* at the base of the spine, the *Svadishthana chakra* at the base of the genitals, the *Manipura chakra* at the navel level, the *Anahata chakra* at the level of the heart, the *Visuddha chakra* at the level of the medulla oblongata opposite the throat, the *Ajna chakra* between the eyebrows, and the *Sahasrara chakra* above the topmost point of the head—symbolically represent an ascending degree of higher spiritual consciousness in an individual. There are also seven chakras below the *muladhara;* these reflect the lower animal tendencies.

Hindu sages also envisaged a system of subtle channels, or

prana, which traverse throughout the body and mind. These are not anatomical channels like blood vessels and nerves. According to learned sages, alongside the physical or anatomical channels of body, there exist the invisible energy channels, through which the vital current of life force, the *prana,* flows. In a subtle and spiritual way, the deep-breathing exercises, the *pranayamas,* have a nourishing effect on the *prana* energy channels. *Prana* channels represent the ultimate micro-tissue life activity. It is believed that *pranayamas* have a major effect on the body through tissue microcirculation at the brain and other parts of the body. Modern medicine has endorsed the beneficial effects of many of these meditation techniques in countering the harmful effects of stress on the human system. Many leading medical authorities now recognize that through the practice of meditation and yoga, one can regulate heart rate, blood pressure, and other vital phenomenon, hitherto considered as beyond the influence of voluntary control.

The best time for meditation is considered to be before dawn, *brahmamuhurta,* when the mind is in its most pure and receptive form. A second meditation before retiring, however, is also highly recommended, as it improves the spiritual quotient significantly.[80] It has been said that while the modern science of psychology delves into the subconscious, traversing through myriad of past guilt and shame, meditation focuses on the super-consciousness, the treasure trove of divine virtues.

Paramahansa Yogananda wrote in his book *The Divine Romance,* more than half century ago: "*The one thing that will help to eliminate world suffering—more than money, houses, or any other material aid—is to meditate and transmit to others the divine consciousness of God that we feel.*" Hindus have an abiding faith that the meditations of sages protect the world in a subtle spiritual manner. Sitting in the high Himalayas and other places in their infinite solitude and purity, these *Rishis* send divine blessings in the form of vibrations, which have a profound and extraordinary effect, even when the *Rishis* appear to be doing nothing!

There have been many research studies on meditation at U.S. universities and elsewhere throughout the world. More evidence is accumulating that this technique "*significantly helps in relieving stress and depression, builds up the positive mood, and actually contributes toward increase in the immune quotient.*" No wonder, then, that in the United States alone, more than ten million adults practice meditation regularly. It is now offered freely in schools, hospitals, law firms, government buildings, corporate offices, and even prisons. There are specially marked meditation rooms at airports. At the Maharishi University in Fairfield, Iowa, even the young students meditate twice daily. There are even reports of brain changes, as observed by MRI (magnetic resonance imaging) techniques, after meditation.[81] Scientists have discovered palpable thickening of some critical areas of the brain cortex in monks who perform meditation over prolonged periods.

The meditation and yoga system involving the *chakras* and *pranayamas* is often claimed to be associated with the attainment of many mystical, supernatural powers, or *siddhas* (miracles) also. In this regard, Charles Robert Richet, who won the Nobel Prize for Medicine in 1913, wrote *"Metaphysics is not yet officially a science, recognized as such. But it is going to be….Our five senses are not our only means of knowledge."*[82] Many yogis have demonstrated astonishing evidence of living without any food or water for extended periods of time. It is believed that they may draw their energy directly from the cosmos, just as plants get energy with the help of chlorophyll.

Modern science has proved that there are over 100 billion thinking neuron cells in human brain. Only 10-20 percent of these cells are in activity, the rest are lying dormant. Till very recently, it was believed that human brain docs not grow after early age. This theory has now been discredited. Marian Cleves Diamond (1926-2017), a noted scientist from U.C. Berkley, studied part of **Einstein's brain**, and discovered that human brain keeps growing with formation of new cells in favorable circumstances, repudiating the old theory that the brain stops growing after a certain age. (LA Times August 19, 2017 Orbituary Notes)

In Hindu philosophy, it is believed from the ancient times, "meditation" at any age, in fact more often in elderly age, may be performed with favorable results, and may bring about changes in the behavior patterns, making the person more spiritual and virtuous, with the regular and extended practice.

The art and practice of "Meditation" has truly been regarded as Hindu philosophy's shining jewel. Its origin has been traced to most ancient prehistoric times, much before the formal establishment of Hinduism. There is evidence of monks practicing "austerity" and "meditation" in the "Sindhu-Saraswati civilization" (Harappa civilization); this was later named as the Sramana ideology. Sraman in Sanskrit means monk.
It is said that in "Prayer", a person talks to God, and requests for

help while in "Meditation", God talks to the person, and prompts him toward the right path. In effect, the purpose of Meditation is to listen to the word of God with utmost attention, and then act in accordance with it in any situation. The most ancient scriptures of Hinduism - the Vedas and the Upanishads are compilations of such "words of God" as heard internally by the sages and Rishis as "Shrutis", after extended meditations on river banks, in forests, and on hill tops. God in Hinduism is conceived as the epitome and embodiment of all truth and wisdom, of righteousness and knowledge. Meditation thus forms the very basis of religion; the search for such divine guidance becomes the purpose life. Hindu scriptures are generally developed and assembled around God's tales in various manifestations, all in different situations and circumstances. Always Keeping God in mind, a human being may meditate to find the answer to all his or her problems and challenges.

In their deep meditation, ancient Rishis connected God with infinite knowledge, infinite virtue, and infinite power, beyond any human understanding. They comprehended that when we meditate and pray to God, we in effect seek His divine guidance in our own life situations. In prayer and meditation, we may seek divine direction and support, and in full faith and sincerity try to carry out our duty in accordance with God's command. Gradually over a period of time, with diligence and practice, we may know what is sanctioned or not sanctioned by God.

In recent times, meditation has become a watchword of human endeavor in all walks of life, and in all places. Although Buddhism has been more associated with the ritual and method of meditation, its origin in Hinduism remains uncontested. Modern science has accepted the art of meditation as an important tool in combating disease and malady of different types. The Hindu concept of union of religion and science has been vindicated and supported by such efforts worldwide.

Spiritual Gems from Mahavira

A day once gone will never return. Therefore, one should be diligent each moment to do good. We reach the goal of good life by pious work.

Blow not thy trumpet. From the root grows the trunk and from the trunk shoots branches, from branches grow the twigs the leaves. And then flowers blossom and the tree bears fruit and juice. It is the root of Dharma (virtue) and Moksha (liberation) is the juice.

Greater will be his victory who conquereth his self than that of one who conquereth thousands and thousands in a valiant fight.

Fool is he who, blinded by his passions, fixeth not his thoughts on his moral progress and welfare but sinketh down through temptations of lust.

Whosoever desireth his own well-being should cast away anger, conceit, deceit and lust. For these four aggravate sin. Anger killeth love, conceit humility, deceit amity, and lust everything. By calmness anger is to be won, by meekness conceit, by straightness deceit, and by content lust.

(Source: Eternal Values, Swami Lokeshwarananda, The Ramakrishna Mission Institute of Culture, Calcutta, 1990)

40 Yoga: Union with the Divine

In Hindu thought, spirituality creates a union with God—yoga. This union is not a physical union but a subtle mental union. When we pray to God and repeatedly think about and meditate on him, there is an intention. The intention behind this meditation on God is to gradually transform our inner mind—*antahkaran*, a very special term in Hindu philosophy—toward godliness. The poet has verily sung, "*O Krishna, may thee color me into thy color.*"

Yoga is basically a system that involves the training of body, mind, and spirit; it is a very integrated program. Often in modern athletic training, the body is exercised but the mind is not attended to. Conversely, in religious or spiritual courses, the physical part is ignored. The ancient concept of yoga recognizes that through a healthy body alone, a healthy mind might be cultivated. The mind must be fixated to the highest and noblest thoughts of virtuous conduct. Thus, man is groomed to attain excellence in all fields of life. Indeed, Hindu seers have always maintained that all disorders and diseases are caused because an individual walks out of the cosmic order into disharmony and discord.

It is to the great credit of these ancient gurus of India that this program has now been adopted by the modern world. Although all schools of yoga do not teach in the same way, the basic structure and philosophy may not tampered with. It should be clearly understood that yoga is not just another physical training program. In essence, it is a training that involves a harmonious blending of the body and mind, aiming toward the highest levels of efficiency in all spheres of activities. By its original definition, yoga is a union with the Divine. In any modified form, if there is no such union, it may not be called yoga. Essentially, yoga is coupled with spiritual and divine qualities.

In the ancient scriptures, yoga has been classified under different forms: *Jnana yoga*: yoga through knowledge; *Bhakti yoga*: yoga through devotion; *Karma yoga*: yoga through action; *Raja yoga*: yoga through deep meditation; and *Hatha yoga*: yoga attained through body postures. In reality, these are not separate divisions but rather many aspects of the same training program. In practice, an individual may opt for more attention to any one or more of these forms of yoga, according to his aptitude and choice.

Even though yoga may not be done in the same way at any two places—there are abundant variations and modifications—yoga is always conducted with a sense of auspicious sacredness. It is usually started with an invocation and chanting of "*Om*" or some other Vedic mantra. Sometimes a candle is lit, and at the end, the yoga is closed with a chanting prayer hymn and a respectful bowing with folded hands—the Indian "*Namaste*". Consider the scene if there is vulgar talk, boisterous loud music, any casual or purposeless video program on TV, or even news broadcast when yoga is going on—it would defile the environment for the yoga.

Hindu sages emphasize holding the spine erect while doing meditation and yoga. The human species is the only creature that can hold the spine erect. Ancient seers probably observed a strong facility of the erect spine and the brain. It would not be wrong to say that yoga has taken the world by storm. In America and Europe, yoga has perhaps become more popular than it is in India today. Swami Vivekananda and Paramahana Yogananda initially brought the concept and philosophy of yoga to the United States in the early twentieth century. B. K. S. Iyengar started many schools of yoga across the country. In recent times there has been a flood of yoga centers across America. There are scores of books, magazines, and Web site programs on yoga. Yoga has found its way into the American lifestyle, not just with adults who want to improve their physical, mental, and spiritual capabilities but also with young children. More than twenty million persons in America alone are, at present, involved in yoga exercises.

Undoubtedly Yoga has gone through many a herculean challenge in USA. Yoga Journal, which is the leading publication for yoga professionals, has branched off into the lucrative area of conferences and retreats. In many Western yoga centers, the proceedings are conducted in a secular, non-religious manner. Physical postures and exercises, together with some breathing exercises (*pranayama*), form Hatha yoga. Yoga exercises have proved very beneficial, as these are balanced with relaxation techniques.

Even though yoga is a child of Hinduism, it has now grown its own strong wings. It has made its mark, beyond the confines of any one religion. Yoga has truly become a citizen of the world!

Today, Yoga has become a household word around the world; the United Nations' Organization has recognized it by

celebrating June 21 every year as World Yoga Day. Like many other ancient Hindu systems of Meditation, Ayurveda etc., Yoga has now earned its long overdue appreciation. Yoga focuses attention on physical, mental, and spiritual aspects in varying degrees. In some places, its spiritual aspect is considerably downplayed, while in other places it is given the highest importance. Even in India, at no two places is yoga conducted in the same manner. This, in fact, lies in accordance with the general liberal attitude of Hindu religion and culture; leaving an individual to practice many activities according to his/her own choice and aptitude. Yoga being an ancient traditional system, there are no formal copyrights on it, yet a natural reference to its Indian origin, avoiding any casual mal-presentation would be most sagacious. In fact, Yoga performed without any spiritual contemplation, by its very definition, would be incomplete and much less beneficial.

Spiritual Gems from Buddha

True happiness comes to those who live at peace with their fellows. The aim of all should be to learn peace and live peacefully with all men.

Guard against evil deeds: control the body. Eschew evil deeds and do good. Guard against evil words: control tongue. Eschew evil words and speak good ones. Guard against evil thoughts: control the mind. Eschew evil thoughts and think good ones.

A word spoken in wrath is the sharpest sword; covetousness is the deadliest poison; passion the fierest fire; ignorance is the darkest night.

Let no one deceive another, let no one despise another, let no one out of anger or resentment wish to harm another.

(Source: Eternal Values, Swami Lokeshwarananda, The Ramakrishna Mission Institute of Culture, Calcutta, 1990)

41 Guru and the Holy Company (*Satsanga*)

"O Shri Rama, an aspirant should take recourse to satsanga (good association). He should nourish his intellect by receiving instruction from the sages and reflecting upon them. Gradually, he should cultivate the great qualities that manifest in enlightened personalities."

—*Yoga Vasistha*

A guru is an integral part of Hinduism. Literally, the word guru means "one who removes darkness." In the Hindu religion, a guru occupies a very prestigious position. It is believed that the guru may pass his knowledge and grace to his disciple both in tangible and subtle spiritual ways: *Danam atma jnanam*—one who gives the knowledge of *Self*, the Divine.

A guru imparts spiritual knowledge out of love and compassion and not for any material considerations. With spiritual knowledge an individual's character is changed. A guru may wield a very powerful influence on the moral values of a large population.

A true guru is himself pure and enlightened. His own behavior is completely free from any blemish. He is above lust, anger, and greed and is forever calm and filled with wisdom. His only motivation is to uplift humanity. His lifelong interest becomes to uplift and educate his disciples, mentally and spiritually, without any personal gain. He does not build any expectations in others, including his pupils, and hence, he is free from any wrath and ill temper. He becomes the embodiment of cosmic love. Guru teaches how to use the senses and the mind in a spiritual manner and in a most practical method, almost as if he were holding his *shishya's* hand. Scriptures tell us the true worth of a guru: "*Guru Vishnu, Guru Brahma, Guru Maheshwara!*" Thus, a guru is elevated to the combined status of all gods. Hindu scriptures mention that even Lord Rama and Lord Krishna had to undergo training with their respective gurus, Sage Vasistha and Muni Sandipani.

At the same time, however, utmost discretion and vigilance is also advised in walking on this path. In the Bhagavad Gita, the Lord clearly instructs Arjuna that after listening to all, he must make his own decision. This, indeed, is the core point of Hinduism. One's own solicitude, judgment, and free will are considered the most important. In the end, we may awaken our own guru, the Divine within. In scriptures this is often called the *satguru*, or the true guru. This is the final destination. Hindus have an abiding faith that the Divine dwells within, and it needs to be sought with a most pure mind.

Also, there are veiled warnings that a true guru, however learned and knowledgeable, must never be trapped in his own ego or his own arrogance. A guru's position is well defined; his limits are clearly marked. As long as he is in the human body, his human weaknesses and vulnerabilities are a part of him. Modesty and not egoism is the mark of a true guru. Harnakash was a most learned guru in his own way, but no sooner did he wear the garb to become God than he was eliminated. The phenomenon of megalomania, the lust for power, is an eternal human weakness. True humility is the sign of a genuine guru. There are some gurus who are not true masters. The highly spiritual gurus do attain very advanced supernatural powers. But even among the highest, the human factor always remains. Have not the scriptures mentioned that even God in the human form falters?

Sudhenshu Mahraj, a renowned Hindu saint of our times, has stated that a guru should always guide and lead his devotees to pray to Almighty Supreme God. He should not himself become the chief object of prayer and devotion.

In the ancient period, it was a common practice that Hindu *Rishis* would recommend another guru for more advanced instruction. Hindu scriptures have also stated that a person should be like a bee, collecting honey from various flowers. In the Srimad Bhagavatam there is mention of Sri Dattatreya, who had twenty-four gurus.

The pupil or *shishya*, too, has certain requirements. There are three basic conditions to be fulfilled: humility (*vinamrata*), true desire (*jigyasa*), and faith (*shradha*). The disciple needs to have faith but not blind faith. He, too, must not be so cynical as to find faults all the time. He ought to be a genuine seeker of truth and knowledge, with an open mind and humility.

In the Hindu spiritual system, a guru is considered indispensable. Hindu scriptures considered a mother to be the first guru, *Matravaan*, until the child is six years old. The father would be the next guru, *Pitravaan*, until the child is nine years of age. Thus, parents have been endowed with the highest honor as well as the responsibility of childcare. Traditionally, every Hindu family ought to have a family guru, *kulaguru*, who is knowledgeable about the flow and movement of the clan in all respects.

A guru is a spiritual guide, but the main responsibility also lies with the pupil to learn as well as assimilate the knowledge. Sri Tapovan Maharaj said, *"To the worthy aspirant, the great spiritual guides impart instruction on the knowledge of truth; but it is the aspiring disciples themselves to follow those instructions and acquire the Divine qualities by strenuous effort."*[83]

Hindu scriptures have also laid great importance in the holy company, the *satsanga*. Indeed, if we leave the holy, we may become involved with the unholy. Man is a social animal; he simply cannot do without some association and fellowship. Hindu sages have repeatedly underscored the value of *satsanga*, the holy company. Man is prompted to attend religious congregations and assemblies, where people talk and think of only pious and spiritual matters. They sing songs in glory of the Lord--*gun gaan*--and thus purify their minds and gradually transform themselves toward a divine way of living. Sri Ramakrishna's advice is pertinent:

"Don't accept anybody as your guru until you examine him or her both by day and night for days together. Then, if you find he or she can stand all these tests and is really pure, you can accept that person as your guru."[84]

The concept of "Guru" is rather unique to Hinduism. Literally, the word "Guru" means the one who removes darkness (of ignorance). Thus a Guru first learns and transforms himself; later he may teach and transform many others toward virtue and divinity. Although it has been mentioned that a Guru is an indispensable requirement—even God-incarnates like Lord Rama and Lord Krishna were instructed by their respective gurus—finding a true Guru, and attaining a constant access in modern times is most challenging. Not all but a few Gurus have their own imperfections and faults; they are trapped in their ego and other sensual weaknesses. In recent times, "Guru" has become a global marvel, attracting persons of great distinction and eminence, across the globe. The Guru occasionally becomes a part of their high color and status, allowing simplicity and austerity to take a backseat. The Guru is invariably in great rush and crowded by many aspirants. Individual and constant attention, a very important requirement of the "Guru" status, is conspicuous by its absence.

Nevertheless the "Guru" phenomenon has been there from most ancient times and has been carried ably throughout millennia by

the most virtuous and spiritual masters, saints and sages of the highest order. Like any other drawbacks of the society, this one too shall find its worthy solution in good time.

42 Ayurveda:
The Most Ancient Medical Science

Ayurveda is a Sanskrit word that means "knowledge of life." It is an ancient indigenous medical science of the Hindu culture, more than five thousand years old. The source of this science lies in Athar Veda. Three most important names are associated with Ayurveda: Dhanvantri, the mythological god is regarded as the divine father of Ayurveda; Sushruta (600 BCE), father of Indian surgery, who performed more than 300 types of surgical operations and invented many sophisticated instruments; Acharya Charaka (100 CE), who wrote the *"Charaka Samhita"*, and is known as father of Indian medicine. It has been said that the Vedic sciences are really *"one integral science, with many windows."* Like many others, this gem of the old Indian civilization is dazzling even today, perhaps more brightly than at any time in the history of mankind. It has come to occupy a position of dignity and honor, which was long overdue. There are number of ayurvedic centers, which now command a health-conscious, nature-loving, and sophisticated clientele. Ayurveda is fast becoming an integral part of many spas, yoga centers, and wellness clinics all over the West.

The ayurveda system is based more on promotion of the physical, mental, and spiritual well-being and balance than on treatment of illness. Modern medicine has long paid attention to the pathological state of various ailments and has been primarily concerned with treatment of the disease and symptoms. Ayurveda, on the other hand, treats the whole being, going to the root cause of the discomfort and its aggravation and giving a basic plan of action for disease prevention. Modern medicine only recently has turned its direction toward preventive aspects.

Ancient *Rishis* of India conceived that our cosmos is made of five basic elements of matter: space, air, fire, water, and earth. Man, too, is made from these five basic elements. According to the modern science of physics, all matter is made of molecules and atoms. More recently, studies have revealed that these atoms may be further reduced to the minutest quantum fluff, which may be ten million to one hundred million times smaller than the smallest of atoms. At the quantum level, energy and matter are transferable; the particles move constantly. At that level, the rock on a mountain is no more a static and immovable entity, but there is a lot of quantum activity going on. The matter and energy are not destructible. These may change shape and form but in reality, they do not decrease or increase. Thus, we may be breathing the very same air that our ancestors breathed five thousand years ago—or perhaps even five million years ago![85]

According to Ayurveda, the interaction of the body humors, called *doshas*, determines the physical as well as the mental makeup of an individual. The therapy is essentially directed at wholesome vegetarian food, a righteous and pure living style, and natural healing remedies. A long and healthy life is essentially linked to a moral and ethical lifestyle that promotes peace of mind.

Ayurveda maintains that human beings are classified in three major groups according to their dosha as: *vata*: space + air; *pitta*: fire + water; and *kapha*: water + earth.

Vata types, like their constituents of space and air, move quickly and lightly. When *vata* is aggravated, it brings on the *vata* qualities of being dry, rough, and mobile, because water is not a part of them. In such cases, people are more likely to suffer from anxiety, insomnia, nervous disorders, arthritis, and constipation. All the *vata* therapies must be directed toward nurturing, moistening, and calming. They may benefit from good rest and sleep. They should avoid over-stimulation and emotionally tense situations. Foods may be warm, tasty, spiced, and with plenty of warm fluids. *Vata* types should avoid iced drinks, sodas, caffeine, and dry, rough foods. Heavy oils, such as sesame, may be used for massage. Meditation, *pranic* breathing, calming and grounding yoga exercises would play a major part in balancing vata.

Pitta types constitute the fire and water and are hot, sharp, and acidic. They are of medium bone structure, muscular, and can gain or lose weight easily. They are pink and oily in complexion. They are irritable and impatient in temperament but are forceful and aggressive in nature. They spend their energies moderately. All the *pitta* therapies should be cooling and calming. They should avoid over-exertion, as they may burn out. They must relax in nature. They are ambitious and have drive. They have a sharp intellect and are prone to anger. They also are prone to rashes, inflammation, and ulcers. They must plan to cool down. Foods that are sweet, bitter and astringent, cooling, and alkaline in nature, such as fruits and juices, would be recommended. Alcohol, tobacco, and coffee must be avoided. Hot spices may be reduced. Massage with cool and light oils, such as coconut and sunflower. Calming *asanas* (yogic postures) are useful.

Kapha types likewise are made of water and earth and are heavy, oily, cold, and steady. They are strong and tend to gain weight easily. They have a heavy and prolonged sleep. They are usually easygoing. They are self-centered but are also loyal and steady. They are lethargic in nature. All therapies are directed toward reducing, stimulating, and drying. They are also more vulnerable to colds, congestion, and diabetes. Dry massage or light oil, such as mustard, may be used. Stimulating *asanas* (yogic postures) are advised.

This classification, however, is not absolute. Combinations of various *doshas* with dominance of any one may exist. A proper evaluation by an expert would be helpful. Special *panchakarma* treatment schedules are prescribed in the ayurveda system, which include an individual customized diet, laxatives, herbal oil massages, sweat therapy, enemas, and nasal irrigations.

In ayurveda, as in all other Hindu philosophies, the main emphasis is on the spiritual aspect. A person is taught to look within, to contemplate, to meditate, to tune himself to the divine wisdom, and to balance in harmony, wherever he finds fault and shortcoming. To achieve this balance and harmony is the main task of an ayurvedic specialist. His role, however, remains that of a guide; the person concerned has to do most of the work himself

In recent times, Ayurveda has gained a prodigious status, with its main emphasis being "natural treatment" in place of chemicals and synthetics used in modern medicine, often accompanied by severe toxic reactions. From the Hindu viewpoint, the secular and the spiritual invariably go hand in hand. In fact, the "spiritual" often plays the dominant and supervisory role. Ayurveda centers are becoming more popular even in Western countries, because of their simple natural methodology.

Ayurveda lays more importance on the "prevention" aspect of disease, rather than its cure. In fact Ayurveda teaches that a person becomes sick mainly because he/she transgresses the natural laws of health. The recent high prominence of organic foods, vegetarianism, massage therapy, yoga, meditation etc. is linked with the Ayurveda philosophy.

Spiritual Gems from Paramahansa Yogananda

"There is a magnet in your heart that will attract true friends. That magnet is unselfishness, thinking of others first.... When you learn to live for others, they will live for you." (Man's Eternal Quest)

"Remain calm, serene, always in command of yourself. You will then find out how easy it is to get along." (The Divine Romance)

"Before embarking on important undertakings, sit quietly, calm your senses and thoughts, and meditate deeply. You will then be guided by the great creative power of Spirit. After that you should utilize all necessary material means to achieve your goal." (The Law of Success)

"Perseverance is the whole magic of spiritual success." (Man's Eternal Quest)

"The true state of meditation is oneness of the meditator with the object of meditation, God." (God Talks With Arjuna: The Bhagavad Gita)

"The way to God is not through the intellect, but through intuition. Spirituality is measured by what you experience intuitively, from the communion of your soul with God. It is so simple if inside you are always talking to Him, 'Lord, come to me!'" (Journey to Self-Realization)

"Knowledge of the scriptures is beneficial only when it stimulates a desire for practical realization; otherwise, theoretical knowledge gives one false conviction of wisdom." (God Talks With Arjuna: The Bhagavad Gita)

(The above excerpts from the works of Paramahansa Yogananda are reprinted with the permission of Self-Realization Fellowship, Los Angeles, CA.)

43 Vegetarianism: The Compassionate Way of Living

From the earliest times, there was a clear call toward vegetarianism in the Hindu society. Yajur Veda calls for kindliness toward all creatures living on the earth, in the air, and in the water. *"You must not use your God-given body for killing God's creatures, whether they are human, animal or whatever"* (Yajur Veda 12.32.90).

Manu Samhita advises: *"Meat can never be obtained without injury to living creatures, and injury to sentient beings is detrimental to the attainment of heavenly bliss; let him therefore shun the use of meat"* (Manu Samhita 5.48-49).

Hindu belief is that all things are rooted in God, and there is God-pervasiveness in every entity.

After the Vedas pronounced that all beings are the family of one God, the Hindu mind became more established toward an attitude of reverence, benevolence, compassion, and auspiciousness toward all creatures. In effect, this certainly aroused people to wean themselves from eating meat. Soon afterwards the concept of non-injury became the model teaching of Hinduism. Manu Samhita stated earliest in the Mahabharata: *"Ahimsa Parmo Dharma:* Nonviolence is the primary religion," and later Mahavira and Buddha adopted this as their main teaching. Soon, vegetarian food came to be considered as the *sattvic* food, which is regarded fit for all spiritual practices. Jainism has always shown greater interest in this direction. Jains not only strictly prohibit their members from eating any animal meat, but they go a step further. They don't allow root vegetables, such as onions and potatoes, lest some germs be attached to them. Buddhists are believers in non-injury but are more accommodating with regard to prohibited foods. Sikhs, too, have a rather soft attitude in this regard. The majority of Sikhs eat meat, but they do not consume it inside the temple.

Hindus have taken to vegetarianism quite well. Even though only about 20 percent of Hindus are complete vegetarians, the majority of the vast population does not consume meat like other communities, such as Christians or Muslims, do. Meat is not a staple or main diet for Hindus anywhere. I have seen with wonder how even small Hindu children in USA observe vegetarianism without any difficulty whatsoever in school lunches or at parties, where they often have to satisfy their hunger with some salad and then come back home to eat the main meal. Those who do not eat meat for long time, in fact, develop a certain dislike and aversion to it.

Meat is is now regarded as a relatively toxic substance for human consumption. Health authorities worldwide agree that heart attacks, cancers, and many other diseases are more prevalent in the meat-eating population than in the vegetarian population. Above all, the longevity of a person is inversely proportional to the amount of his meat intake; the more meat one eats, the fewer years one may live. Vegetarian food provides potassium to the body, which is considered a beneficial element. It also has a more alkaline base that is beneficial to good health in many ways. Vegetarian food is considered a complete diet, especially if there are sufficient dairy products and nutrient foods like soya in the diet. Some may consider milk products as non-vegetarian food, as its source is animals, but this is not acceptable to the Hindu point of view. Dairy forms the essential part of the Hindu diet, and it is therefore labeled as lacto-vegetarian. The average combined vegetarian meal contains a sufficient amount of the protein and other constituents needed by the body. Some people feel that vegetarian food is not easily available in most restaurants in the West, but now, with the increasing demand for the vegetarian meals, the restaurant industry is responding with many positive options.

Human anatomical and physiological evidences lean in favor of vegetarianism—a human being's teeth, digestive tract, and other bodily mechanisms are akin to plant-eating animals, not the carnivorous ones. Beyond that, there is also strong evidence that meat production is becoming a costly affair. There is also an important ecological reason that is now becoming increasingly persuasive—destruction of ancient rainforests is significantly related to creating pasturelands for livestock meant to provide the meat for human consumption. Studies at the University of Chicago showed that a typical American meat eater is responsible for nearly 1.5 tons more carbon dioxide a year than a vegan! It is said that one hundred million people could be adequately nourished, if only the Americans reduced their meat intake by a mere 10 percent.[86]

All in all, there is undoubtedly a celebration in the vegetarian camp. For many Hindus, vegetarianism is a passion. There has been a gradual increase in the non-meat-eating population all over the world. At present, a rough estimate is that there are over ten million people in the United States who are vegetarians.

In America, there seems to be a strange phenomenon. Fire engines may be called to save a bird when it is caught in electrical wires, or perhaps an entire town will come forward to rally around a dying whale that is beached on the shore. But these same people would have no problem sitting at their dinner tables and eating birds, animals, and fish without hesitation. Many Muslims are now completely or mostly vegetarians. The former president of India, Abdul Kalam, was a vegetarian. The vegetarian movement is undoubtedly marching ahead with great force. Sadhu Vaswani's birthday on November 25 is celebrated as International Meatless Day, when millions of people around the globe pledge not to eat meat. One of the giant literary figures of the twentieth century, George Bernard Shaw, wrote: "*My stomach and body are not a crematorium or cemetery for killed or dead animals. While we ourselves are the living graves of murdered beasts, how can we expect any ideal conditions on this earth?*"

Hindus regard all life as sacred, human life as well as other beings. In their search for alternate sources of food in the very early periods of history, they discovered that some of the animals that were killed for food could be harnessed to co-operate in producing the non-meat meals for them. The cow was identified as the most important animal in this regard. Its nourishing milk established its status of mother or goddess. According to the Hindu mythology, the foremother of all cows, *Surabhi*, emerged from the primeval ocean of milk to bless the world with plenty.[87] She earned the status of goddess, alternating her form with Mother Earth and Shri Sita of the Ramayana. The male bull would be used for plowing the land for agriculture. Soon India became an agricultural country, which it remains to this day. The humble appearance and nature of the cow has given her added grace and dignity. She has been granted the symbol of divinity as *Kamadhenu,* the wish-fulfilling cow! In recognition of her invaluable services to humanity, Hindus in India have built thousands of cow homes, or *gaushalas*, all across the country, where weak and infirm cows are lovingly taken care of in their later years. This in itself is a unique phenomenon to be noted only in the Hindu society.

Mahatma Gandhi, whose teachings of non-violence resonate even with the most hardened people all over the world, wrote in regard to cow protection, "*Cow protection to me is not mere protection of the cow. It means protection of all that lives and is helpless and weak in the world.*" Compassion is a teaching of all religions. All sentient beings have feelings. Vegetarianism is a cause for millions of non-speaking members of the global community who are driven mercilessly toward the slaughterhouses, day in and day out, through no fault of their own. It is believed that an average meat-eating human being consumes the flesh of nearly one hundred animals in his lifetime. More and more people now protest against the various types of cruelties involved in the killing of animals for procuring their meat. To a Hindu mind, however, any killing without a valid reason is an act of brutality. Hindus, who believe in the absolute theory of karma, consider the act of slaughtering as sinful, but they also dread the consequences of such acts very seriously. Vegetarianism has a great symbolic significance in Hindu society.

Vegetarianism in recent times has become a "wonder" word all over the world. Hindus were the first ones to adopt vegetarianism; the rest of the world until very lately, considered meat as an essential part of their diet. In fact till only half a century ago, medical curricula taught that the "essential amino-acids" were present in meat only. Tables have now turned; in the medical domain, mcat is now considered to be relatively toxic. In Hindu philosophy, the secular is often overshadowed by the spiritual; vegetarianism in Hindu society was regarded as religious and a divine feature, rather than a scientific and material advantage. In ancient Hindu scriptures, longevity of one hundred years or more has been repeatedly emphasized. Perhaps in no other society such longevity was known so early in human history.

Of late, there has been much talk about environmental pollution, carbon dioxide emissions, green forest depletion, etc. causing serious health concerns and other problems, even proclaiming danger to the very existence of the universe. Global food shortage caused by the destruction of rainforests is mainly attributed to the heavy consumption of meat. The cause of vegetarianism stands fully vindicated now!

The Belgian city of Ghent has become the first in the world to go vegetarian at least once a week. Ghent means to recognize the impact of livestock on the environment; hence Ghent's declaration of a weekly "veggie day". The rapid spread of vegetarian and vegan foods in many restaurants all over the world is an indirect testimony of the impact of the Hindu viewpoint.

44 Hindu Society Today
The Dynamic Patterns in Motion

There are at present more than one billion Hindus in the world, mainly in India. But they are also present in many other countries. Hinduism is the most predominant religion in India (974,000,000) and Nepal (23,000,000). They are also in significant numbers in the United States of America (2,400,000), Canada (685,000), Cuba (24,000), Martinique and Guadeloupe (50,000), Jamaica (31,000), Panama (10,000), Colombia (9,000), Trinidad (402,000), Guyana (318,000), Suriname (144,000), French Guyana (2,900), Brazil (3,000), Argentina (5,000), the United Kingdom (966,000), Germany (98,000), Belgium (7,600), Austria (9,600), France (65,800), Spain (23,000), Portugal (56,000), Greece (6,000), Switzerland (30,000), the Netherlands (175,000), Norway (25,000), Denmark (6,000), Sweden (11,000), Lebanon (10,000), Egypt (1,000), Gulf States including Dubai (3,877,000), Ethiopia (4,000), Libya (10,000), Nigeria (20,000), Uganda (254,000), Zambia (39,000), Malawi (30,000), Botswana (7,000), Ghana (12,000), Zimbabwe (13,000), Mozambique (43,000), Rwanda (11,600), Seychelles (4,000), South Africa (805,000), Madagascar (20,700), Reunion (177,000), Mauritius (640,000), Tanzania (389,000), Kenya (386,000), Somalia (2,900), Yemen (157,000), Pakistan (3,500,000), Sri Lanka (3,100,000), Malaysia (1,737,000), Singapore (203,000), Hong Kong (41,000), Japan (8,000), Bhutan (167,000), Cambodia (40,000), Bangladesh (15,800,000), Myanmar (2,336,000), China (16,000), Vietnam (5,500), Thailand (68,000), Philippines (47,000), Indonesia including Bali (5,200,000), Brunei (6,000), Fiji (293,000), Australia (158,000), New Zealand (75,000), Slovakia (5,400), Ukraine (46,000), Uzbekistan (3,000), Kazakhstan (3,300), and Iran (15,000) (adapted from *Hinduism Today, Oct-Dec 2011*). In smaller numbers, they are spread in almost all countries of the world.[88] It is believed that more than sixty million Hindus live outside India. Although Hinduism originated in India, it has spread now all over the world through mainly by the process of migration of Hindus to other countries, rather than by conversion of other religious people into Hinduism. The Angkor temples of Kampuchea (formerly Cambodia) gives evidence of

Hinduism in the South East Asian countries around 12th century. This temple was built by king Suryavarman, obviously a Hindu name, suggesting that Hinduism was the main religion of the region in that period. The inhabitants of this region were vastly influenced by India since the 1st century or even earlier. They had very close contacts with India, and also adopted the Hindu religion. In more recent times, British who ruled India sent large number of Hindu laborers to many of their colonies like West Indies, Mauritius, Fiji, Guyana, South Africa and many other counties to serve in the agriculture fields. After the end of the colonial rule, many Hindus also got opportunity to migrate from these countries to U.K. and other similar colonial countries as they obtained the visa facility. The first large batch of Sikh farmers migrated to U.S.A. in the 18th century when similar job opportunity was offered. Small trickles of Hindus migrated thereafter, but main influx of Hindus to USA occurred after 1960s as the migration rules softened.

Together with the followers of Buddhism (360 million), Jainism (10 million), and Sikhism (23 million), which may be considered as the companion faiths and which share very considerably the religious philosophy with Hinduism, the total number swells to a staggering 1.5 billion world-wide for this whole group of religions—almost a quarter of the total population of the world.

Hindus are generally known to be tolerant and non-violent people; undoubtedly there are exceptions too. India has been home to people from all almost every religion, philosophy, and cultural heritage who have lived together harmoniously for thousands of years, creating a vibrant tapestry of more than 2000 ethnic groups. It has more than 1650 languages as mother tongue of different groups; most of them have their own script. India has 22 languages recognized by the constitution; both Hindi and English accorded as official languages.

There is no doubt that the ancient philosophies of the Hindu culture are now regarded with great respect and enthusiasm. Yoga is taught in many universities and other teaching institutes in India and abroad, especially in the United States. Modern medical faculties all over the world have acknowledged and recognized the concept of the *Ayurveda*, the ancient health science of India. The ecological conduct of the Hindu philosophy has become a world issue. Reverence for life and vegetarianism are hailed with respect. Meditation is a household word in the United States and many other countries. But above all else, it is the recognition of the root concept of the Vedic teaching that all beings, human and others, are the children of one Supreme Divine, whatever our faith. Underlying this ancient philosophy of India is the vital ethical principle of non-violence—*ahimsa*. In tomorrow's world, this principal doctrine of equality of all creation may well become an important Torch bearer.

Hindus have performed generally very well in most countries where they have settled. They have earned a high reputation for attaining a good academic education, maintaining a superior family system, a low crime rate, and big economic progress.

It has been perhaps one of the greatest challenges for Hindus living outside of India to integrate and adapt themselves to different cultures, while at the same time retaining their own identity of religion and tradition. Hindus cannot afford to throw away their long-cherished heritage, but some useful changes may be needed periodically. Human evolution is a saga of such endeavors, where the good and worthy is accepted and the harmful and unworthy is dropped.

Only fifty years ago, the Hindu swamis and gurus lived a very austere and simple life. They lived in ordinary cottages, ate the simplest food, traveled in lower class, and did not enjoy any luxuries of the modern world. All this has changed considerably. The *sanyasin* who has pronounced renunciation now would consider this vow as a vow of mental rather than physical abnegation. This change, however, may not necessarily be regarded as a serious shortcoming. It may be accepted more as a sign of the changing times, although a sense of propriety is essential. Even so swamis, sadhus and sanyasins do play very important role in Hindu society. Many personally guide the lives of hundreds of families; others run institutes that provide social service. Even those who live reclusive lives in the mountains, by their deep meditations, send spiritual vibrations for the good of mankind. Priests, who conduct the rituals and ceremonies in the temples and homes of the devotees, are not always well trained and professional in their behavior. As there is no code for their curriculum etc., the variations abound. A judicious supervision and guidance in this regard may be called for. In recent times, there has been a perceptible change in the conduct of spiritual teachings and ceremonies. Swami Vivekananda declared boldly that the ritual and worship ceremonies may not be in the sole hands of *brahmins* and heredity priests; anyone with aptitude and proper training may do so with impunity. In US all church ministers need to undergo full course in university or some recognized institute; similar arrangement is being worked out for the priests in Hindu temples also. The continuing shortage of man power in this field only enhances the need for such professional approach.

Hindus are much more family-oriented than most other religious communities. Starting and maintaining a family is considered a religious duty, which is well defined in the *Grahastha Ashram*. Sacrifice is the bedrock of good living. Hindus basically endorse the family lifestyle in preference to an individualistic one. Sharing and caring are virtues of greatest importance in Hindu society. Children are often given the highest attention in their formative years. The need for the children to learn the basic discipline of the traditional Hindu family, however, cannot be overemphasized. Most youngsters do well in education and conduct. Parents teach best by example.

Elders have enjoyed very respectful position in Hindu society for millennia. The Vedic teachings *"Treat your mother as God, and treat your father as God"* gave high status and dignity to the elderly. Even though the parents don't generally live with children now, they often arrange to live near to each other. In olden times, the elders occasionally had undue dominance over the youth, especially the daughter-in-law of the family. In some urban places, the tables have turned, and it is the elderly who are pushed to the wall and have become targets of humiliation and abuse by the young. Undoubtedly, a harmonious balance is needed for healthy survival of the family and society.

Women have enjoyed a twisted status in Hindu society. In the Aryan patriarchal society, at the beginning, women were pushed down along with the lower castes to remain ineligible to learn the Vedas. This was later rectified, and they were given equal standing in all Hindu rituals. The prevalence of the dowry system, in direct or indirect manner, still continues in certain areas, occasionally with dire consequences. The plight of widows in many places remains pathetic and shameful. The women in Hindu society are, of late, becoming very vibrant and awakened of their rightful position.

Although traditionally Hindu women are not encouraged to work outside their homes, the modern setup has changed that option considerably. Typically Hindu women in the past gave lot more attention to make homes places of serenity and joy, while men folks worked outside. While more and more women are now working to supplement the home income as well as to fulfill their own dreams, men have not yet taken to domestic chores enough as yet.

Divorces are not favored by Hindu society, but they are becoming more common than before. More and more women are now working. Their contribution to the economic structure of the family has increased significantly. Although the divorce is not sanctioned in the Hindu religion, many suggest changes while keeping in view the dynamic nature of Hindu theology. Swami B. V. Tripurari said, *"If a husband abuses his wife and this cannot be resolved, she should not remain with him. Any woman who finds herself in such a situation should get out of it for her spiritual and material well-being."*[89]

Sex has never been considered a sin in Hindu philosophy. The open expression of sexuality in some of the temples and the detailed descriptions in the scriptures, especially the *Kama Sutra*, is an indication that sex is accepted as a natural activity of human beings. Sex outside wedlock, however, is not sanctioned in Hindu society. There are some cultural differences also; for example dating is not traditionally allowed, even married couples do not hug or kiss in open public, and in mixed company women often remain in the background and do not participate in conversations and arguments along with men. Some changes are of course happening, but these may be done with discretion and wisdom. Respect and pride for one's own culture is a necessary ingredient for good and happy life. Hindu society generally has a tolerant attitude toward sex. It largely leaves the choice of birth control and many other sexual decisions to the individual and family. It does not extend any condemnation or code of harsh punishment in matters related to a person's sexual behavior. Hindus recognize that life starts at the time of conception, but they generally have a tolerant attitude toward abortion. This may have been a result of their progressive attitude of adjustment, according to the present situations and needs of society.

Suicide is not sanctioned in Hinduism. An individual is expected to complete his mission of fulfilling all his karmas in its natural course. In case of a terminal condition of life, a voluntary fast (*vrat*) until death is sometimes accepted as a spiritual option, especially amongst the Jains.

The present time seems to be a period of transition for Hindu society. Undoubtedly, the rituals are an essential part of Hinduism. They have an important role to play, creating an eternal bonding with religion and culture. Their contribution, however, needs to be modified to suit the modern age of science and technology. Lengthy rituals performed without any understanding may be better molded to make them precise and purposeful. In America, at present, the Hindu priest usually explains the meaning and significance behind each step of the ritual associated with most wedding and death ceremonies. A judicious combination of ancient Sanskrit as a traditional culture, along with the regional language, Hindi, or English as a practical language, may be a prime requirement in years to come.

The ravages of the caste system have not yet completely disappeared. Raja Ram Mohan Roy and Swami Dayanand Saraswati started the crusade against the caste system. Mahatma Gandhi spent his lifetime in services of the low castes, calling them *Harijan*—the people of God. Bhimrao Ambedkar (1893–1956) waged a war against this evil, which also gave birth to a vertical division of Hindu society. Even though he was directly involved in writing the new Constitution for free India in 1950, he soon became frustrated by the slow pace of change. The changes in the laws alone do not bring about the changes in the hearts and attitudes of the people. The real solution lies not in blaming, quarrelling, and bringing down those who are in the superior position but, as Swami Vivekanananda said, *"...in uplifting the downtrodden."*

Hinduism has always been a dynamic religion, absorbing changes and modification as the situations and circumstances demand. Any violence and hatred by a religious organization or individuals however is unbecoming. Some take the position that protecting religion and God is an ordained duty; this responsibility may be best performed by the dully assigned personnel. They may also remember what Swami Vivekananda recalled in similar circumstances, when he heard the divine voice of Mother saying, *"Do you protect me? Or do I protect you?"*[90]

Despite several hurdles, Hindus outside India have maintained a very close connection with their religion and culture. They have built an enormous number of temples, some of which are most gorgeous and elegant. At home, most Hindus carry on their daily routines in a more traditional manner. They also observe many Hindu festivals and customs fairly well, although with some modifications as suitable. It is rather interesting that in some places Hindus are even more conventional and orthodox than Hindus in India. As an example:
Bali is a province of Indonesia, a country with biggest population of Muslims in the world. Even so Bali has maintained its unique Hindu image; 93% of its population is Hindus, names of Hindu Rishis like Markandeya, Bharadwaja, and Agastya are properly taught in history books in schools, none is allowed to enter

Hindu temples without wearing Dhoti, Trikala Sandhya and Gayatri Mantra are practiced daily by the children in class!

Hindus are now present in most countries of the world. Occasionally, they are also treated unfairly in foreign countries. In some places, there is racial prejudice; in schools it may be because of the usual bullying habit of some children, or there may be unnecessary damaging comments about the Hindu religion or culture in text books. Hindus may need to address these issues on various planes, both at individual as well as community levels. Most importantly, Hindus must themselves know and appreciate the positive and glorious aspects of their own religion, and also bring about the same awareness in their children. The strength of such awareness can not be underestimated.

Marriages in Hindu society are often still "arranged", although with some modifications. The would-be bride and bridegroom usually meet and discuss their options and plans for the future more freely than before. Westerners often wonder how "arranged marriages" work and succeed. But the fact is that these "arranged marriages" often succeed more than the so-called "love marriages" without any parental council! In Hindu society, it is said, "To separate the marriage is to displease God".

Rituals still do form an important, rather indispensable part of the Hindu religion. However there is no pressure on how to perform the same; in some places these are performed in a symbolic manner, and in others these may be very prolonged and laborious. Rituals are performed in Sanskrit language, but they are also explained in the local or English language, especially in foreign countries.

Women in Hindu society are becoming more and more free and liberated. Even so the old habits of male dominance are not completely gone. Husbands still do not extend an equal helping hand in home chores, child care etc. even when their wives are very busy and have fulfilling careers. In the presence of guests, many men feel shy to carry out any tasks, because of the culture's patriarchal social attitudes.

Divorces are not yet common in Hindu society, but are no longer regarded as a disgrace on women. Although Hindu religion and culture stress on saving the marriage to the utmost as a matter of spiritual duty, and the consideration of children remains uppermost in the minds of parents, divorce by no means is totally ruled out. It is now accepted in a more positive manner; even the religious leaders seem to give tactical support by remaining silent on the issue.

Caste system is nearly becoming extinct. The new problem now is about the quarrel over who should get the benefit of the "special advantages for the low caste". Many compete to be included in the category so that they may take those fat doles!

45 Hindu Wedding—Nuptials for Eternity

The Hindu seers of the ancient times invented a very ingenious method of tying the wedding knot. There is perhaps no other example of creating a bond that goes beyond the mortal life on this earth than with the Hindu man and his wife. According to Hindu scriptures, marriage is a duty. Non-performance renders the individual as incomplete. It is based on the principles of love, sacrifice, and service to build a good family and lay a strong foundation for noble society. Hindu marriage is often an elaborate affair. It is believed that a Hindu wedding is not just a relationship of two individuals; rather, it is a relationship of two families. Participation of the family members is very deliberate and vocal.

Even though the Vedic society was considered paternal in the beginning, it soon recognized the esteem of the woman and accorded the highest status to her, on par with the man. The wife was called *ardhangini* (half-body) or *sahadharmini* (partner in spiritual life). In the long voyage of the married life, the Hindu wife becomes her husband's true and honored partner. There is no family occasion, religious ceremony, or a spiritual ritual where she is not a major participant. The high status, which a Hindu wife earned more than five thousand years ago, is way ahead of most women in other cultures of the world.

The parents generally arrange Hindu marriages. Even when the man and woman seek each other directly, the family usually endorses the wedding. Nowadays, the involvement and influence of the parents and elders has been reduced in the choice of selection, especially in the urban sector.

Traditionally, the wife comes to live in the husband's home after the marriage, leaving her parent's place. It is also expected that she would adapt to the religious and social customs of her new family. Hindus, therefore, prefer that their daughters be married in their own religion and sect so they may carry the spiritual disciplines smoothly and guide their own children evenly. The Vedas state, "*United your resolve, united your hearts, may your spirits be one that you may long together dwell in unity and concord.*" In present times, many weddings do take place outside the faith, entailing an extra sense of maturity and self-restraint from both spouses.

189

The dowry system is common in Hindu weddings, when the bride's parents offer gifts and money to the bridegroom and his family. Even though the law now bans it, this custom nevertheless still prevails in Hindu society. In some cases, it takes an ugly and even tragic toll.

At the beginning of the ceremony, the bride's family and guests welcome and receive the bridegroom and his family outside the place of the wedding. Traditional *shehnai* music is played to augur the auspicious event. This music is called the *baraat*, which signifies the arrival of the groom's party. The bride's mother greets the groom and performs *aarti*, a religious prayer of blessings. The priest invokes the divine *mantras* to herald the ceremony.

Even though the majority of Hindus do not understand the ancient Sanskrit language, the wedding ceremony is always performed in this dialect, even in foreign countries. Nowadays, the presiding priest usually renders a simultaneous translation in English or the local Indian language. The Sanskrit word for marriage is *vivah,* which literally means "what supports or carries" a man and woman throughout their married life, in pursuit of righteousness, the *dharma.*

As previously noted the bridegroom arrives at the bride's place and is welcomed by the bride's parents and relatives. This is known as *Var Agaman.* The bride customarily wears a red dress, signifying abundance and fertility. The bride and groom garland each other in a ritual called *Jai Mala,* to the accompaniment of loud applause by all the guests.

Ganpati Puja—Lord Ganesh—is worshipped. It is customary to say prayers to Lord Ganesh at important occasions to remove any obstacles that may come. This is often followed by an invocation to the Supreme Lord or to one's own favorite god, the *isht devta* and the *navagrah puja*—invocations of the blessings of the nine planetary gods.

Havan—lighting of the sacred fire for the ceremony, the worship at the sacred fire, *Agn kund,* is an important ritual that is never missed.

Kanyadan—bestowing the bride's hand in marriage to the groom by the bride's parents is considered the most essential part of Hindu wedding.

Granthi bandhan—tying of the nuptial knot, symbolizing the eternal union, is performed soon after.

Parikrama (mangal pherra) —a ritual that marks the symbolic union of the bridegroom and the bride, when they both take four rounds together around the sacred fire: In the first three rounds, the bridegroom leads the bride. The first three rounds signify the three activities of a Hindu life—*dharma*, or religious duty; *artha*, or prosperity; and *kama*, or fulfillment of desires. In the fourth round, the bride leads the bridegroom. The fourth round signifies the last activity of a Hindu life, *moksha*, or salvation. Though the bride leads only in the last round, it is the most vital and sacred activity; hence, her position becomes elevated.

The bridal couple then takes *satpadi*—seven steps together for the seven vows:

Together we will share in the responsibility of the home.
Together we will fill our hearts with strength and courage.
Together we will prosper and share our worldly goods.
Together we will fill our hearts with love, peace, happiness, and spiritual values.
Together we will be blessed with loving children.
Together we will attain self-restraint and longevity.
Together we will be best friends and eternal partners.

In the seventh and the last step, the bridal couple point toward the star; the star is the virtuous *Arundathi*, who was never separated from her husband, *Rishi Vasistha*.

The bridegroom adorns the bride with *Mangal Sutra*, by putting the auspicious black-beaded ornament around her neck.

Panigrahan—holding hands to accept the vows and exchanging the places—is a ritual of sacred vows. The bridegroom applies *sindoor*, vermillion, in the parting of the bride's hair as an auspicious symbol of her married status, followed by *Shantipath*—the peace invocations.

The bride and the bridegroom seek the *ashirwad*—the blessings—by touching the feet of all the elders. Serving of snacks, lunch, or dinner follows the wedding ceremony.

Hindu scriptures implore upon every man to love and care for his wife, despite any shortcomings. He is forbidden to strike or speak harshly to her or ignore her needs. Traditionally in the Hindu society, the responsibility of providing financially remains with the husband. He is expected to provide not only for the necessities of life but also for many fine things, such as a good house, decent clothes, jewelry, and many other things to make her feel comfortable and secure.

According to the Vedas, it is the duty of the husband—*purusha dharma*—to provide for the spiritual, economic, physical, mental, and emotional security of the entire household. The wife, in return, is expected to extend full cooperation and support to her husband and take care of the family and children. She is expected to present her husband with a serene corner where he can return after a day's work and find the peace and joy of the household. A wife in the Hindu culture is expected to play her role with modesty and humility. She must let the husband be in the forefront and accept his final decision as the head of the family. Dominant and aggressive women are not regarded highly in Hindu society.

Hindu theology regards the ideal marriage as a spiritual journey, where the man and woman must complement and help one another toward divine realization. The path is often long and arduous; the spiritual awakening comes through many experiences on the physical plane.

Often, weddings in Hindu families are a protracted affair, involving the participation of extended relatives and friends, over number of days with great festivity and fun! Even in foreign countries, a Hindu wedding often invites the attention of many locals, who marvel at the number of guests attending, and the high expense incurred on such events. Family members and close contacts freely dance vigorously with loud music on the open public road. The Punjabi Bhangra style dancing is now being adopted by many non-Punjabis also; Bollywood film styles are freely combined and fused.

Even as more and more weddings are being arranged directly by the would-be bride and the bride-groom, because of the ease provided by services available on the internet, the parents and families are usually the main task bearers. The heavy expenses involved are more often than not borne by the family even in foreign countries; this is in stark contrast to the system prevailing in the Western society.

The wedding ritual continues to be traditional, involving the "Fire Ceremony", and all other routines. Even so Hindu weddings are also evolving on other fronts: the traditional "Horoscope Sharing", "Caste Considerations", and "Direct Dowry Deals" are now gradually becoming extinct. In foreign countries, inter-religious and inter-racial marriages are becoming commoner; often two sets of ceremonies are performed-one Hindu and the other non-Hindu. Probably time will tell whether this arrangement will be beneficial or otherwise for Hindu society.

46 Hindu Mythologies: The World of Sacred Fantasies

Hindu mythology is fascinating, but it is also intricate and difficult to comprehend. It is basically an art form through which various aspects of religion are expressed. By its very definition, it is not a factual presentation; it is in the design and arrangement of allegories and symbols. The myths act as a bridge between that which we perceive and what we cannot know.[91] To the believer, however, a myth is as real as it can be. There is a vast scope of variations in interpretation and understanding of this medium. In fact, as in any other art, the artist often displays a vigorous expression of feelings of the subconscious and unconscious, which may otherwise remain quite restrained in society.

One of the earliest mythological figures is that of Lord Vishnu, the god of preservation. His skin is blue. He has four hands. In one, he holds a conch trumpet; in another, a discus-shaped boomerang. The other two hold a lotus and a mace. He reclines on the coils of a serpent, named as *Adi Shesh* (*Adi* means the beginning, and *Shesh* means the end). His image in temples is adorned with silks, gold, pearls, perfumes, sandal paste, peacock feathers, and bright flowers. His rituals are associated with beautiful music, communal dance, and sweet food cooked in clarified butter. His blue color represents the ether that pervades all space. The serpent he rests on represents time, coiling and uncoiling itself with unfailing regularity. His vehicle is the sun itself. With the trumpet, he blows the breath of life and warns wrongdoers to return to the path of *dharma*, or the orderly conduct of righteousness. With the mace, he would strike those who do not listen and obey.[92]

In Hindu mythology, the earth is represented as a cow. When tired of being exploited, she takes her woes to Lord Vishnu, who reassures her, "*I will descend on Earth and relieve you of your burden.*" Thus, the Lord came down as Rama, Krishna, and in other forms to mitigate the sufferings on Earth. To Hindus, this narration and presentation has always inspired beyond limits. They feel enriched and empowered. The cow is the earth itself, whose milk sustains life. In exchange, she must be taken care of. The practice of cow worship, the taboo against beef, and eventually, vegetarianism may have roots in this belief.[93]

One of the most important considerations in Hindu mythology is the status of man and woman. Man was presented as the spiritual being and the woman as his earthly complement. Man would not be able to manifest without the partnership and alliance of woman. In Hindu temples, therefore, God is often accompanied with the goddess. The man and woman in Hindu society became complimentary aspects of one another. In Shiva temples it is Parvati; in Vishnu temples, it is Lakshmi; in Krishna temples, one finds Radha; in Rama's temples, there is Sita. Thus the inseparable pairing of male and female became established in Hindu philosophy. So much was the force of this cohabitation of the male and female that Lord Rama had to make use of a golden effigy of Sita to conduct the rituals of a *yagna,* when the Lord abandoned her, after returning to Ayodha.

There are thousands of mythological tales in Hindu scriptures, especially in the Bhagvat Purana. Often, these are symbolic representations of the Divine and its many manifestations, which have been given animate characteristics to make them alive and tangible to the common person.

The sacred River Ganges is known as a consort of Lord Shiva. According to the legend, she was brought down from the heavens, passing through the hair of Lord Shiva, by King Bhagiratha to purify the ashes of his ancestors. Ever since, Hindus always consider the Ganges as a holy river and immerse the ashes of their ancestors into it. The Ganges and other rivers are often worshipped as a divine mother because of their enormous contribution toward the prosperity of the land. The mythological representations have cultivated mammoth devotion in Hindu society; these representations have become the icons of the Divine in full measure.

Despite the abundance of mythological tales found in Hindu scriptures, they are more like allegories and parables, rather than actual facts. They reflect religious and cultural viewpoints and perspectives in a symbolic manner; one may accept them accordingly. In olden times, these mythological tales were regarded as authentic and thus accepted in a much serious manner; in the modern era, however, most people do revere and respect them as icons of religion and spirituality, but do not become very rigid and obsessive about these legends.

47 Symbols and Icons in Hinduism

Hindu seers were among the earliest and the greatest artists of the world. They would often convey their observations and thoughts in the concealed language of symbols and icons. The richness and variety of symbolism used in Hindu scriptures is unrivalled! Few examples may be recalled to capture the beauty and significance of the symbols in the Hindu pantheon.

The portrait of Lord Shiva has deep symbolic significance. The matted hair proclaims the length and intensity of his austerities, or *tapas*, and the cobra around his neck signifies that even the most poisonous snake becomes harmless because the one who has identified with the Supreme has gone beyond all the effects of matter on his senses and organs. The third eye in the middle of the forehead represents the concentration of knowledge, or *jnana*, and it embodies the absolute power to destroy the sloth, *tamas*, and all its manifestations. The ashes that besmear the body recall to us that this body of which we are proud and obsessed is ultimately bound to end up merely as ashes.

With Lord Shiva, the dancing pose, *nataraja*, is symbolic of the cosmic dance. The Lord dances over the body of the demon *Apasmara*, who represents the ego. *Nandi*, the snow-white bull facing the Shiva temple, represents the human soul, the *jeev atman*, who is separated from the Divine due to animal tendencies but is attracted to God by divine grace.

The elephant head of Lord Ganesha signifies the highest intelligence, *buddhi*. It represents the largest brain matter. The trunk of Lord Ganesha signifies the discretionary power. He can pick up a needle from a heap of grass. The large ears of Lord Ganesha signify the importance of hearing—to accept what is good and reject what is not useful to us. The small eyes of Lord Ganesha symbolize concentration and the power to focus our attention on what we should while shutting out the rest. The Vedas of Lord Ganesha signify the importance of knowledge in our lives.

The famous mythological legend, of the churning of the ocean by gods (*devas*) and demons (*asuras*), is symbolic of churning the mind. Attainment of the nectar of immortality stands for the essence of wisdom.

The epic scripture, the Mahabharata, is studded with many symbolic presentations. The blindness of Dhritarashtra in the Mahabharata is the blindness of our minds, which cannot see right from wrong. So, too, is the war of the Mahabharata considered as a war within ourselves. There is a constant war in our minds as to whether we should go by the right path of God or the wrong path of Mammon.

The five Pandavas represent virtues that are few; the hundred Kauravas represent vices that are many in number. Draupadi represents our honor, when she was being undressed in the court of Duryodhana. Draupadi later asked the Lord, why he did not help her earlier; the Lord replied that as long as she was looking for help from others, he would not come. But as soon as the devotee wholeheartedly looks toward God and asks only his help, the Lord comes immediately. In the Hindu pantheon, the Supreme Lord always resides within one's own self as the supreme wisdom. One must constantly strive to connect and unite with this eternal wisdom of the Divine, to conquer worldly problems. When Arjuna and Duryodhana went to the Lord before the commencement of war, the Lord declared, *"On one side would be I without any material possessions and the army; on the other side would be all my wealth and army, but not I."* Arjuna--the man of virtue-- preferred God, his counsel, and moral support; while Duryodhana--the man of vice--preferred the wealth and army.

Krishna is portrayed as the universal husband. The husband in the traditional Indian society is the symbol of provider, caretaker, and defender. The maids, or *gopis*, represent all human beings who look at this super model of a husband. He has all the qualities that a dependent, weak, and vulnerable wife would seek in her husband. They even turn their backs on their conventional husbands and seek his company. Human beings, weary from the conventional and material possessions, finally turn to God for the eternal support! Lord Krishna's flute is the symbol of the soothing and comforting voice of God. We may listen to God's divine music from within and become peaceful. We may also emulate the Lord, and bring peace and joy to others by our soothing and harmonious words

In Southern India, Deepavali marks the victory of Lord Krishna over the mighty *asura*, the demon Narakasura. It is after this victory that the Lord married the 16,008 wives. In this story, the 16,008 damsels represent our numerous desires. When we work selflessly, however, dedicating our actions to a higher goal, the desires remain in check and, most important, get sublimated through the blessings of the Divine.

Hindus have a special regard for the lotus flower, *padma*. Its one thousand petals have been associated with the mental convolutions, the chakras, finally culminating into *sahasrara,* the highest stage of spiritual evolution. The lotus, which arises from mud roots and blooms in beauty, is a symbolic reminder of the emancipation of the mind from the low to the high.

The *swastika* is the four-angled figure, formed from the shape of a cross, with the arms bent to the right, signifying auspiciousness and peace. There is evidence to suggest its presence in the ancient Sindhu-Saraswati culture, and it was later adopted as symbol by the Brahamin caste in Aryan rituals.[94] Swastika is a Sanskrit word, where *Su* means good or auspicious. It is believed that this ancient Indian symbol, with slight modification, was misused as the anti-Semitic sign during the Nazi period. The saffron color of the flags on top of Hindu temples and the robes worn by Hindu seers represent the sun's life-giving glow and purity.

NOTE: This chapter is mainly adapted from Nityanand Swami, *Symbolism in Hinduism*, Central Chinmaya Mission Trust, Mumbai, India, 2001.

Spiritual Gems from Dada J. P. Vaswani

"Happiness does not depend on what happens to us
 but on how we react to what happens to us."

"There are three ways of handling anger:
By expression,
By Suppression
and By forgiveness.
The right way to overcome anger is by forgiveness."

"Ask yourself these things before you speak:
Is it true?
Is it necessary?
Will it hurt anybody?"

(Source: Sadhu Vaswani Mission, Pune-India)

48 Hindu Customs

Customs form over a long period. In the beginning, there is a purpose for whatever started as a custom. Over a period of time, however, the purpose is sometimes downplayed, even as the practice is continued. This makes it an empty ritual.

Om is the Hindu icon for the Divine:

Om became the Hindu symbol of the transcendental Divine. It is very commonly used as a beginning of all ceremonial mantras and *slokas*.

Shaanti Shaanti Shaanti:

Shaanti, or peace, is regarded as a most auspicious word. Hindus repeat it thrice to make it more emphatic and assertive.

Hindus wear a forehead mark:

Historically, both men and women wore a mark on the forehead, but nowadays most men prefer not to apply a mark, except during religious or auspicious ceremonies. Hindu women continue to wear the mark, which has become famous as the *bindi*. It is applied between the two eyes and is usually red in color. This mark, or *tilak*, as it is mentioned in the ancient Sanskrit scriptures, symbolically represents the third eye, the spiritual eye. With this mythological eye the person may acquire the inner sight that is not perceived with the physical eyes.

Namaste or *Namaskar:*

A traditional Hindu way of greeting with folded hands is now becoming popular even among non-Hindus. It is spiritual; it conveys, "I bow before the Divine in you!" It is, indeed, a more hygienic, non-aggressive, and graceful way of greeting than the Western custom of shaking hands or hugging.

Touching feet of the guru, parents, and elders:

Hindus have raised the status of mother and father to the level of God. In traditional Hindu families, it is a common practice to bow down and touch the feet of parents and elders and seek their blessings, or *asheervaad*. Although many do not observe this practice in modern society, others continue to do so with great warmth and enthusiasm, even when they settle in Western countries.

Tiruvadi:

Hindus worship the sacred sandals worn by saints, sages, and *satgurus*.

Hindus worship *Tulasi*, the basil plant:

Tulasi occupies a very exalted position in Hindu mythology. *Tulasi* becomes wedded to Lord Vishnu. It also represents an honor to the agriculture product in Hindu society. Ayurveda has described many good benefits accruing from the use of the basil plant.

The coconut is used in the worship ceremony:

Kalasha, a husked coconut circled by mango leaves on a pot, is used in puja to represent any God; especially Lord Ganesha. The breaking of a tough coconut shell is compared to breaking the ego.

Rudraksha:

Hindus revere and worship with rosary, *mala*, made of the *Rudraksha* seeds. It is especially associated with prayers for Lord Shiva:

Hindus often light the wick of an oil lamp in the evening:

This may be substituted by burning an incense stick, *agarbati* or *dhoop*. The light is symbolic of a spiritual inner awakening. Lighting a lamp is symbolic of removing the darkness and bringing the knowledge of spiritual wisdom. Now many prefer battery candles to avoid fire.

Hindus offer prayers before meals:

It is customary for Hindus to offer prayers before starting their meals. Food is considered as *Prasad,* the Divine blessing, and therefore is considered very auspicious and sacred in Hindu society.

Shoes:

Many Hindus do not wear shoes inside the home; shoes are regarded impure and unhygienic for temple and home. Even those living in foreign countries often observe this custom, occasionally in very severe cold weather also!

Hindus observe *vrat*, or fasting:

It is common for Hindus to observe vrat, or fasting, on some religious days, such as *Ekadasi*. Essentially, it is a token of a self-restraint. It may be in other forms, such as a vow to observe silence (*maun vrat*) for one or more days, as Mahatma Gandhi often did. It is a self-willed determination, *sankalpa*, to purify oneself with some type of physical austerity. It is also a period of time when one remains dedicated to the virtue of God and refrains from any evil thought, word, or deed. v

Hindus have earmarked special days for each deity:

Monday is Lord Shiva's day of prayers and fasting.

Tuesday is for Lord Ganapati.

Thursday is dedicated to goddess Lakshmi and Sai Baba.

Friday is devoted to Santoshi Mata.

Saturday is sanctified as Lord Hanuman's day.

Havan Kund:

This is a temporary fire made by burning pieces of wood in a specially erected platform. It is the legacy of the ancient ritual of Vedic period.

Sacraments, *samaskars*, associated with various life stages:

For the Hindu, life is a sacred journey in which each milestone, marking major biological and emotional stages:

Ceremonies associated with childbirth:

Hindu society has given the highest importance to the upbringing of children:

The *namakarana*-naming ceremony-occurs in the temple or home, eleven to forty-one days after birth.

Head shaving (*mundan* or *chudakarana*) is performed at the temple between the child's thirty-first day and fourth year.

The *annaprashana* celebrates the child's first solid food, when sweet rice is fed to the baby.

Upanayana:

The thread ceremony is performed to herald puberty and adolescence of the male child. It is equivalent of the baptism in the Christian religion. In early times, the boy would be initiated in the training of sacred scriptures. Thus, it would be hailed as the time of being *twice born*. The second birth coincides with spiritual training.

Last rites:

Hindus have a fascinating relationship with death. According to the Hindu philosophy, the physical body is considered unreal self, as compared to the imperishable soul, which is regarded the eternal and undying self. The phenomenon of death of the body, however, is always regarded as most sacred and eventful in the family. Traditionally, a person is brought home when the end is in sight so that the death occurs among loved ones in the family, rather than in the alien atmosphere of the hospital. A lamp is lit near the head, and mantras are chanted, such as *Aum Namo Narayana* or *Aum Namo Shiva*. At the very last moments of life, holy water—*Ganagjal*, water from River Ganges—or few drops of milk and honey are trickled into the mouth. The holy songs, *bhajans*, or tapes of spiritual instrumental music are played in low volume to purify the atmosphere. Hindus generally cremate their dead. The body of the departed is given a bath and dressed in fresh clothes. Fragrant sandalwood paste is applied to the corpse, which is then decorated with flowers and garlands. Traditionally, after scriptural chants and cremation rituals (*antyeshti*) by the priest, the body is placed on the funeral pyre. Nowadays, cremation is done in the electric crematorium in many urban places and in foreign countries. Embalming is usually not favored, but is commonly performed in the foreign countries.

Shraddha—the ceremony in memory of the departed souls:
Hindus perform a ritual ceremony in memory of their deceased parents. They invite their family priest to conduct the rites, which are followed by family meals together. Many Hindus have discarded this ceremony, although some observe it very solemnly. There are others who do not call the priest, but family members get together and partake of meals after doing worship, or *aarti*.

For Hindus, life is a sacred journey in which each milestone is sanctified with sacraments and rites. The holy ceremonies are meant to empower spiritual perspective in individuals and families. Some customs have a harmful effect, too. The poisonous custom of inequality among castes, gender, and other attributes are a slur on Hindu society. Sri Tapovan Maharaj said, "*Alas! Think how customs get the better of man and enslave him! Every intelligent man ought to know that customs are made for man, not man for custom.*"[95]

Customs do form an important part of Hindu society; with time, these "customs" have evolved. Om has remained an icon for the Divine, and, continues to be used emphatically. People often use "HariOm" while addressing each other.

Use of "Tilak" has reduced significantly in public, although its use during the "Puja" ceremony is still quite popular.

"Namaste" as a word of greetings, is getting popular even in Western countries. It is less aggressive, more meaningful, and very spiritual.

Touching feet of the guru, parents, and elders etc. is an ongoing tradition in the Hindu society. Some people follow this tradition earnestly even after growing old and acquiring high positions.

Oil lamps are now occasionally replaced by battery operated lights to avoid any fire accidents, especially in homes.

Offering prayers before meals in homes remains in vogue, although not by majority.

Removing of shoes before entering is observed very firmly in Hindu temples. However, some temples in foreign countries like the "Vedanta" temples allow the wearing of shoes inside their premises. Many modern temples make suitable arrangements in covered areas for devotees to remove their shoes while sitting comfortably on chairs; the shoes are kept in a place well-protected from rain etc. A carpet passage is usually provided to protect devotees from cold and accidental injury.

Vrat, or fasting on "special religious days" is still quite popular. Some occasions like "Karwa Chauth"-when women observe a fast as a prayer for their husband's long lives-have become more like community festivals and are celebrated with fun, mirth, and lot of food afterwards.

"Havan Kund" remains quite popular in many places. The "Fire" is nowadays reduced to avoid accidents and smoke.

Sacraments—samaskars--associated with various life stages are observed with variation. The Namakarana-naming ceremony, Mundan or Chudakarana-the Head shaving ceremony, the Upanayana-the thread ceremonies etc. are becoming less popular, although some do observe them very religiously.

"Last rites" after the death are observed faithfully by most. Often a big Puja, followed by serving food to many guests is organized in memory of the departed. Feeding the "Brahmins" as per old traditions is becoming less popular. Even the yearly "Shraddha ceremony" is performed by many with some modifications.

In Hindu society, customs are usually performed softly, according to one's individual choice and preference; no pressure is felt from religious authorities.

The Legacy of Sri Ramakrishna Paramahamsa —Harmony of Religions

(Contributed by Swami Sarvadevananda, Minister, Vedanta Temple, Hollywood-Los Angeles. He can be contacted at sarvadevananda@gmail.com)

Sri Ramakrishna did not study philosophy, or books – but we are surprised to see how his realization echoed the experience of the Vedic sages: Ekam Sat Viprah Bahuda Vadanti – Truth is one, sages call it by various names. Thus spirituality like science brings one perfectly to the realization of the nameless sages of pre historic age and the experience of Sri Ramakrishna. He was the unique historical figure of the 19th century India, who re-lived this harmony of religions, its practices, its experiences and presented the truth before the skeptics of the modern time.

Many writers, scientist, philosophers, teachers, actors, musicians and famous people from all walks of life, were influenced by this message of Oneness, Divinity, Peace and Harmony. The interfaith movement has become a very important theme of modern times. Vivekananda, the Vedanta monastics and lay devotees are at the back of this movement, and are silently contributing like unseen dew drops to this harmony. Not to proselytize but to inspire everyone to follow his own religion and to be a better Christian, Muslim, Hindu by realizing God –is the legacy. Not to criticize, not even toleration but acceptance of every path as varied and true is the real message of harmony. Vedanta societies through the monks and devotees as also many Vedanatic traditions of India, along with the leaders of other faith traditions of great world religions are trying to carry on the flag of Sri Ramakrishna's legacy through meetings, dialogues and respectful understanding each other. This is the good news of hope, as it is gradually bringing peace and harmony and becoming a force to counter act distention and disharmony.

49 Hindu Festivals

Hindus celebrate their religious occasions with great enthusiasm and revelry. True to the liberal style of their functioning, these religious festivals have much variation. Hindus count the historical events by the traditional calendar, *Vikram Samvat*, which is fifty-seven years before the Common Era.

Common Hindu festivals celebrated all over India:

Diwali, or Deepawali, as it is often called, is the festival of light. Undoubtedly, it is the most popular festival of Hindus. One billion Hindus celebrate this auspicious event with gusto and religious sentiment in all parts of world. Diwali signifies the return of Lord Rama, after completing his fourteen years of exile in the forest and winning victory over the wicked King Ravana. In South India, Deepavali marks the victory of Lord Krishna over the mighty *asura*, the demon Narakasura.

Holi is the festival of colors, which Hindus celebrate as an event of divine incarnation of their most cherished god, Lord Krishna. The gaiety and mirth of this festivity is unique, as no other ethnic group in the world has anything similar to this event. It is a celebration signifying the joy and mirth of the community. Holi is also celebrated to mark the day when the infant Lord Krishna killed the demoness Putana and as a symbolic day when the demons were destroyed by the Lord anywhere. Bonfires Hola are organized on the eve of Holi to celebrate the death of the demons.

Mahashivratri is the great celebration of one of the three most important gods in the Hindu pantheon, Lord Shiva. Many fast for the whole day and in the night they line up to bathe the Lord with milk. The chanting and worship continues for most of the night, as devotees herald the happy advent of their most adored Lord.

Shri Krishna Janamasthmi, the birthday celebration of Lord Krishna, is a festival of great revelry. In some places, especially in Maharashtra, the occasion is marked by processions of youngsters, dancing and singing their way in the neighborhoods and breaking the pot containing butter, reminiscent of the Lord's style in his childhood.

Raksha Bandhan is a special day for sisters to tie colorful cotton bands on their brothers' wrists. The brothers, in return, give a gift and token money to their sisters, but also it signifies a spiritual pledge that a brother gives to his sister for protecting her from any harm at any time. **Ram Navami** is Lord Rama's birthday. The festival is marked mainly with fasting and worship in the temples. Many fast on this auspicious day as a mark of reverence for the Lord.

Dussehra Vijaydashtmi is one of the most important Hindu festivals; it celebrates the victory of Lord Rama over wicked Ravana. In many places large effigies of Ravana are burned to symbolize the ultimate victory of goodness over evil. It follows another festival of nine nights of worship of goddess Navratri, culminating in victory on the tenth day. (*Vijay* means victory, and *dashtmi* is tenth day.)

Kumbh Mela is associated with a fascinating spiritual legend. *Kumbh* (literally, pot) is the pot of eternal nectar, promising immortality. Lord Vishnu announced that the nectar would be given away to the winner between the gods and the demons, after the nectar is derived from the ocean. In the struggle, part of the nectar of immortality was spilled onto four different corners: Allahabad, Haridwar, Ujjain, and Nasik. The Kumbh Mela takes place once every three years; in rotation in these four places, so that each place celebrates it once in twelve years. Allahabad, where there is a confluence of three rivers—Ganges, Jamuna, and the deep, invisible Saraswati—is considered the most auspicious. Over thirty million pilgrims attend the festival in one season of forty-one days, making the world's largest assemblage of mankind. Many visitors also come from foreign countries to witness this mega-religious fair.

Ekadasi is the eleventh day after every new moon (*amavasi*) and also after every full moon (*poornima*). Thus, there are twenty-four *Ekadasi* days in every year. This day is considered auspicious, and fasting on this day brings many boons. The *Vaikuntha Ekadasi*, which falls in November or December, is most sacred, and many Hindus all over the world fast on this day.

Guru Purnima is celebrated on the full-moon day in July to honor the Hindus spiritual preceptor. The gurus are garlanded and showered with many gifts, almost all of which are utilized for spiritual causes.

Regional festivals are many in the Hindu culture. In addition to the common national festivals, Hindus have many festivals that are unique to their own regions. These regional celebrations are often associated with the harvest season and also mark the beginning of the New Year.

Onam, Pongal, Makar Sankrati, and **Baisakhi** are regional festivals, mainly associated with their respective harvest season, and are marked as New Year's Day, which may vary from one place to another. **Onam** is the most important festival of Kerala. It is celebrated every year to honor the mythological god Mahabali. Homes are decorated with floral designs, boat races are organized, and family gatherings are held with festive dinners. **Pongal** is celebrated with much fanfare in Tamil Nadu. It is held in the month of January or February to coincide with the harvest of rice. **Baisakhi** in the northern state of Punjab is its equivalent. **Makar Sankrati, Gudi Padva,** and **Cheti Chand** are the New Year's days in some other regions.

Navaratri is a nine-day festival, followed by the tenth day of victory, *vijayadasmi.* This festival is celebrated in honor of three most important Hindu goddesses. Only the combined force of all three divine deities, manifested as the female form *Mahishasura Mardini,* was able to destroy the powerful demon *Mahishasura.* During the first three days, goddess *Shakti,* in her aspect as Parvati, is worshipped as the personification of power and vanquisher of evil. During the next three days, she is worshipped in the form of Lakshmi, signifying wealth and beauty. In the last three days, she is worshipped as Saraswati, signifying knowledge. The festival is celebrated with many regional variations; most prominent among these are the Durga Puja in Bengal and worship of goddess Amba in Gujarat, where the Navaratri is celebrated with the worship of goddess Amba, who is the mythological goddess representing the union of the three goddesses described earlier. The worship ceremony is followed by great tuneful dances of *Garba* and *Dandia.* Men and women, young and old, dance, accompanied by loud folk music and singing, until dawn, for the ten days before the Dussehra.[96]

Ganesh Chaturthi It is an important Hindu festival but especially so in Maharashtra. It was national leader Bal Gangadhar Tilak who first conceived the idea of celebrating this festival on a mass scale, just like Durga Pooja is celebrated in Bengal. Large idols of Lord Ganesh are worshipped in thousands of places. Weeklong celebrations finally culminate in huge processions of taking out the Ganpati idols, singing and dancing all the way, for immersion or *visarjana* in the sea or other water ponds.

Rath Yatra is the festival that is celebrated in the eastern state of Orissa; it has attracted world attention by its most vigorous and colorful *Rath Yatra,* the journey of the Lord's chariot. In the Jagannath Temple, massive floats of the temple carts are hand-drawn by more than four thousand persons over a distance of half a mile, accompanied by very rhythmic singing and dancing. Many tourists come from all over the world to witness this inspiring festival.

Chhat Puja is celebrated mainly in Bihar and Uttar Pardesh. Women of the town or village worship the sun as God. This worship is performed in winter, when the women take baths in the cold water, looking at the sun for protection. Similar festivals are also celebrated in different seasons as Bahag Bihu, Kati Bihu, and Magh Bihu in Assam.

Durga Puja is the biggest Hindu festival in Bengal. Goddess Durga is worshipped with pomp and dedication throughout this celebration. Large edifices and idols of the goddess are made, with artistic designs and ingenious craftsmanship. On the final day, the goddess is given a most affectionate farewell by immersion in the holy river. The festival coincides with the Dussehra celebration.

Kali Puja is also popular in Bengal. Kali Puja is performed on the night of Diwali. Kali, the black, four-armed goddess, is the symbol of Mother Nature.

Saraswati Puja is the celebration of Saraswati, goddess of knowledge, who grants boons in regard to education, music, and other fine arts.

Thaipusam is celebrated in the month of January and commemorates the immortal dance of Lord Shiva. This festival is especially important for Hindus settled in Malaysia.

Thiruvembavai is celebrated in the month of December and marks the arrival of Tamil saint Manikavasagar in Thiruvennamalai. He sang twenty soul-stirring hymns, calling on the maidens to rise early for a bath in the river and then worship Shiva, so as to be blessed with good husbands.

Hindu religious festivals are now celebrated across the globe, wherever Hindus have settled. With new technologies and an improvement in the financial status, many of these functions, both in India and abroad, are very huge and stunning. Bollywood and other entertaining programs are often mixed up with religious and spiritual elements; these then turn out to be gala events. Many programs are free for public, albeit some outside the temple area also ticketed presentations that demand fat fees for the entrance. Hindus have no inhibition of such fraternization of the spiritual with secular; an individual may opt according to one's personal choice.

Many highly reputed saints and spiritual leaders participate in these mammoth gatherings, delivering most worthy divine talks and rendering bhajans and kirtans. Hindus are generally very liberal in sponsoring such religious occasions at huge costs, often spending millions of dollars. For many common people these religious festivals provide the best opportunity of their life to revere God and also enjoy at the same time.

Occasionally there may be some elements who exploit these spiritual festivals also for their selfish purpose. Human nature has shortcomings; there is no substitute for vigilance at all times.

Spiritual Gems from Vishnu Purana

Desire cannot be pacified by the enjoyment of the objects of desire. On the other hand, it goes on increasing still more like the fire through the oblations (of clarified butter). Even the entire produce of the earth, the corns, gold, animals, and women are not sufficient (to quench the desire) of a single man. Therefore (taking this into view) one should give up all desires.

50 Hinduism and Interfaith The Future Trends in Our World

At the World's Parliament of Religions, held at Chicago in 1893, Swami Vivekananda quoted a beautiful verse from ancient Hindu scripture, Shiva Mahimna Stotra:

"As different streams having their sources in different places all mingle their waters in the sea, so, O Lord, the different paths, which men take through different tendencies, various though they appear, crooked or straight, all lead to Thee."[97]

He concluded his address by summarizing the message of his master, Sri Ramakrishna: *"Criticize no one, for all doctrines and creeds have some good in them. Show by your lives that religion does not mean words, or names, or sects, but that it means spiritual realization."*

There are two ideologies in the world today: the ideology of one religion or faith, and the ideology of multiple faiths. The believers in one religion feel strongly that their faith is the only one that leads to spiritual evolution and salvation of man. The believers in multiple faiths have a more open-minded approach and feel that mankind may attain spiritual wisdom through many different paths. There are many gradations of attitude, however, in this second category. Some practice tolerant exclusiveness; they tolerate other beliefs but do not wish any more closeness. Others believe in interfaith dialogue. They maintain a good communication with other faiths. Yet there are those who go beyond that to practice interfaith enrichment: They have a mutual respect for and an interest in learning from other faiths. Inter-religious tolerance is not enough; inter-religious respect is needed.

In modern times, the talk of one religion being superior to other religions is gradually fading. Most don't accept that one religion is right and another is wrong; they are simply different! As all races of the world are considered to be equal and free, so too are the various religions. The world at large is coming to terms with religious pluralism. It is important to realize and accept the fact that for any individual, his or her own faith is the best; there is simply no point for competition or confrontation among various religions.

There is undoubtedly a growing awareness of the interfaith approach. The youth, especially, appear to be more inclined toward this new direction. In recent times, America and other Western countries have witnessed an unusual phenomenon—many people are not giving up on God, but they are not interested in empty rituals and labels. They see a unity in the diversity of many religions. Hinduism has a unique status in this regard. Its origin itself is suggestive of a conglomeration of many spiritual vistas in the ancient era in the subcontinent of India.

The Hindu concept that the entire world is but one family lays great emphasis on the unity of all religions. At the same time, Hindu seers and saints have distinguished themselves consistently and emphatically in the belief that all different religions, as well as the religious sects, are sacred and must retain their individual identity. The Vedas explain, *"Let us have concord with our own people and concord with people who are strangers to us."*[98]

Mahatma Gandhi, too, strived all his life for unity among the various religions but not for uniformity. When confronted with failures and insurmountable difficulties, he would often surrender to the Supreme God for guidance, and pray:

"Let us ask for help from God, the All-Powerful, and tell Him that we, His tiny creatures, have failed to do what we ought to do. We hate one another. Let us ask Him to purge our hearts of all hatred in us. Let us ask God in all humility to give us sense, to give us wisdom."[99]

Swami Vivekananda's participation and his famous speech at the World's Parliament of Religions in 1893 have been hailed as a landmark and a turning point in the organization of the interfaith movement. His thundering words truly echo the concepts of Hindu philosophy:

"I am proud to belong to a religion which has taught the world both tolerance and universal acceptance."[100]

Paramahansa Yogananda adopted this open-door attitude to great advantage. He founded new and unique meditation centers, which adapted many ideas from the Western style of functioning. The Ramakrishna temples, spread all over America, also embraced a new system to a considerable extent. Devotees sit in comfortable chairs and may enter without removing their shoes; they even have no problem with keeping a picture of Christ in the main worship place. Participating and celebrating in each other's religious festivities may be a great joy!

For Hindus, interfaith is a sacred heritage. In fact, it is incorporated in the ancient teachings of the Vedas and Upanishads: *Ekam Sat, Viprah Bahudha Vidanti*—there is only one truth; sages call it by different names. This age-old maxim is the intrepid recognition of the plurality of faiths. Sri Ramakrishna said, "*As many faiths, so many paths to God, there can never be a single religion for all humanity. Each faith has distinct characteristics and has a definite significance in economy of an enriching divine life.*"[101]

In the ancient period, Emperor Ashoka created the Council of Religions, where representatives of various faiths met and discussed different issues in a cool, deliberate manner. None would be permitted to speak ill about other religions. Hindu sages have also repeatedly professed not to talk pretentiously of other creeds and sects.

A pertinent question is often raised as to what Hinduism has to offer in regard to the emerging concepts of interfaith. Hinduism may be considered as a living link between the ancient tribal system and the organized religions of the later periods. The ancient concept of Mother Earth is also the basic Vedic theme. A unified vision of the world as one family has been ingrained as *Vasudhaiva Kutumbakam*. Hinduism has thus carried forth the tradition of the early tribal religions, when tolerance of other religions was astonishingly high as compared with the organized religions of the later period. It has been said that in this war-torn age, only the ancient Indian spiritual teaching of unity and harmony can be a true savior.[102]

Said Sadhu T. L. Vaswani, one of the most prominent saints of the last century:

"*There are so many who can believe only one thing at a time. I am so made as to rejoice in the many and behold the beauty of the One in the many. Hence my natural affinity to many religions: in them all I see revelations of the One spirit. And deep in my heart is the conviction that I am a servant of all prophets.*"[103]

Hinduism was originally formed by the conglomeration of the spiritual wisdom of many ethnic tribal communities of the ancient past. All along its course through millennia, it has retained its pluralistic character with great diversity, by its representation of God in many different forms and names, in its ways of worship, and in its rituals and customs.

At no time has any Hindu saint or leader claimed that Hinduism is the sole way to God. Hindus have generally adopted a soft attitude toward other faiths; in many temples and places of worship, bhajans and hymns, containing the names of other religious messiahs are recited without any demurral. In some places even the pictures or idols of Christ, Buddha, or Guru

Nanak are positioned along with Hindu gods without any protest! This is not to say that there are no fanatic elements in the Hindu community; human nature betrays its weakness time and again.

Many non-Hindu world philosophers and scholars, through the ages, have recognized the positive impact of Hindu religion, and even boldly opined that the ancient Hindu teaching of "Ekam Sat, Viprah Bahudha Vidanti—there is only one truth; sages call it by different names", may perhaps help us out of the many conflicts and quarrels grappling the modern world.

51 Hinduism and Fine Arts

There is a close association between Hinduism and fine arts. From the ancient period, when Hinduism was not yet formally established, the proto-Hindu culture of the Sindhu-Saraswati civilization exhibits an abundance of artistic skill and craftsmanship. As long as five thousand years ago, the direction in which the people were moving was clear by their activities: the design pattern of the housing in the upper and lower regions of the city, the ingenious drainage system, the large community baths, the storage facilities for agricultural products, the seals, the aesthetically beautiful sculptures, the production of ultra-fine clothing, and the large variety of aromatic spices for their gourmet cooking.

The inception of the Vedas has been considered as man's first attempt to create organized literature. The world of poetry, music, dancing, sculptures, painting, and many other forms of fine arts grew steadily and swiftly. The earliest Hindu scriptures, Vedas and Upanishads, are regarded as divine inspirations. As there was no written language at that time, these were produced in poetic lyrics. These lyrics were then rendered to very haunting melodies to make them easy to recite and remember. The vast canvas of the Hindu scriptures is a testimony of the literary zeal among the followers. The free flow of written word is but a projection of a free mind. In this golden cradle of civilization were born so many new ideas and philosophies. The poets had a green pasture from which to feed themselves. Much of the early scriptures, including the Ramayana and the Mahabharata, were rendered in lyrical style. The Bhagavad Gita literally means the "song of the Lord."

In the period of Chandra Gupta II (375–415), India produced her finest poet and dramatist, Kalidasa. His most popular works include *Shakuntala*, *Meghdoot*, *Kumarasambhava*, *Malavika*, and many others. These great classics have become the world's heritage—there has been unprecedented interest in the Kalidasa's *Shakuntala*. In the nineteenth century, no fewer than forty-six translations of this masterpiece—in twelve different languages—were published in Europe.[104]

In the twelfth century another brilliant poet, Jayadeva,

composed the Sanskrit epic song *Geet Govinda,* which immediately became popular throughout the country. Chandidasa, in the fourteenth century, and Vidyapati, in the fifteenth century, soon followed his example.[105] The devotional aspect of Sri Radha, the Krishna zealot, often has been colored with sensuous moods, making Hindu religion unique in its abundance and passion. The love play expressed in these songs, however erotic, was still of pure type (*prema*), in contrast to the worldly type that is full of physical desires (kama).[106]

The songs of other saints—Thirukural and Chivavakkiyar (Tamil), Bhagat Namdev, Chaitanya Mahprabhu, Sant Kabir, Bhagat Narsi Mehta, Guru Nanak, Bhagat Surdas, Sant Haridas, Goswami Sant Tulsidas, Sant Mirabai, and many others—also have become extant and popular. For more than five thousand years, places of worship have been steeped in the deep melody and enraptured tunes of chanting the Vedic prayers (*mantras*), devotional songs (*bhajans*), and chorus singing (*kirtan*).

As extension of the Vedas, the Upavedas were created, which were mainly concerned with various human arts and sciences. For example, Sama Veda has its Upaveda, Gandharva, which deals with the art of music. Carnatic (sometimes called Karnatic) music is the original classical music of the Hindu culture, which started the basis of the *sa, re, ga, ma, pa, dha,* and *ni* musical notes. Carnatic, which translates as "older," may be related to the ancient Dravidian culture. Soon afterward, the art of dance took hold in Hindu society. It is said that Lord Shiva composed the first syllables of *bhav* (emotion), *raga* (melody), *tala* (rhythm), and *rasa* (mood). He thus came to be called *Nataraja,* the King of Dancing. A separate scripture, *Natya Shastra,* was compiled between the first and third centuries and was dedicated to this fine art. Dance became the most prominent temple activity in ancient times. Dancing maids, or *devadasis,* performed in front of the *murti* (idol) of God, and all devotees cherished the worship through this medium. The sexual exploitation of these *devadasis* has been yet another tragic tale of human weakness, but the flower of civilization blossoms by cutting the weeds, not by uprooting the plant itself. Today, Hindu women have taken to dancing, both as art and profession, in a mature and serious manner.

Seven prominent classical dance styles are in vogue: *Bharat Natyam* of Tanjore, South India; *Kathak* of Uttar Pradesh, North India; *Kathakali* of Kerala, South India; *Manipuri* of Assam, East India; *Mohiniyattam* of Kerala; *Kuchipudi* of Andhra; and *Odissi* of Orrisa, East

India. There are also many folk dance forms, such as *Chhau* of Orrissa, *Raas Garba* of Gujarat, *Bhangra* of Punjab, and *Lavani* of Maharashtra. The richness of these dancing arts has been admired in art circles all over the world.

Sculpture and painting became the foremost features in Hindu temple construction. From ancient times, these arts have dominated the temple scenario. The terra-cotta art of earthen pottery, as well as bronze, copper, silver, gold, and marble work, all have drawn the attention of Hindu society from all walks of life. The extraordinary display of these arts in many Hindu, Jain, and Buddhist temples is a testament to this concept. Even today, Hindus expend their wealth and other resources for art, with great passion and intensity. The Hindu temple is often a work of art and beauty in itself, both the outside and inside. The legend is that near the famous pilgrimage of Orcha in Madhya Pradesh, there is a beautiful hilltop shrine of goddess Shakti, which is known as *Maihar*. According to the ancient scriptures, this Shakti goddess is associated with the fine arts.

Apart from the permanent structures in the temples, Hindus started the custom of creating very large, highly artistic, and alluring idols of gods, especially during the *Ganpati* and *Durga* festivals. These idols were ceremoniously immersed in the sea or water tanks after the conclusion of the gala religious events, thus ensuring an ongoing support and patronage for the artists and craftsmen. Every year new idols with current ideas and designs are created.

Fine arts and religion have been intricately connected in the Hindu society through ages. Even, in the modern period, the classical dance patterns of Bharat Natyam, Mohiniyattam, Kuchipudi, and the folk dances of Navratri, Raas Garba etc. are linked to the religion in a meaningful manner. In recent times, these art forms have touched new heights; they have become very popular in many countries outside India. With an international outreach and Bollywood connections, these arts now have frequently mind-boggling budgets. Often, the country's most celebrated artists perform with worship rituals, dedicating their art to deities in a most devoted manner. All over the world, Hindu temples exhibit exquisite and spectacular forms of fine arts. The gorgeous and elegant forms of their architecture, sculpture, and painting etc. are unmatched. The idols of deities during Ganpati and Durga Puja are sometimes so colossal and magnificent nowadays that it becomes almost impossible for visitors, especially the non-Hindus, to imagine that these would be simply immersed in water and dissolved after the end of the ceremonial period of only a few days!

52 The Evolution of Hindu Temples

The history of the growth of Hindu temples is indeed very vibrant—the roots are found somewhere in the Stone Age. In the Megalithic period, people buried their dead by constructing monuments of stone over them and worshipping the departed. The transition from worshipping ancestral spirits to revering a personal God was marked by the creation of icons of deities with specific attributes. The terra cotta seals found in the ancient Sindhu-Saraswati civilization give evidence of this trait. There is mention of copper and bronze work in the Rig Veda, and the discovery of the bronze figures and carvings of goddesses in the same period, with tremendous sophistication and artistry, would become the precursor of many presentations of excellent pieces of sculptures in Hindu temples.

In the Vedic period, worship was conducted in open air. A platform was raised, a holy fire lighted, and the priest performed the chanting and oblations. These rituals of worship were called *agni havan,* where the devotees offered sacrifices of different materials into the sacred fire, with one or more priests conducting the ceremonies.[107] It was in the period of great emperor Ashoka (270–232 BCE), that the earliest Indian architecture could be traced. Some of the earliest Buddhist *stupas* (a pillared mound-like structure) of this ancient period are still visible. The Sanchi Stupa (shrine) built in 3rd century BCE to early 1st century CE, is perhaps the earliest architectural structure in India. The dome shaped structure of the Buddhist Stupa has its origin inspired from the primitive, stone-covered earthern burial mounds. Buddhist started the cremation method of disposing the dead after the cremation of Buddha, and later his relics were preserved inside the dome-shaped stupa in the same pattern as the dead bodies were buried under the stone-covered earthern mounds.

The Gandhara School of Art, in existence from 50 BCE through CE 500 and extending from the northern state of Punjab to bordering Afghanistan, became famous for Mahayana Buddhism. A new school of sculpture, markedly showing the combined influence of Persian, Greek, Roman, Saka, and Kushan regions, also defined this period. The energetic and vigorous nature of Indian culture became more noticeable. The rich carvings of the Buddha idols of this time became famous all over the world. The Mathura School of Art, which contributed heavily in the creation of most refined Buddhist figures (and later, seductive feminine idols), also became established around this time.

The cave temples, with their unique styles (created between the second century BCE and the CE second century) became highlights of Buddhist-Hindu architecture of this era.[108] The Gupta era (320–600) is considered the zenith of Indian culture. Many temples of Shiva, Vishnu, Krishna, the sun god, and Durga, with beautiful sculptured idols, evolved in this period. Starting from the sixth century, the southern Hindu architecture flourished under the patronage of Chalukyas, Pallavas, Gangas, Cholas, Hoysalas, Pandyas, and the rulers of the Vijaynagara Empire.[109] Away from the repeated invasions of the Muslim rulers, the Hindu temples flourished unhindered in the South, due in part to the large patronage of the Hindu kings, who built new cities around the grand temples, which then became appropriately popular as the temple cities. In the tenth and eleventh centuries, the Chandella rulers of the Madhya Pradesh in central India built the most notable temples of Khajurao, which today attract tourists from all parts of the globe. These temples are decorated with elaborate sculptures.

The passion for building temples has only intensified in the modern era. Not only in India but also in almost all countries where a substantial number of Hindus live, some of the most beautiful worship centers have been built to serve their spiritual and cultural needs. Jain temple art is unrivalled; Jains built beautiful marble temples in Rajasthan, Madhya Pradesh, Maharashtra, Karnataka, and Uttar Pradesh. The major Sikh shrines, or *Gurudwaras*, were built toward the end of eighteenth century, when Sikh rulers came to the power.

The conical dome, called *shikhara*, characterizes the Northern Indian temples, whereas the decorated gate tower, the *gopuram*, distinguishes the Southern temples.

Hindu temples are often built on hilltops to mark the place of God, high up toward heaven. A devotee may reach the place after a long and steep walk, suggestive of the effort for the purpose. When the temples are built on the plains, the height of the *shikhara* or the *gopuram* compensates for the hilly situation. The dome or steeple inner chamber is where one or more images (*murtis*) of the deities are installed. In Shiva temples, dome-shaped stone or marble (*Shiva lingam*) is invariably erected at the entrance of the inner chamber, the *garbha-griha,* where the deities are placed. In some of the Vishnu temples, a similar stone image, *shaligrama,* is installed.

For Hindus, the temple is pivotal to all spiritual and religious activity. It is often constructed with great care and planned in accordance with the codes mentioned in the *Shilpa Shastra,* the ancient Hindu book of architecture. The *Agamas* contain several references for temple construction. Even the site of the temple is chosen carefully, which must be auspicious, or *shubha.*

The whole process is started with worship rituals in which the artisan, or *shilpi,* offers prayers and undergoes a process of purification before embarking on this sacred task. Vedic rites are performed to install the idols (*vigrahas* or *murtis*) in the temple. During these rites, the deities are given a ceremonial bath (*abhisheka*). After the *murtis* are made, they are installed with a touching ceremony of *Nyasa.* Finally, by elaborate mantra recitations, the breath of life, or *prana,* is infused in the deity.[110]Grand inaugural ceremony is often called the *Kumbhabhisheka,* when the water for bathing the *murtis* is collected in a special receptacle, drawn from a holy river or other pious source.

In many Hindu temples, the idols of the nine planets (*nav grah*) are also installed: *Surya* (Sun), *Chandra* (Moon), *Sevvai* (Mars), *Bhutan* (Mercury), *Viyalan* (Jupiter), *Sukran* (Venus), *Sani* (Saturn), *Rahu,* and *Kethu.*

There has been undue harsh criticism of idol worship in Hindu theology. Ancient Hindu sages propounded both the God without form, *Nirguna,* and the God with form, *Saguna.* The *Saguna* concept became more easily acceptable for the vast majority of people. *Saguna* became the tangible manifestation of the Divine.

For a Hindu, a temple is not just a worship place; it is a shrine infused with holy vibrations. A devotee goes there, in faith, to meet the Divine, and he prays for both material and spiritual benefits. The Hindu temple, or *mandir,* as it is known in the vernacular, is a place where one realizes the inner dimension of one's mind (*Ma* =mind; *andir* = inner). For Hindus, visiting the places of pilgrimage is considered very auspicious. A Hindu never outgrows the temple service; whatever may be his spiritual advancement. As long as he lives, he must visit and pray in the temple. For Hindus, visit to temples and holy places (*Tirath Yatra*) is one of the five essential spiritual practices (*panch yajna*). Along with reading the Holy Scriptures (*Swadhya*), uttering God's name (*Japa*), worship (*Puja*) and rituals (*Charya*), visit to the temple (*Tirath Yatra*) is considered as a necessary spiritual practice (*Sadhana*).

Hindu temples occupy a place of great privilege in the Hindu society. Through the ages, they have grown from simple mounds in the prehistoric proto-Hindu period to the most magnificent and grand structures. In the Vedic period, open air platforms were used to conduct "Agni Havan"-the Fire Puja. This most ancient worship ceremony still remains active in the Hindu society, and is performed regularly on many important occasions, sometimes in a very elaborate manner with a number of priests participating together in a spectacular atmosphere. Vedic hymns are chanted in haunting original tunes even today. With the growing number of elegant sophisticated temples, this ancient simple ceremony is occasionally performed in a stylish, tasteful way, erecting temporary decorative pillars around the "fire", and placing ornamental "kumbh" pots in vertical columns. This has become the pattern in Hindu culture; the old are not totally discarded, but they are subtly modified.

From the early prehistoric period, different art forms, especially sculptures carved out of stone became an important part of the Hindu Temple. With the transition of diet from the consumption of meat to vegetarian food, tools earlier used for hunting were suitably modified to become useful for cutting stones and sculpting.

The Hindu Temple soon became a major patron for different forms of art through the centuries. The Gandhara School of Art, The Mathura School of Art, and other art forms involving the combined influence of Persian, Greek, Roman, Saka, and Kushan regions etc. contributed in the earlier period. Toward the beginning of the Common Era, Cave Temple art grew both in Hindu and Buddhist temples. The Gupta era (320–600) is considered the zenith of Indian culture, erecting temples for different Hindu and Buddhist gods; a generous plural attitude under which the art flourished freely. During the same period, away from the harsh onslaught of the Muslim rulers, many Southern state rulers like the Chalukyas, Pallavas, Gangas, Cholas, Hoysalas, Pandyas, and the Vijaynagara Empire etc. patronized the Hindu temples of Dravidian art forms, creating a wave of temple cities.

In the tenth and eleventh centuries, yet another form of temple sculpture grew; erotic figures decorated the outer walls of the temples in Khajurao and later in Konark Sun Temple etc.

Although these sensual images drew huge crowds, and still continue to attract visitors from all over the world, they are probably considered by the Hindu society as inappropriate to be placed within temple premises. As such, such images have no longer been seen in temples that have been constructed more recently.

NOTE: This chapter is adapted from Kolapen Mahalingum. *Hindu Temples in North America*. Winter Park, Fla.: Titan Graphics andPublications, 2002.

Common types of Meditation as practiced in the U.S.

Mindfulness:
This type of meditation, being studied by the National Center for Complementary and Alternative Medicine (NCCAM), is part of the Buddhist religion. During this meditation you may learn to concentrate on your breathing. As you follow your breathing, you try to become completely focused and present in each moment. Your thoughts pass out of your mind without judgment, called nonjudgmental awareness. Over time the goal is to learn how to experience everyday life with greater acceptance, balance, and perspective.

Transcendental:
This form of meditation, also being studied by NCCAM, is from the Hindu religion and involves the use of repeated words, phrases, or sounds — called mantras. By repeating a mantra, the meditator can block distracting thoughts and achieve a deep state of "restful alertness."

Vipassana:
Vipassana means "to see things clearly" and has been taught as a way of healing the body and the mind. Also called insight meditation, vipassana is said to have been taught by the Buddha. Vipassana requires focusing on the deep connections between the body and the mind, while remaining calm and detached.

Zen:
In Zen meditation, you close your mind to thoughts and put your whole being into the meditation, to achieve a state of concentration and realize your true inner-self.

At present in the West, Yoga is mostly known for its asana tradition, while Buddhism is more known for its meditation tradition of Zen and Vipassna.

53 The Abode of God is the Heart of Hinduism

The temple is the heart of Hinduism. In Hindu society, the temple has occupied a pivotal position, not only the spiritual aspect of it, but also because it has been the focal point of social and cultural activities. It has been closely associated with developments of fine arts, such as music, dancing, painting, architecture, sculpturing, and many other crafts. The Hindu temple has had a strong base of many philanthropic and charitable projects.

In recent times, the example of the Tirupati Temple in Andhra Pradesh is perhaps the most impressive beginning of such activities. With a huge income from the donations of the devotees, it supports a number of educational institutes, hospitals, and other worthy causes. The other major religious organizations include Sri Rama Krishna Mission, Swaminarayan *Sanstha,* Sathya Sai Baba Temple, Hare Krishna Temple (ISKCON), Chinmaya Mission, Sadhu Vaswani Mission, Mata Amritanadamayi "Amma" and Swadhya Parivar and many others.

In the traditional Hindu temple, the worship ceremonies are conducted with an organized set of rituals. Temple rituals are usually performed by one or more its own temple priests, who are, by convention, hereditary in lineage of a particular sect and are trained from early childhood in the intricate liturgy of the temple rites by reciting many *mantras* and *slokas* in special manner.

In the early morning, singing and chanting hymns perform the waking ritual of the deities. In Hindu temples, *Murti Puja* is conducted in very elaborate manner. Usually, the deity is given a sacred bath twice a day, followed by decoration with beautiful clothes and ornaments. Incense or *Agarbati* is burned, and the priest chants to the Deity in Sanskrit, describing all these acts, and beseeching blessings.

There may be five or six main worship ceremonies (*pujas*) through the whole day. In present times, the main ceremonies have been reduced to twice daily in many temples. Lighting a lamp (*diya*) signifies the light within our inner self. *Aarti* is regarded as one of the sixteen steps of worship ceremony. Hindus often perform *pujas* on important and auspicious occasions in the family. After the *puja* or the *aarti*, there is usually a divinely blessed food (*prasad*), which is first offered to the Lord and then distributed to the rest of the devotees. The ritual of the symbolic offering of the *prasad* to the Lord recognizes his supremacy in all respects. The devotees partake of it with humility and without complaint, whatever is offered. Almost every Hindu visits a temple, but there is no code or compulsion about these visits. A Hindu temple is usually open for long hours of the day, so the devotees may come and go at their convenience. A bell is often present, which the devotees ring as they enter. Individual cash donations are offered in specially placed boxes (*hundi*). New temples, and especially those in foreign countries, are usually clean and hygienic, but some of the old temples are not properly maintained. Most big temples are involved with social and charitable activities, apart from the religious ceremonies and *pujas*. Some of the very large temples have ongoing projects, such as running hospitals, educational institutes, or even universities, and many other social projects. Devotees enter the temple after removing their shoes outside. Many perform circumambulation (*parikrama*) around the *murtis* before starting the worship, thus making God the central focal point around which all activities are done. Some even perform the *parikrama* around themselves, recognizing the Divine within. The temple priest or *pujari* performs the worship ceremony in accordance with the codes in the *Agamas*, although variations and modifications abound. A special worship rite (*archana*) is performed by the priest, in which the name of the devotee, his ancestor lineage, names of other family members, and home address is intoned to the Divine before starting the main ritual. One hundred eight names are often recited to highlight the divine attributes of the presiding deity.

The Hindu temple is mainly a product of the Puranic tradition. The Puranic tradition evolved from a synthesis of the Sanskritic (mainstream) tradition and the regional or vernacular (little) traditions. For example, the cult of Vithoba in Maharashtra, a survival of an early pastoral deity absorbed as a form of Krishna in mainstream Hinduism, still retains its tribal and folk origins and traditions; there are numerous such examples. Hindus usually have a personal god, the *isht devta*, whom they invoke as a preferential god. This *isht devta* is often the family or community god, but an individual may choose his or her *isht devta* on the basis of personal choice.

Temple services have undergone periodic changes over the years. Today, more emphasis is on the real teachings of religion, rather than the formalities and customs. Animal sacrifices are omitted in most places. Many temples offer classes for children and youth to give orientation in the Hindu religion and philosophy. Temples are often the main locations for organizing various social and service activities, thus making these places the community cultural centers. The problem of language in the temple ceremonies has remained unresolved to a great extent, especially in foreign countries. Lectures are usually given in English or one of the Indian languages commonly understood by the devotees in the particular area, but the ceremonies and rituals are often conducted in Sanskrit, as a tradition. It may be interesting to note that in America, various European communities did start their church activities in their respective languages, such as German or French, but later were changed to English. The sentimental and emotional attachment to the languages can be understood, but it may not be allowed to become an impediment in the practical conduct of affairs.

Hindu temples play a major role in the lives of all Hindus, regardless of their religious, social, or financial status. They simply do not overgrow the "temple"; even the spiritual masters of the highest authority are found prostrating in the temple. Apart from the religious ceremonies, temples have played an important role in facilitating art, social service, and philanthropic activities etc. Many large "Temple Organizations" associated with various temples have undertaken mega projects that involve running big multi-discipline hospitals, charitable clinics, educational institutes, free food distribution, natural disaster service, homes for the underprivileged, orphanages, medical and surgical camps and many other activities. These have proved to be invaluable for the poor and needy and very often supersede similar services provided by the government. In recent times, these "Temple Organizations" have sometimes rendered these services in India of such magnitude and quality at low costs, sometimes even free of charge that even the most advanced Western nations simply cannot match. This is indeed a great achievement in modern times. Many of these high-tech medical services have skyrocketed in costs, and have become unaffordable for the poor and middle class people.

NOTE: This chapter is adapted from Kolapen Mahalingum, *Hindu Temples in North America*, Winter Park, Fla., Titan Graphics and Publications, 2002

Vegetarianism-Extra

The Belgian city of Ghent has become the first in the world (outside India) to go vegetarian at least once a week. Ghent means to recognize the impact of livestock on the environment. The UN says livestock is responsible for nearly one-fifth of global greenhouse gas emissions, hence Ghent's declaration of a weekly "veggie day".

The concept of 'Vegetarianism' is an evolutionary phenomenon in mankind. The earliest proto form of the human being, who walked on the two hind limbs instead of the four as his predecessors had done, came into existence as long as 6 million years ago. That proto human being probably ate raw meat also. The cooked food with fire started about 1.9 million years ago, although its common use occurred only 50-100 thousand years from now with the development of modern brain in human being. Although mankind ate all types of wild plants earlier, the planned agriculture products became possible less than 10 thousand years ago. Undoubtedly the prehistoric cultures of India were amongst the earliest when the mankind opted for farming in place of hunting as evident from the excavation of Sindhu-Saraswati civilization. Hindu society continued to make rapid strides toward 'Vegetarianism' philosophy. However it is more likely that the Vedic rituals of the animal sacrifices were real and not just symbolic as some would like to believe. With the march of time, the animal sacrifices have almost disappeared. Hindus in Nepal, Bali and in few pockets in India still carry out the animal sacrifices in religious ceremonies.

54 A Pilgrimage through India

Pilgrimage, or *tirthyatara*, is very different from an ordinary sightseeing trip. *Tir*, which in Sanskrit means "other side," refers to the journey toward the Divine. It is the spiritual preparedness and mental outlook of sacredness of the visit, which makes the person conducive to receiving the holy vibrations. Pilgrimage done with utmost faith and purity of mind may yield the most gratifying benefits.[111]

Some of the most important sacred places, which also include Hindu, Jain, Buddhist, and Sikh shrines, are included here. Hindus frequently visit the pilgrimage places of these allied religions as well as their own. For want of space, only the names and few details are given; more details may be obtained from internet and other sources.

The North Region has many sites associated with the origin of the Vedas and Hinduism:

Mount Kailash, considered as the abode of Lord Shiva and his consort, Sri Paravati, is high in the Himalayan range. It is also called Mount Meru. The Himalayas, which literally means "Home of snow," have been the eternal abode of sages and *Rishis* throughout millennia. For Hindus, the Himalayas and the Divine are inseparable!

Yamunotri, Gangotri, Kedarnath, and Badrinath, located northeast of Rishikesh in an area known as Garhwal, are four sacred Hindu pilgrimage sites. Yamunotri is at the source of sacred River Yamuna (Jamuna), and Gangotri is at the mouth of River Ganges, *Gaumukh*. The mountaintop Shiva temple at Kedarnath is at an altitude of 11,750 feet. Badrinath is dedicated to Lord Vishnu and is at a somewhat lower height. It is believed that no place in the world can match the grandeur of these regions. Sri Swami Tapovan Maharaj wrote, "*In the valley between the two mountains Nara and Narayana there shines a celestial mass of light called Badareesa, which is the seed of this entire universe.*"[112]

Ladakh is the location of the Buddhist monastery, Spitok Gompa, and it is built at an elevation of more than ten thousand feet.

Shri Vaishno Devi Temple is situated high in the Himalayas; this temple lately has attracted a number of devotees. They throng in thousands every day to journey up to the site, singing *Jai Mata Di* all the way. According to the legend, Vaishno Devi, who was a devotee of

Lord Vishnu, defeated a demon called Bhaironath at this temple site.

Ganga Maa, the river Ganges, figures most prominently as the most sacred river. Taking a dip in Ganga is believed to wash away the sins of a lifetime. It is mentioned in the scriptures that Ganga originated from the feet of Lord Vishnu, traversed through the matted hair of Lord Shiva, and was brought down to Earth by sage Bhagiratha to perform the worship ceremony in honor of the ancestors.

Har ki Pairi Ghat, Haridwar, or "abode of the Lord," as it translates is one of the most popular pilgrimages of Hindus. Situated in the foothills of the Himalayas, it is located on the banks of sacred Ganges.

Varanasi Ghats, also known as Kashi or Benares, is the oldest holy city of Hindus. Hindus consider it most auspicious to die in this sacred place. Varanasi has been a center of 'learning' for over 2000 years.

Allahabad (Prayag), Sangam is the confluence (*sangam*) of three sacred rivers—the Ganges, the Yamuna, and the invisible heavenly Saraswati. It is the site where the most famous *Kumbha Mela* is held once every twelve years. This is also a most favored place for immersion of ashes after cremating the dead.

Ayodha, the birthplace of Lord Rama, the Jewel of the Solar Kings, is regarded as one of the holiest places. There are temples and shrines in every quarter of this small city on the banks of holy River Sarayu.

Mathura, the birthplace of Lord Krishna, and **Brindavan,** where he was reared in childhood and played many a *raas leela* with *gopis,* are regarded as very sacred places for Hindus.

Golden Temple, Amritsar, the world-famous Sikh temple, was first built in 1577, but was destroyed by the Mughal emperor in 1761. It was rebuilt in 1764. In 1802 the roof was covered by gilded gold plates, which gave it a unique image. It houses the original copy of the sacred scripture *Sri Guru Granth Sahib.*

Anandpur Sahib Temple, or "City of Bliss," as it is literally translated, is another equally holy Sikh shrine, situated on the bank of River Sutlej in Punjab.

Chitrakut is the holy spot, where Lord Rama stayed for some time after his exile. The place became especially significant because his beloved brother Bharata came to meet him here to persuade him to return. Rama then explained the concept of duty and observance of one's father's vow, *pitruvakyaparipalana.*

Lakshmi Narayan Mandir is located in New Delhi. The Birla industrial family built it in 1939. This is the first of its own type, where multi-deity worship was adopted. It houses the shrines of many different Hindu and non-Hindu gods.

The Akshardham Monument, the new Swaminarayan temple in Delhi, which was opened in 2005, is a landmark in the Hindu temple movement. The Akshardham Monument, built without steel, is entirely composed of sandstone and marble. It consists of 234 ornately carved pillars, nine imposing domes, twenty quadrangle *shikhars*, a spectacular *gajendra* (plinth of stone elephants), and twenty thousand *murtis*.

Central India, Madhya Pradesh and Chhattisgarh:

Khajurao Temples in Madhya Pradesh, built between CE 950 and 1050, are undoubtedly among the most popular temples for visitors. Out of eighty-five original temples of rare sculptural beauty, only twenty-two remain. Hundreds of figures decorate the walls in perfect and flawless patterns. These temples are also famous for their erotic sculptures. There have been many debates on why such overtly sexual poses have been admitted in religious places. Whatever may be the reasons, the fact remains that the Hindu society did not consider it appropriate to have such erotic figures in the temple premises in the later periods.

The Great Stupa, Sanchi, the dome shaped *stupa,* or ancient sculpture, may perhaps be the earliest religious site in India, as it's thought to have been built between the first century BCE and the Common Era first century. It is a Buddhist sanctuary with four intricately carved gates on four sides.

Ujjain in Madhya Pradesh occupies a very special status in the holy map of India. It is one of the four places where the *Kumbh Mela* is held in rotation, once every three years.

The East-West Bengal, Sikkim, Orissa, Bihar, and Jharkhand:

Kali Temple at Dakshineshwar, Kolkata, was built in 1847. It has become famous because the God-realized soul Shri Ramakrishna Paramhans was associated with this temple. The black image of goddess Kali represents God in the aspect of eternal Mother Nature.

Konark Sun Temple is situated about forty miles from Bhubhenshwar. This world-famous temple has been designated as a United Nations World Heritage site. Constructed between 1238 and 1264, it is famous for its huge, intricately carved chariot wheels, which form the base of the temple.

Jagannath Temple is situated at Puri, only twenty miles down the coast from the Konark Temple, and is equally famous. Jagannath has become most popular for its grand *Rath Yatra*—every summer, on the auspicious occasion of Lord Krishna's birthday, *Janmashtami,* devotees and visitors witness a massive procession of temple carts drawn by more than four thousand persons.

Mahabodhi Temple, Gaya, Bihar, attracts crowds because it is here that Lord Buddha attained enlightenment after meditating under the banyan tree. Mahabodhi Temple, built in eleventh century is well known for its impressive gilded Buddha idols.

Brindavan is famous for the many temples dedicated to Lord Krishna. It is in the gardens of Brindavan, where the Lord played *raas leela* with the *gopis.* Brindavan has become the convergence point for all Krishna devotees who throng to this simple town.

Rajasthan:

Jain Temple, Ranakpur, built in 1439, is the largest Jain temple in India. Inside, 1,944 pillars of most intricate and enchanting carvings support twenty-nine halls. The roof and walls are covered likewise with many marble designs of exquisite beauty. The temple is hailed as a feast of art.

Pushkar is located near Ajmer, at the foot of a mountain around scenic Pushkar Lake. This peaceful, holy town affords a magnificent view to the devotees and visitors. It is also famous for the only single temple anywhere dedicated to Lord Brahma.

Jain Dilwara Temple of Abu was built between 1032 and 1233. This marble temple is among the finest Jain architecture in India. The delicacy of the interior of this and the more important Vimla Sha Temple takes marble carvings to unsurpassable heights.

The West:

Dwarkanath Temple, at a seaside location in the western part of Gujarat, has tremendous importance for the Hindu devotees. This is where Lord Krishna had his kingdom. Recent excavations have shown that the sea has submerged five settlements earlier and the present one is the sixth.

Somnath Temple is considered to be a very sacred shrine; here lies one of the twelve original *jyotirlingas.* It is ancient, and is mentioned in the Rig Veda. The temple was destroyed repeatedly by Muslim invaders and reconstructed. The present magnificent structure is the seventh temple on the original site, built in 1995.

Ajanta and Ellora Caves were built between the second century BCE and the Common Era seventh century. These world-famous caves are situated about two hundred miles from Mumbai in Maharashtra. Ajanta Caves are the earlier ones.

Ellora caves are more famous for their superb stone sculptures. Here, the caves are of mixed variety. Twelve caves are Buddhist, seventeen are Hindu, and five are Jain. The caves themselves have been hollowed out from the rocks, thus requiring meticulous planning in their execution. Unlike the conventional architecture, here the success depended on what was to be removed, rather than what was to be constructed.

Holy City of Nasik is situated about one hundred miles from Mumbai. It is full of temples. The Tryambakeshwar Temple, containing one of the twelve original jyotirlingas, is an ancient Shiva temple, which attracts pilgrims from all over India. There is also the ancient site Panchvati, which is on the bank of the sacred River Godavari, where Lord Rama stayed during his fourteen years of exile, *vanvas*.

Jain Temples, Palitan, where the hilltop Jain sanctuary is one of the most holy pilgrimages of India. Built in the eleventh century, these temples were destroyed by Muslim rulers in the fourteenth and fifteenth centuries. The existing temples are from the 1600s through the present.

Modhera step-well Temple, 65 miles northwest of Ahmedabad, is famous for its spectacular step-well, interspersed with multiple shrines, and image of sun-god *Suray*. Nearly 3000 such step-wells with intricate archeological designs were constructed from seventh to nineteenth centuries, primarily to hold the water to descending levels, till the year end and then get again filled in the rainy season.

Ambaji Temple, situated on the Arasur hill near Mount Abu, is one of the most important pilgrimage sites. Dedicated to goddess Ambaji, it is recognized as an original *Shakti Pitha.*

Shri Swaminarayan Akshardham Temple, Gandhinagar, is the new temple, which combines the traditional stone architecture with modern technology. Golden *murti* of Lord Swaminarayan is the chief attraction of this holy place.

Mahalakshmi Temple in Mumbai is the oldest temple in the metropolitan city. It is dedicated to Sri Lakshmi, the goddess of wealth. The temple is situated on small hill overlooking the Arabian Sea.

Shri Siddhivinayaka Ganapathi Temple, Mumbai, had humble beginnings in 1801. It housed the black stone idol of Lord Ganpathi. Over the years, it has grown enormously and now attracts huge crowds.

South India:
The culture of South India has its own nostalgia. The deep, thick forests have divided the North from the South since ancient times. Muslim rulers never got a strong foothold in the South, and hence, the Hindu temples were spared from repeated onslaughts and devastation. The architecture of the southern temples has retained more pure form.

Tiruvannamalai, the Arunachaleshwar temple dedicated to Lord Shiva and goddess Parvati, is decorated with giant gate towers, *gopuras,* which are visible from a long distance. The *ashram* of the famous spiritual master Raman Maharishi in the vicinity has lent additional aura to this sacred place.

Kanchipuram in Tamil Nadu is regarded as one of the seven sacred cities for Hindus. It is a city studded with many beautiful temples. The Ekambareshwara Shiva Ganesha Temple has a massive temple tower, which is 192 feet tall.

Mamallapuram (Mahabalipuram), located thirty-seven miles from Chennai, it is a seaport with many Hindu temples constructed by the Pallava dynasty. Among the important sites is an immense relief carved on the face of a huge rock, depicting the descent to earth of the sacred River Ganges through the matted locks of Lord Shiva's hair.

Chidambaram was a Chola capital from 907 to 1310. Among the many temples is the Nataraja Shiva Temple, with 108 classical postures of the Lord as the cosmic dancer. An impressive fire ceremony conducted by the priests is the highlight of this temple.

Thanjavur (Tanjore), the famous Rajarajeshvara temple built about CE 1000, is considered to be the masterpiece of South Indian architecture. The city also has the shrine dedicated to the famous Saint Tyagaraja (1767–1847), who is regarded as the greatest musical composer of South India.

Lord Babubali Sarvanabelagola is one of the oldest and most popular Jain pilgrimage centers. This temple is famous for a huge statue of Lord Bahubali. The fifty-one-foot-high statue of the Jain saint can be seen from a long distance. It was built in the tenth century; in 1981 there was a big celebration to commemorate its thousand-year anniversary.

Tirumala and Tirupati Temples, built in the tenth century, is one of the most popular temples of India. Crowds queue to get a looks at the *darshan* of the Lord. The temple is dedicated to Lord Venkateswara, a

Vishnu incarnation. On special auspicious days the number of pilgrims may swell to one hundred thousand in a day. Many have a deep abiding faith in Tirupati.

Shree Minaksi Temple, Madurai, a Shiva temple built in the seventeenth century, attracts thousands of devotees and visitors every day. It is dedicated to fish-eyed goddess Minaksi.

Rameswaram, built in the twelfth century, is another fine example of the Dravidian art of South India. Its magnificent corridors are lined with beautifully carved pillars. One of the corridors is four thousand feet long, the longest in India. It is a Shiva temple, where Lord Rama, who is Vishnu incarnate, worshipped Lord Shiva in penance for killing Ravana, a Brahmin and a Shiva devotee. This reflects the mindset of Hindu philosophy, where gods worship each other, and war does not breed any enmity or hatred.

Kanyakumari is the southernmost point of India, where three oceans meet. The Bay of Bengal, the Indian Ocean, and the Arabian Sea merge here. Vivekananda Memorial Temple was built on two rocky islands in 1970. The imposing beauty of this temple is enhanced by its natural surroundings.

Ayappa Sabarimala Hills, one of the most popular temples of Hindus, is situated in Kerala. Those who come here must walk through animal-infested jungles to keep their vows after receiving the divine favors. In this temple, the deity is the mythological god Lord Aiyappen, son of Lord Shiva and Mohini, the female form of Lord Vishnu.

There are also many more important temples run by different religious organizations, such as Swaminarayan, Hare Krishna (ISKCON), Shirdi Sai Baba, Radha Swami, and Satya Sai Baba sects in different parts of India.

NOTE: This chapter is adapted from Arnette Robert. India Unveiled. Georgia: Atman Press, 2006

Legacy of Bhagwan Sri Satya Sai Baba
(Contributed by Prem Sadani)

The Vedas exclaim from time immemorial, *Ekam Sat Vipra Bahudha Vadanti*, Existence is One, Sages call it by different Names (Rig Veda, 1-164-146). God, Brahman, Allah, Isvara, Jehovah, Ahuramazda, etc., is one. I offer my worship to that Supreme Being the One eternal homogeneous essence, indivisible mass of bliss and intelligence whom sages describe in a variety of ways through diversity of intellect.

Bhagwan Sri Satya Sai Baba has further elaborated it beautifully. The truth proclaimed by all religions is one and the same. The ultimate goal of all religions is the same. The primary object of religion is to cure man of his follies and make him a real human being. Equally, religion aims at promoting righteous conduct by transforming the mental attitude of man. Religion is concerned with developing in man faith in the Spirit, besides his preoccupation with the needs of the body. For all religions the foundation is morality. If morality declines, humanness will decline together with the eclipse of religion.

55 Hindu Temples in the United States and Canada

The first Hindu Vedanta temple in the United States was built in San Francisco in 1906. Paramahansa Yogananda started the Self-Realization Fellowship in 1920, which constructed a string of elegant worship centers, mostly in California. These earlier religious establishments, however, although philosophically related to Hinduism, had their own codes. These were not typically Hindu organizations. The main purpose of these earlier places of worship was to cater to the local populace, the majority of which was non-Hindu. These institutes have continued to render most admirable service in acquainting the devotees with the basic principles of Hindu philosophy for over a century. After the large influx of Hindu immigrants in the latter half of the twentieth century, traditional Hindu temples were built. In the United States and Canada alone, there are more than eight hundred Hindu temples. Most of these have been built in the last two or three decades.

Dr. V. Ganpati Sthapati of Tamil Nadu, India and others from the United States and India have contributed enormously toward erecting magnificent Hindu temples in North America. Many of these temples have been built according to the traditional *Vastu Shastra* of the Vedic period. There have been modern adaptations also. Although there was initially strong resistance from the local communities at some places, the courts of law often prevailed and gave permission after satisfying themselves with some basic requirements. In few places, however, the leading Christian churches supported the cause of the Hindu temples. These new temples in America have a large community basis. Spacious halls have become part of the temple premises, which are used for weddings and other socio-cultural functions.

There is also generally a good mix of various sects and communities from different parts of India. In most temples, there may be one presiding deity, such as Lord Shiva or Lord Vishnu, but other major and minor deities are usually also recognized. In a few places, the deities of Jain, Buddhist, and Sikh faiths also have been accommodated in the same temple. Although this practice may have become necessary to meet the demands of various sections of Hindu populations in a foreign land, there appears to be a hidden advantage in bridging the unnecessary gulf among the different sects.

For want of space, only the names and few details are given; more details may be obtained from internet and other sources.

Sri Meenakshi Temple, Pearland, Texas, like the one at Madurai, India, is dedicated to goddess Meenakshi, symbolizing the female power (*shakti*) aspect of the Lord.

Sri Viswanatha Temple, Flint, Michigan is dedicated to Lord Shiva. The scenic situation of the temple on the shore of a lake has enhanced its spiritual value.

Hindu Sabha, Brampton, Ontario, in which the main deity is goddess Durga as *Jagdamba Mata,* contains idols of other deities also.

Hindu Temple, Dayton, Ohio, has as the main deity the boon giver, *Sri Satyanarayana,* whose idol in black granite occupies the central place.

Connecticut Valley Hindu Temple has as its main god Sri Satyanarayana, who is considered as *Mahavishnu,* the giver of boons.

Sri Rajeshwari Radha Rani Temple, Austin, Texas, is a large establishment of 230-acres, which has been converted as the land of the great saint of the Lord, *Shree Radha.*

Venkateshwara Temple, Bridgewater, New Jersey, has Lord Venkateshwara as the presiding deity, whose granite image measures seven feet in height.

Hindu Temple of Greater Chicago, Lemont, Illinois, has Lord Shiva as the main deity in the form of Shiva Linga.

Hindu Temple of St. Louis, Ballwin, Missouri, has been acclaimed as an architectural marvel for its artistic designs and superb sculptures.

Palace of Gold, New Mathura, and Vrindavan, Moundsville, West Virginia, is monument of golden domes and stained glass, an architectural wonder accomplished by the devotees of the Hare Krishna Temple, located among the scenic winding hills of West Virginia.

Shiva-Vishnu Temple, Livermore, California, has one entrance guarded by a majestic gate, *rajagopura,* which opens into a spacious hall, *mahamandapa,* leading to two main shrines of Lord Shiva and Lord Vishnu.

Sri Lakshmi Temple, Ashland, Massachusetts, was built initially with the help from the Tirumala Tirupati Temple of India.

Ganesha Temple, Richmond Hill, Ontario, houses Lord Ganesha and Lord Murgan, also known as Subramanya or Kartik.

Sri Ranganatha Temple, Pomona, New York, situated deep in the wooded valley of Pomona in Rockland County, New York, this beautiful temple is dedicated to Lord Ranganatha.

Sri Siva Vishnu Temple, Lanham, Maryland, is situated twelve miles from Washington DC. It has been richly incorporated with Mayan, Pallava, Vijayanagara, Kerala, and South Canara styles of temple architecture.

Sri Maha Vallabha Ganpathi Devasthanam, Flushing, New York, has a logo, adapted from Sri Satya Sai Baba's ecumenical symbol—a light surrounded by insignias of several religions with "Om" on top, which represents the fundamental unity as the core point of all religions.

The Hindu Temple of Atlanta, Riverdale, Georgia, first installed the idol of Lord Ganesh. Images of Sri Venkateshwara, Sri Devi (Lakshmi), Sri Bhudevi, Sri Durga, and others are also housed here.

Hindu Jain Temple, Monroeville, Pennsylvania, has on the main axis the Lakshmi-Narayan temple, with two subordinate temples of Sri Radha Krishna and Sri Ram Pariwar.

Hindu Temple, Loudonville, New York, represents a blend of the modern and the traditional, the new and the old, in a smooth manner.

Sri Prasanna Venkateswara Swami Temple, Mamphis has Lord Prasanana Balaji as the presiding deity.

Sri Ganesha Temple, Nashville, Tennessee, has Sri Ganesha as the main deity.

Sri Shiva Vishnu Temple, Davie, Florida, is a large structure with two entrance towers, *rajagopuras*, and two sanctum towers, *vimanas*.

Sri Venkateshwara Temple, Penn Hills, Pittsburgh, is one of the earliest Hindu temples in the United States, and has been called the Tirumala of the Western Hemisphere..

Hindu Temple, Las Vegas, Nevada, serves the spiritual and cultural needs of the Hindu community and is visited by many travelers. The main deities are the Sri Radha Krishna, Sri Shiva Parvati, Balaji Padmavati, and Sri Ram Pariwar.

Sri Venkateshwara Temple of Greater Chicago, Aurora, Illinois, is excellent blend of the ancient temple architecture, according to the *Shilpa Shastra,* and modern design.

Malibu Hindu Temple, Los Angeles, California, is a spiritual landmark for the Hindu community of the metropolitan Los Angeles area. This temple is dedicated to Lord Venkateshwara. There is separate Shiva temple also in the same premises.

Hindu Samaj Temple, Wappingers Falls, New York, received a gift of the idols of Lord Venkateshwara and Sri Laksmi (Padmavati) from Tirumala Tirupati Devasthanams in India.

Kauai Aadheenam, Hawaii, is also known as Kauai's Hindu Monastery. It is a traditional South Indian-style monastery/temple complex on the mystical garden island of Kauai, Hawaii, spread over 458 acres of tropical lushness.

Sanatan Dharam Temple, Los Angeles, California, has become a landmark of numerous religious and cultural activities in the thriving Hindu community.

BAPS Shri Swaminarayan Temple, Houston, is regarded as the first traditional Hindu mandir in the United States and is built entirely of stone and marble. Spread on twenty-two acres, this elegant place of worship houses thirty-three thousand carved pieces that were shipped from India.

Ekta Mandir, Irving, Texas was inaugurated in 1991 to serve the needs of Hindu community residing in the metropolitan areas of Dallas/Fort Worth.

Vedanta Society Temple, Seattle, Washington, along with the spacious Vivekananda Assembly Hall in the adjoining premises, has been an active Hindu worship center since 1938.

Lakshmi Narayan Mandir, Riverside, California, is situated on the eastside of Los Angeles. Spread on four acres, it has activities throughout the year.

Radha-Krishan Temple, Los Angeles, California, is one of the oldest Hindu temples in Southern California and is very close to the buzzing Indian community and trade center.

Sindhu Center, Los Angeles, California, started by the Sindhi Hindu community, houses the beautiful idols of Sri Radha/Krishan, *Ram Parivar*, and Lord Shiva/Parvati along with Lord Ganpati in three sections.

BAPS Shri Swaminarayan Mandir, Chicago, Illinois, also known as *Shikharbaddha Mandir*, is spread over thirty acres and is considered as the largest stone and marble traditional Hindu temple in the United States.

Chinmaya Mission Center, Los Angeles, California, has now a spacious center Rameshwaram at Tustin, which combines both the Lord Shiva and Lord Rama idols.

Vedanta Society Temple, Los Angeles, California, started around

1930. This temple has served the local American and Indian communities for over seven decades.

BAPS Shri Swaminarayan Mandir, Los Angeles, California, is built on a twenty-acre site; the temple has an imposing and artistic structure, with adjoining Haveli Cultural Center.

BAPS Shri Swaminarayan Temple, Toronto, Canada, was recently inaugurated by Shri Pramukh Swamiji, and was a gift to all the communities of Canada.

Hindu Temple of Atlanta, Georgia, was built at a cost of $19 million in the Lilburn suburb of Atlanta. The white temple covers an area the size of two and a half football fields. The idols in the temple include those of Bhagwan Swaminarayan, Radha/Krishna, Sita/Ram and Shiva/Parvati.

BAPS Shri Swaminarayan Temple, New Jersey, the largest Hindu Temple outside of India was inaugurated by Pramukh Swami in August 2014. Built on 160-acre premises, 134 feet long and 87 feet wide with 108 ornate pillars, is expected to be fully complete by 2017.

Many other Hindu temples are run by the Vedanta Society, Chinmaya Mission, Swaminarayan Sampradaya, ISKCON, and other Hindu organizations in major cities (and some minor ones) in North America.

NOTE: This chapter is adapted from Kolapen Mahalingum. *Hindu Temples in North America.* **Winter Park, Fla, Titan Graphics and Publications, 2002.**

Paramahansa Yogananda's Legacy to World Harmony and Unity
(Contributed by Lauren Landress, Self-Realization Fellowship, Los Angeles)

"If we had a man like Paramahansa Yogananda in the United Nations today probably the world would be a better place than it is."
– Dr. Binay R. Sen, former Ambassador of India to the U.S.

Throughout his 32 years of public ministry in the West, Paramahansa Yogananda devoted himself to fostering greater harmony and cooperation among all religions, races, and nationalities; and to helping people realize and express more fully in their lives the beauty, nobility, and divinity of the human spirit.

Sri Yogananda took every opportunity to foster interfaith understanding, brotherhood, and world peace – through the many interfaith conferences that he organized or participated in; the founding of the Self-Realization Fellowship Worldwide Prayer Circle, an international network of those who regularly pray for the physical, mental, and spiritual well-being of others, and for world peace and harmony; and the establishment of spiritual sanctuaries open to people of all religious backgrounds, including the SRF Lake Shrine with its Mahatma Gandhi World Peace Memorial.

Among his greatest contributions to the world was his instruction in the science of God-realization, including techniques of meditation for developing a direct, personal experience of God. He said, "I believe that if every citizen in the world is taught to commune with God (not merely to know Him intellectually), then peace can reign; not before. When by persistence in meditation you realize God through communion with Him, your heart is prepared to embrace all humanity."

56 Hindu Temples in the Rest of the World

Hindu temples are now in all corners of the world. Whenever there is sizeable population of Hindus, the temple activity becomes imperative. The local community takes up the project under the leadership of one or more enthusiastic leaders, and usually the response is encouraging. Undoubtedly, the Hindu community needs these sacred premises, not only so they may be spiritually uplifted but also so that they may maintain their identity and social structure. The temples have become the most important cultural centers around which all other activities are organized.

In many Hindu temples, the multi-deity worship has become a common practice to accommodate the sentiments of different sections of the community. The temples, however, which are organized under the umbrella of the parent institutes, such as **ISKCON**, the **Swaminarayan** sect, etc., maintain their individual form and style. In the recently opened Swminayarayan temples, the multi-deity worship has been adopted. Fortunately, in none of the Hindu temples is there a total polarization, nor is the Hindu community rigidly divided on the basis of their temple affiliation. Hindus often visit temples of separate sects and organizations, although they usually have a preference for one of their choice. They normally sponsor their own family functions in the temple of their allegiance.

Hindu temples are established on all five continents. In Africa, these are present in Botswana, Kenya, Nigeria, and South Africa. In Asia, apart from India, Hindu temples are present in Nepal, Pakistan, Bangladesh, Sri Lanka, Malaysia, Indonesia, Singapore, Japan, China, and Cambodia. Hindu temples are established in many cities of Australia.

Hindu temples are present in many countries of the Caribbean islands—Barbados, Fiji, Guyana, and Jamaica. In Europe, Hindu temples are established in the UK, Denmark, France, Ireland, and the Netherlands. In North America, there are Hindu temples all across the United States and Canada. In South America, Hindu temples are in Argentina, Bolivia, Brazil, and Chile. **Hastinapur, the city of wisdom, in Argentina** is a unique temple of its kind. **Swaminarayan temples** have been established in Africa, the UK, and in many cities in America, such as Boston, Los Angeles, Houston, and Chicago. **ISKCON temples** are in many places, such as Nigeria, South Africa, Australia, Denmark, Ireland, Netherlands, North America, Argentina, Bolivia, Brazil, Chile, China, and Japan.

The Chinmaya Mission has set up temples, apart from India, in the United States, the UK, Australia, Sri Lanka, and France. **Swaminarayan Temple** in London occupies a place of pride, as it attracts not only the Hindus but also many persons of other faiths because of its artistic architecture and extensive marble and wooden craftsmanship. The **ISKCON temple** and **Balaji Venkateshwara temples** are other important Hindu shrines. The spectacular **London Hindu Sri Murugan Temple** is popular landmark.

In Australia, the **ISKCON** and **Swaminarayan temples** are there along with temples of South Indian origin, such as the **Venkateshwar Balaji, Murgan, Balasubramaniam**, and **Siva temples**. **Murugan Temple** in Sydney, Australia is an important landmark, especially for the Tamil Hindu community. **Shiva-Vishnu Temple** in Melbourne is very popular.

In Malayasia, Singapore, and other Southeast Asian countries, temples of South Indian origin abound, as more persons from that region of India have migrated there. **Sri Perumal Temple** is one of the oldest temples in Singapore. **Velmurugan Gnana Muneeswarar Temple**, Rivervale Crescent Sengkang in Singapore is also very popular. Malaysia's population includes 20 percent Hindus of Dravidian origin. **Sri Maha Mariammman** temple, founded in 1873, is the *Shakta* temple, dedicated to goddess Parvati. It is the most famous Hindu temple. **Sri Subramaniaswamy Temple**, or the **Batu Caves Temple**, as it is commonly known, is equally popular. Many devotees and tourists visit this temple, situated high up in the mountain, with elegant steps leading upwards. The **Arulmigu Sri Rajakaliamman Glass Temple** is a major Hindu temple as well as one of the oldest temples in Malaysia.

Indonesia, too, has witnessed enormous temple activity, especially in the province of Java. **Sukuh Hindu Temple** and **Penataran Hindu Temple Complex** in Indonesia, along with **Temples of Phanomroong and Muangtam** in Thailand, and **Rishikesh Complex of Ruru Kshetra and Ram Janaki Temple in Nepal** are currently on the "Tentative List" of UNESCO World Heritage Convention nominated by their respective countries waiting to be inscribed on World Heritage List. Currently, the World Heritage

List is made up of 911 properties "having outstanding universal value", which includes four Hindu temples: **Konark Sun Temple in** Bhubhenshwar, **Hampi and Pattadakal temples** in Karnataka (India) and **Prambanan Temples** in Indonesia. The **Mother Temple of Besakih**, or *Pura Besakih*, in the village of Besakih on the slopes of Mount Agung in eastern Bali, is the most important, the largest and holiest temple of Agama Hindu Dharma in Bali.

The famous temples of Angkor in Cambodia, are very similar to the ancient Hindu temples of India.

In Nepal, which is an overwhelmingly Hindu country, there are many diverse Hindu temples. **Pashupatinath Temple** in Khatmandu is the most famous **Shiva temple** in Nepal. **Gushmeshwari Shrine** is one of the eighteen *Sakti Peethas*, dedicated to goddess Sati.

Pakistan, which had a sizeable Hindu population before the partition in 1947, has a number of diverse Hindu temples. Bangladesh has many Hindu temples of different types. Sri Lanka has a large Hindu population and has many temples of the South Indian style all across the country.

Hindu Temples have evolved through millennia, from the most simple structures made of small earthen mounds in the ancient times, to most elegant, highly architectural and artistic structures, housing stunning sculptures, paintings, and imposing "murtis" of deities, through different periods of time.

Hindus have demonstrated greatest interest and importance towards temples, investing heavily in building and maintaining them. Many Hindu temples were systematically destroyed during the Muslim rule; with equal enthusiasm, if not greater, quite a number of them were rebuilt.

In present times, Hindu temples are built in all corners of the world. Many non-Hindus too, visit these temples, sometimes due to their genuine interest in the religion and philosophy, but often also out of curiosity towards the temples' magnificent architecture, sculptures, and the elegant Murtis. Hindus usually welcome all without any distinction, and no effort is made to convert any one into Hinduism. Hindus too visit the worship places of other communities freely.

Many Hindu temples now have mega assets; often, they build big spacious halls where thousands of devotees, at one time, may attend the religious ceremonies, "Spiritual Talks", Bhajans and Kirtans etc. Sometimes these spacious halls are also used, with suitable restrictions, for social occasions like "Wedding Functions" etc. by the devotees

Bal-Vihars and Youth Centers, where children and youth may participate and learn about Hindu religion and culture are now becoming common in many Hindu temples, especially those in foreign countries.

Sitting arrangements inside the temples are now mixed; usually chairs/benches are provided for the elderly and handicapped. Individual sitting arrangement on the floor is not yet organized as in some of the Buddhist temples in foreign countries.

Some Hindu temples now provide excellent arrangements for removing and keeping shoes in protected area. Chairs are kept for the devotees to remove and put on shoes comfortably. The shoes are kept in a proper safe area away from rain etc. The shoe room is also inside the main temple area, and a carpet is provided for the devotees to walk safe and warm after removing the shoes. However, there are still many temples that do not have such good facilities.

Hindu temples are now gradually gearing up to organize their programs in a more professional manner. An advance time-table of the events is mailed, and every effort is made to keep punctuality. Manyt temples, however, lag behind on this score.

Albeit some Hindu temples are now equipped with very modern restrooms; they are also kept clean and hygienic, most Hindu temples are not yet ready for this.

Many Hindu temples, especially in foreign countries, are now multi-deity, keeping the Murtis of many Hindu gods, with one or more as presiding deities. Even those Hindu temples, which were previously very sect specific, are now accommodating other deities; either in the same room, or in separately-built chambers. Some Hindu temples also keep the pictures or Murtis of other religion gods/messiahs in a suitable place. Satya Sai Baba temples keep the logo of all the world religions as their emblem. Hindus are usually more liberal in such matters.

NOTE: This chapter is adapted from www.Mandir.com

57 Hindu Prayers:
The Trail of Divine Unfoldment

All religions believe in the power of prayer. God, however, is not only omnipotent and omniscient; He is also our most benevolent mother and father. Only He would know what is best for us at a given time. Accepting the will of God is indeed part of a good prayer. When we pray with utmost sincerity, there is always a change of our heart toward divinity and virtue. This is indeed the most secure benefit, which never fails to occur from a forthright and genuine prayer. Prayer brings a treasure of blissful joy. Doctor Swami, an esteemed saint of the Swaminarayan sect, says *"Prayer is both the exercise and rest for the soul. It is the essential food, too, and the cleansing shower. Prayer may take time to show the result, but no sincere and truthful prayer ever goes unheard."*[113]

Prayer is the most important tool of any religious activity. We may perform many good and noble deeds, but these would not be considered spiritual until we add a touch of the Divine to these. A brilliantly clever person may do amazing things but could be, at the same time, a good or a bad person. A truly spiritual person, however, is always a noble being. Hindu seers of the yore created a very intimate connection with the Divine by prayers and meditation.

Hindu sages have prompted mankind to pray for the divine guidance so that we may walk on the right path. We may also pray to know our personal duty *'svadharma'* in any situation. We may visualize mentally the picture of our *ishta-devta* for more effective help and guidance.

Hindu seers envisaged that we need God's grace for the emancipation of our soul. Good and noble deeds alone are not enough. With prayer and worship, in utmost sincerity and humility, and with total surrender at the lotus feet of the Lord, we may obtain His grace. According to Hindu philosophy, God does not intervene until a special request is made. Prayer renders purity. When we sincerely pray, we cannot, at the same time, think nor do anything impure. To pray and simultaneously hate anyone is incompatible. Nor we may scheme to cheat when we are in the midst of a truthful prayer. It is said that God will answer the prayers of those who are pure in mind and body.

Said Pramukh Swami:

If someone has harmed or hurt you, don't retort in the same manner. Instead, respond with calmness and with goodwill and prayers. Pray that the other person should see the divine light and understand properly. Pray for his welfare. The vibrations sent spiritually will always bear powerful results, both to the person who is thus praying and sending the good wishes, as well as to whom these are directed. This is the principle of religion and spirituality in everyday life.[114]

Prayer also makes us humble. When we kneel down before God, we at once dispense with our pride and arrogance. Ego and arrogance are closely associated. With prayers, we may be rid of both of them. Prayer is empowering. Time and again we come across the futility of confronting the odds in our lives. We simply become helpless spectators, even as tragedies flow past us. With prayer, we get connected to the infinite power of the Divine and use it for our great benefit. Prayer brings peace and a sense of security. With total surrender to our Supreme Lord, we attain the serenity and quietness, even when tough life situations surround us. In some mystical way, God always helps a person who sincerely prays. This is borne by the experience of most great persons of the world. There simply are no bounds and limits to the infinite treasures of the Divine.

Medical practitioners, scientists, and politicians alike have repeatedly kneeled down and endorsed the high value of prayer. Sages regard prayer as a spiritual substitute for worry, our most potent enemy! In estranged relationships, prayer becomes our soothing repose. Prayer, however, is not just for mystical benefits; rather, it yields tangible results in most trying circumstances. Often, as we are not able to contain the evil of others, we might pray for them. *Prayer is the magical link with God*, in the opinion of Paramahansa Yogananda.

Hindu sages sought God for different reasons, in different ways, and in many different forms. They sang of the Lord's praises in abundance and with passion. But the *Rishi* was constantly aware of the unity of all manifestations in one Supreme Being, as is clearly stated in this hymn of the Rig Veda: "*They call Him Indra, Mitra, Varuna, and Agni. The being is one, but sages call him variously.*"[115]

Hindu sages composed many beautiful universal prayers:

"Common be your prayer,
Common be your desires,
Common be your hearts,
United be your intentions,
Perfect be the union amongst you."
—Rig Veda X, 191–3, 4
The universal nature of the Hindu faith is very visible in this prayer.

"Gods, May we hear with our ears what is auspicious.
O Ye adorable ones, May we see with our eyes what is auspicious.
May we sing praise to ye and enjoy with strong limb and body the life allotted to us
by the Gods."
—Vedic
Auspiciousness and goodwill (*sadbhavna*) has been a marked feature in Hindu philosophy.

"May there be peace in heaven. May there be peace in the sky.
May there be peace on earth. May there be peace in the water.
May there be peace in the plants. May there be peace in the trees.
May there be peace in the Gods. May there be peace in Brahman.
May there be peace in all. May that peace, real peace, be mine."
—Vedic
Peace, or *shanti*, is invoked repeatedly with great passion.

"May the winds bring us happiness.
May the rivers carry happiness to us. May the herbs give us happiness.
May the night and day yield us happiness.
May the dust of the earth bring us happiness.
May the heavens give us happiness.
May the trees give us happiness.
May the sun pour down the happiness. May the cows yield us happiness."
—Taittiriya Aranyaka X, 39
All nature gods are invoked to grant us happiness and prosperity.

NOTE: All prayers are adapted from Swami Yatiswarananda. *Universal Prayers.* **Chennai, India: Sri Ramakrishna Math, 200**

Spiritual Gems from Swami Chinmayananda

"Success or achievement is not the final goal. It is the 'spirit' in which you act that puts the seal of beauty upon your life."

"The tragedy of human history is decreasing happiness in the midst of increasing comforts."

"A successful man is one who can lay a firm foundation with the bricks that others throw at him."

"What you have is all His Gift to you. What you do with what you have is your Gift to Him."

"In life to handle yourself, use your head, but to handle others, use your heart."

"The cultured give happiness wherever they go. The uncultured whenever they go."

"The highest form of grace is silence."

"We may often give without love, but we can never love without giving."

"To give love is true freedom; to demand love is pure slavery"

(Source: Central Chinmaya Mission Trust, Mumbai)

Conclusion: A Legacy for Hindu Youth Diaspora

The birth of Hinduism coincides with the superior development of the human mind, *sumati*. With the advent of higher brain about fifty thousand years ago, man took longer strides toward mental awakening and spiritual consciousness. There is evidence to suggest that various prehistoric tribes passed through India around this period. Harnessing the mind in a spiritual manner to make it noble, *sattvic*, and non-hurting has been prompted by Hindu *Rishis* through the ages.

Hindu culture is the immaculate quintessence of a profound ancient philosophy. Promoting an open-arm culture, it allows for freedom within the bounds of responsibility.The sense of duty and sacrifice is the foundation of Hindu culture. It inspires compassion, love, respect, humility, and modesty in all spheres of activity.

There may be some controversy regarding the origin of Aryan community that is associated with the creation of the earliest scriptures of the Hindu religion. But there is no contest that the seed of Hindu thought sprouted first in the holy land, *Punya Bhumi,* of India. Chains of *Rishis* meditated on riverbanks, mountaintops, and in the forests. In their deep sojourns, they established a secure communion with the Divine. From this spiritual union, they heard the inner voice of God and created thousands of sacred hymns, which would then form the eternal Vedas. The Vedas were not written by a single author but by many highly enlightened and virtuous masters. These scriptures attained supreme authority, one which is still considered sagacious. Hindu theology, however, soon charted a new direction. The old teachings were respected and revered but subtly changed as the situation and circumstance demanded. Dynamic character became visible, but no force or violence was deployed.

Changes came in succession through the Upanishads, the Bhagavad Gita, the Srimad Bhagavatam, and many other Holy writings. Through more such changes, new religions like Jainism, Buddhism, and Sikhism came into being. Many new sects, or *sampardaya,* also organized. New ideas percolated, giving an impetus to grow and survive through oncoming challenges. The dynamic character of Hinduism became well established, with a free flow of ideas and philosophies. Jain scriptures stress the phenomenon of different points of view—*anekta*— making way for a more restrained and rather non-dogmatic approach to various problems—a crying need for our contemporary situation. In our own times, the energetic roar of Swami Vivekananda became the bugle of another major reform movement. He boldly carried the message of his guru Sri Ramakrishna that all religions are but manifestations of one supreme truth. He reaffirmed that true religion lies in the transformation of our inner being (*antahkaran*); service of the poor and needy became more valid and relevant than empty, prolonged rituals. He regarded service as *karma yoga*. Any form of good and useful service rendered with sincerity and unselfishness merits as good karma, and spiritually rewarding. He also taught that religion need not be in the hands of a few learned priests; we all may learn the principles of religion and use these in everyday living. These changes are not new as these were described in the ancient Vedas, too, but we often need wakeup calls. The great swami even proclaimed, *"There is nothing like a closed book on Vedantism. Something, which is considered useful to human society, may be adopted at any time."* [116] Hindu Society today has the good fortune to be guided by many living sages, saints, and swamis. Lately, India has taken giant strides in economic fields. It has adopted a secular constitution, guaranteeing freedom of religion to all subjects. Just as science has brought many material benefits to the people, it is religion that enhances the quality of the mind. A truly religious person, belonging to any faith, would always abide by the spiritual values of truth, love, and compassion. Science has grown due to the sharing of its knowledge among different countries of the world. The new spirit of interfaith, too, may be of use to human beings once its spiritual values and principles are shared.

Hindus are at the threshold of a major transformation. After centuries of subjugation, they are now making bold and mammoth progress in various fields. They live in most countries of the world, and their contribution toward religious development is obvious in all places. Hindu temple activities have made a tremendous impact in recent years all over the globe. A Hindu temple is regarded as the home of God, where any devotee, Hindu or non-Hindu, may walk in and find solace and peace. Religion always plays a major role in the lives of Hindus. Living a good material life alone, however, is not the end in itself; it is rather imperfect—*apara*. But aiming to live a virtuous and moral life by using the tools of material and scientific advantages would be considered a perfect goal—*para*.

The future decades may prove to be challenging for Hindus in many ways. Synthesizing modern science with traditional religious activities may bring forth golden opportunities previously unimagined. Hindus would do very well to build ultramodern, hygienically superior and finely comfortable places of worship, where they may spend most of their spare time in search and practice of higher values of the Divine. The mega temples of yore are a clear inspiration in this direction. The serenity, which is the heart of the temple, may not be compromised by the ostentatious and glitzy decor. The day has perhaps dawned where Hindus now boldly adopt the look of a new age, discarding the ragged and dilapidated appearance of yesteryear, reminiscent of slavery and poverty. They may even accept the good practices of other faiths without feeling embarrassed. Learning from any source is always a sign of progress; not learning is shameful ignorance.

Maintaining a sense of brotherhood and love for others is the basic principle of Hindu spirituality. Helping and serving others, whatever may be their religion, is the moral duty of every Hindu. Prejudice, hatred, and undue criticism for people of other faiths are seriously harmful for our own growth. Hindus may do well to remember the lessons of tolerance and kindness *(Daya)* taught through ages by their own seers and saints. Respecting others and maintaining harmony and peace—*shanti*—are some cherished values of the Hindu philosophy. We should always treat the whole world as God's one large family, *Vasudhaiva Kutumbkam*. Only then will we earn true joy—*ananda*—in our lives.

This book is especially dedicated to the Hindu Youth Diaspora that is now settling in many countries. There are some protocols and conventions that all immigrants should follow when they choose to live in other lands. Loyalty and integrity form the basis of such conventions. Observing the laws of the land is mandatory for all, perhaps even more so for immigrants. Hindus in foreign countries should conduct themselves as virtual ambassadors of India. They may serve and love their new country with complete sincerity and honesty without disrupting the roots with the country of their origin.

True spirituality, simply stated, is living a life of virtue and ethics. Tolerance (*sahan Shakti*), not confrontation, has always been the watchword of Hindu philosophy. They may do well to recall the old decree of Mahabharat: *Tasmat tikshnataram mridu*— "*By gentleness one can overcome the greatest difficulty in the world.*" Religion teaches us to remain patient and restrained in all situations. Criticizing and condemning often makes things worse. There may be many customs and rituals in our own faith as well as in the faiths of other people that do not appeal to us. Hindu society has always adopted a soft attitude of tolerance in this regard. Religion is essentially a very personal and private matter. Any interference is, therefore, not called for.

Our scriptures also do not commend self-praise. In fact, any pleasure in listening to one's own adulation is severely discouraged. Modesty is valued in Hindu society. Doing noble and good deeds, which win other people's acclamation, is hailed as a virtuous act.

Despite some inevitable mistakes, there are several noble and glorious achievements that the Hindu culture can brag about. The book attempts to acquaint the Hindu Youth Diaspora of their grand heritage and restore their pride and confidence in their own ancestry. True religion brings out the highest values in an individual. The spiritual virtues taught in the Hindu religion, as in all other religions, are our best assets in life, more than secular education, financial security, and military strength. Every generation acquires many traditions—the best of the past that has been carried forward for the future. It then becomes the responsibility of the future generation to handle these traditions with wisdom and maturity. Albeit some changes are inevitable, they may be implemented only for the better with care and discretion. Respect for elders is a keystone of Hindu culture. Hindu *Rishis*, throughout millennia, have always stressed the spiritual values of truth, integrity, love, forgiveness, compassion, and humility. Often, we run after material possessions, compromising our moral and spiritual principles. We may liken this to the old saying, "*collecting the dust, and throwing away the gold!*" For Hindus, the moral teachings of religion have always been the bedrock of good living.

Religion—*dharma*—is basically like a classroom, a school, or a university, where we receive instruction for the moral and virtuous pedagogy. Ultimately, however, it is we who are responsible for learning and understanding these spiritual teachings properly and putting them into use in everyday living. Moreover, we may imbibe dharma deep into our mindset (*antahkaran*), so that we think in a moral and spiritual manner, harboring no hatred, ill will, or harm to others. Is it easy? No, it probably is not easy, but the rewards are incredible and fabulous. In a world where we are always searching for a moment of peace and joy, a question was put to Revered Pramukh Swami Maharaj, the great saint of the highest stature in our own time: "*You have a master key; as a result, you are always happy and at peace, no matter what difficulties you face. What is the secret?*"

He replied, "*Sarvamangal--one who is always happy--has the master key! It is to obey the command of God at all times, to be tolerant, humble, and to serve everyone.*"[117]

Spiritual Gems from Sri Sarda Devi

One should not hurt others by words. One must not speak even an unpleasant truth unnecessarily. By indulging in rude words, one's nature becomes coarse. One's sensibility is lost if one has no control over one's speech.

If you want peace of mind, do not find faults with others. Rather see your own faults. Learn to make the whole world your own. No one is a stranger. The whole world is your own.

(Source: Eternal Values, Swami Lokeshwarananda, The Ramakrishna Mission Institute of Culture, Calcutta, 19)

Bibliography

Abhedannada, Swami. *Spiritual Sayings of Ramakrishna*. Kolkata, India: Ramakrishna Vedanta Math, 1985.

Aiyangar, S. K. *Ancient India*. Madras, India: Lucaz & Co, 1911.

Amrutvijaydas, Sadhu. *Divine Memories (Part 3)*. Ahmedabad, India: Swaminarayan Aksharpith, 2003, p 82.

Arnette, Robert. *India Unveiled*. Georgia: Atman Press, 2006.

Asha, Dayal. *Bharat jaa Bhagat* (Sindhi Language). Madras, India: Veena Devidas Mirpuri, 1981.

Bellani, Deepchander. *Ved Prakash* (Sindhi Language). Ajmer, India: Akhil Bhartiya Sindhi Arya, 1979.

Bhaskarananda, Swami. *The Essentials of Hinduism*. Seattle: Viveka Press, 1994

Bhaskarananda, Swami. *Meditation*, Seattle: Viveka Press, 2001.

Bowker, John. *Cambridge Illustrated History of Religions*. Cambridge, U.K.: Cambridge University Press, 2002.

Brahmadarshandas, Sadhu. *Karamasddhant & Punarjanmavad, Part-II*. Ahmedabad, India: Swaminarayan Aksharpith, 2003.

Chellaram, Lachman. *Navrattan*. New Delhi: Dada Chellaram Publications, 2002.

Chopra, Deepak. *Quantum Healing*. New York: Bantam Books, 1989.

Dharmaratnam, Dr K. *Questions and Answers on Hinduism*. Kuala Lumpur: Visal Print Service, 1997.

Dodeja, Lokram P. *Srimad Bhagavad* (Sindhi Language). Bombay: Noble Stationery Mart, 1950.

Dalai Lama, *The Universe in a Single Atom*. New York: Morgan Road Books, 2005.

Editors of *Hinduism Today* magazine. *What Is Hinduism?* Hawaii: Himalayan Academy, 2007

Flood, Gavin, *An Introduction to Hinduism*. Cambridge UK: Cambridge University Press, 2005.

Gandhi, M. K. *An Autobiography*. Ahmedabad, India: Navajivan Publishing House, 1927.

Gidwani, Bhagwan S. *Return of the Aryans*. New Delhi, India, Penguin Books, 1994.

Hemenway, Priya. *Hindu Gods*. San Francisco: Chronicle Books, 2003.

Jagdeesan, J. Kuala Lumpur, Malaysia: TRAC Publication, 2002.

Jung, Carl G. *Modern Man in Search of a Soul.* New York: Harcourt Brace & World, 1933.

Kolapen, Mahalingum. *Hindu Temples in North America.* Winter Park, Fla.: Titan Graphics and Publications, 2002.

Knapp, Stephen. *Proof of Vedic Culture's Global Existence.* Detroit, Mich.: World Relief Network, 2000.

Muller, Max F. *The Upanishads.* New York: Dover Publications, 1984.

Nityanand, Swami, *Symbolism in Hinduism.* Mumbai, India: Central Chinmaya Mission Trust, 2001.

Osborne, Arthur. *For Those With Little Dust.* Carlsbad, Calif.: Inner Directions, 2001.

Parikh, Vastupal. *Jainism and the New Spirituality.* Toronto: Peace Publications, 2002.

Parmananda, Swami. *The Upanishads.* Cohasset, Mass.: Vedanta Centre Publishers, 1981.

Pattanaik, Devdutt. *Indian Mythology.* Rochester, Vermont: Inner Traditions, 2003.

Prinja, Dr. N. K. *Hindu Dharma.* UK: Vishwa Hindu Parishad, 1996.

Radhakrishnan, S. *The Hindu View of Life.* Boston: Unwin Paperbacks, 1980.

Robb, Peter. *A History of India.* Palgrave, 2002.

Ronan, Colin A. *The Natural History of the Universe.* New York: Macmillan Publishing Company, 1991.

Sachchisanand, Swami, *My Experiences.* Ahmedabad, India: Gurjar-Anada Prakashan, 1989.

Sanghave, Dr Vilas A. *Aspects of Jaina Religion.* New Delhi, India: Bharatiya Janpith, 2001.

Saradananda, Swami. *Sri Ramakrishna: The Great Master.* Chennai, India: Sri Ramakrishna Math, 1952.

Sharma, R. S. *India's Ancient Past.* Delhi: Oxford University Press, 1920.

Singh, Chitralekha. *Hindu Goddesses.* New Delhi, India: Crest Publishing House, 1995.

Sivananda, Swami. *May I Answer That?* Shivanandnagar, India: The Divine Life Society, 1999.

Sivananda, Swami. *Science of Pranayama.* Shivanandnagar, India: The Divine Life Society, 2001.

Smith, Huston. *The World's Religions.* San Francisco: Harper, 1958.

Srikantananda, Swami. *Human Excellence*. Hyderabad, India: Ramakrishna Math, 2001.

Srimad Bhagavad Geeta. Delhi, India: Shree Geeta Ashram, 1985.

Sullivan, Bruce M. *The A to Z of Hinduism*. New Delhi, India: Vision Books, 2003.

Swahannada, Swami. *Vedanta and Ramakrishna*. Kolkata, India: Ramakrishna Mission Institute of Culture, 2003.

Tapovan, Maharaj Swami. *Iswara Darshan*. Bombay, India: Central Chinmaya Mission Trust, 1983.

Tapovan, Maharaj Swami. *Wanderings in the Himalayas*. Bombay, India: Central Chinmaya Mission Trust, 1996.

Tathagatananda Swami, *Light from the Orient*, Mayawati, India: Advaita Ashram, 2005

Tathagatananda, Swami. *Journey of the Upanishads to the West*, Mayawati, India: Advaita Ashram, 2005.

Tathagatananda, Swami. *Meditation on Swami Vivekananada*. New York: The Vedanta Society, 1994.

Tejomayananda, Swami. *Hindu Culture*. Mumbai, India: Central Chinmaya Mission Trust, 1994.

Thus Spake Lord Mahavir. Mylapore, Chennai, India: Sri Ramakrishna Math, 1998.

Thus Spake Lord Buddha. Mylapore, Chennai, India: Sri Ramakrishna Math, 1998.

Thus Spake Sri Sankara. Mylapore, Chennai, India: Sri Ramakrishna Math, 1998.

Turlington, Christy. *Living Yoga*. New York: Hyperion, 2002.

Vaswani, J. P. *Dada Answers*. Pune, India: Gita Publishing House, 2002.

Vaswani, T. L. *The Bhagavad Gita: The Song of the Supreme*. Pune, India: Gita Publishing House.

Vedic Prayer. U.K.:Kuldip Mangal.

Viswanathan, Ed. *Am I a Hindu?* San Francisco: Halo Books, 1992.

Vivekananda, Swami, *The Complete Works of Swami Vivekananda*. Calcutta, India: Advaita Ashrama, 1970-1973.

Vivekananda, Swami. *Lectures, From Colombo to Almora*. Calcutta, India: Advaita Ashrama, 1997.

Yatiswarananda, Swami. *Universal Prayer*. Mayawati, India: Sri Ramakrishna Math, 2001.

Magazines and Journals:

Editors. Where Hindus Live. *Hinduism Today*. Oct-Dec 2006, p 52
Klugger Jeffrey. Is God in Our Genes. Vol. 164, No. 17. *Time*.
October 25, 2004, p 62-68
Matlani Dr. Baldev. The Labor of Sindhis. *Hindvasi Sindhi Weekly*:
April 8, 2007, p 10-11
Panjwani Ram. Supreme Court of India and Rig Veda. *Hindvasi
Sindhi Weekly*: April 22, 2007, p 5
Panjwani Ram. Secular. 5. *Hindvasi Sindhi Weekly*: May 6, 2007, p 5
Prabhananda Swami. Sri Sarda Devi's Journey. Vol.IX, No 3. *Global
Vedanta*: Summer 2004, p 2-4
Prabhananda Swami. Treasure From the Attic. Vol.XI, No.2. *Global
Vedanta*: Spring 2006, p 4-5
Shandilya and Varuha Upanishads. Hinduism's Code of Conduct.
Hinduism Today, April-June 2004, p XIII-XVI, p . XIII-XVI
Stein Joel. Just Say Om. Vol. 162, No.5. *Time*. August 4, 2003, p
48-52.
Swaminarayan Prakash (Gujarati language), Aksharpeeth
Swaminarayan, Ahmedabad, India, March 2007
Tathagatananda Swami. A Young Frenchman's Odyssey in Quest of
Wisdom. Vol. XII, No. 2. *Global Vedanta*: Spring 2007, p 2-3

Web sites:

1. http://beyondbelief.freedomblogging.com/2008/02/06/
maharishi-mahesh-yogi-pioneered-transcendentalmeditation
2. http://www.himalayanacademy.com
3. www.Beliefnet.com
4. www.Shakunarayan.com
5. www.Mandir.com
6. www.indiatimes.com

Glossary

In most places, the meaning in English is described where any Sanskrit word is used in the book for the first time. Some particularly important words appear here for immediate reference.

Abhay: Fearlessness

Abhyasa: Practice

Abhisheka: Ritual bathing of the deity's image

Acharya: Spiritual preceptor

Advaitya: Non-duality or monoism

Agamas: Scriptures of rituals and temple construction

Agni: Hindu god of fire

Ahimsa: Non-injury or nonviolence, in thought, word, or deed

Akasa: Free open space, sky, ether

Amrita: Nectar of immortality

Ananda: Divine bliss

Anekta: Different points of view

Antahkaran: Inner being

Apara: Imperfect

Archana: Personalized temple worship

Artha: Property, wealth

Asana: Body posture

Ashrama: Place for learning, hermitage

Asura: Evil spirit, demon

Atman: Soul

Aum or *Om*: mystic symbol (icon) of the Divine

Avtara: Incarnation of God in earthly form

Ayurveda: Ancient Hindu science of life

Bhakti: Devotion of God

Brahmacharya: Divine conduct, controlling lust when unmarried

Brahman: Supreme Being, Transcendental Absolute

Brahmand: Represents solar system or galaxy in Hindu scriptures

Brahmin: Person with divine knowledge, used as higher caste

Buddhi: The determinative faculty of mind

Chakra: Subtle center of consciousness at different levels

Chit: Consciousness

Dasanami: Ten renunciate orders founded by Sri Shankaracharya

Daya: Compassion

Deva: Shining One, refers to God or deity

Devi: Goddess, *Shakti* deity

Dharma: What sustains, way of righteousness, religion
Dhyana: Concentration, meditation
Dipavali: Row of lights, Hindu festival to celebrate the return of Lord Rama from exile
Ganges: India's most sacred river
Grihastha ashrama: Householder law and family code of conduct
Guna: Strand, quality (inherent from birth)
Guru: One who removes darkness of ignorance, spiritual preceptor
Hatha-Yoga: A school of yoga that chiefly aims at physical well-being and exercises
Ida: Feminine psychic current flowing along the *Kundalini* energy
Ishta Deva: Chosen family or personal deity
Japa: Recitation of Lord's name
Jnana: spiritual knowledge or wisdom
Kalpa: Time period in Hindu scriptures
Karma: Action, deed, in Hindu philosophy it refers to the consequences of the deeds performed
Kartikeya: Son of Lord Shiva, also known as Skanda, Murgan, Subramanya
Kriya: Religious rite or ceremony
Kundalini: Coiled latent cosmic serpent power, awakened with yoga practice
Mahaprasthna: Great departure, death
Mahatma: Great, enlightened soul
Mahayuga: Time period in Hindu scriptures
Mantra: Mystic sound syllable endowed with spiritual energy, Vedic hymn
Mauna: Vow of silence
Maya: Illusion, God's ever-changing manifestations of the creation
*Moksha: S*alvation, in Hindu philosophy liberation from recurrent birth/death cycles
Murti: Image, icon, or effigy of God
Niruna: (God) Without attributes and form
Nirvana: Absorption in the Absolute Transcendental, liberation
Nirvikalpa samadhi: The realization of Self, a state of oneness with Supreme
Ota-prota: pervading in all the creation
Papa: Wickedness or sin
Para: Perfect
Paramhansa: Highly evolved soul

Pingala: Masculine psychic current flowing along the *kundalini* energy

Prakruti: Primordial nature, the material substratum of the creation

Prana: Vital energy, life principle, also refers to breath

Pranayama: Breath control by yoga technique

Prayaschitta: Penance, acts of atonement for mitigating the effects of *karma*

Puja: Worship and adoration ceremony

Pujari: Hindu temple priest, anyone who performs the worship rituals

Punarjanma: Reincarnation, taking birth again and again

Punya Bhumi: Holy land

Punya: Virtuous, auspicious actions

Purana: Ancient lore of Hindu folk narratives

Rajsic: Active, materialistic

Rishi: Enlightened soul with spiritual wisdom

Rita/Ruta: Hindu god of order

Sadhana: Religious or spiritual discipline and meditation toward super conscious God-realization*Sadhu*: Holy man, Hindu monk

Saguna: (God) With attributes and form

Sahan-Shakti: Tolerance

Samadhi: Ecstasy, communion with God

Sampardaya: Sect

Samsara: The phenomenal world fraught with recurrent birth and death cycles

Samskara: Hindu sacraments and rites marking significant stages of life, creating mental impression

Sanatana Dharma: Eternal religion of Hindu philosophy

Sanyasa: Renunciation, refers to those who have renounced household aspirations and obligations

Sanyasin: One who has renounced, Hindu monk, swami

Sanskrit: The classical language of sacred Hindu scriptures

Sanstha: Organization

Saraswati: Goddess of arts and learning, sacred river of ancient Hindu civilization

Satguru: Spiritual preceptor of highest attainment

Sattvic:Noble auspicious

Satya: Truth

Self: Refers to the Supreme Being at the core of every soul

Self Realization: Direct knowing of the Supreme God, the ultimate spiritual experience

Seva: Service, selfless work considered an integral part of spiritual path

Shanti: Peace

Shastra: Scripture

Shraddha: Faith and reverence

Siddha: A perfected one, who attains supernatural powers

Sloka: Holy hymn in Hindu scripture

Sumati: Good auspicious mind

Swadharma: One's own set of duties

Swami: Hindu monk, who knows spiritual knowledge, one who is master of one's senses

Swastika: Hindu sign of auspiciousness

Tamsic: Indolent, lethargic

Tapas: Austerities and penances associated with spiritual purification

Tilaka: Marks made on forehead with red clay, ash or sandalwood.

Varna: Group, caste in Hindu society

Vasudev Kutumbkam: God's universal family

Vastu Shastra: Hindu scripture dealing with building construction

Veda: Literally means (spiritual) knowledge or wisdom. Hinduism's most authentic scripture

Vedanta: Final culmination of the Vedas, refers to the ultimate wisdom and spiritual knowledge

Yajna: Worship sacrifice, offerings in sacred fire altar *agni havan-kund*

Yama-niyama: Hinduism's fundamental ethical codes

Yoga: Union with the Divine

Endnotes

1 Colin A. Ronan. *The Natural History of the Univers*. New York: Macmillan Publishing Company, 1991.

2 J. P. Vaswani. *Dada Answers*. Pune, India: Gita Publishing House, 2002.

3 John Bowker. *Cambridge Illustrated History of Religions*. Cambridge, Mass.: Cambridge University Press, 2002, 10.

4 Dalai Lama. The Heart of Compassion. Wisconsin: Lotus Press, 2002, 2.

5 Baldev Matlani. *Hindvasi Weekly* (Sindhi Language). Bombay, India: April 8, 2007.

6 Bhagwan S. Gidwani. *Return of the Aryans*. New Delhi, India: Penguin Books, 1994, 82.

7 John Bowker. *Cambridge Illustrated History of Religions*. Cambridge, Mass.: Cambridge University Press, 2002, 48.

8 Swami Tathagatananda. *Light from the Orient*. India: Advaita Ashram Mayawati, 2005, 13.

9 S. Radhakrishnan. *The Hindu View of Life*. Boston: Unwin Paperbacks, 1980.

10 S. Radhakrishnan. *The Hindu View of Life*. Boston: Unwin Paperbacks, 1980.

11 Swami Tathagatananda. *Light from the Orient*. India: Advaita Ashram Mayawati, 2005, 17.

12 Swami Tathagatananda. *Light from the Orient*. India: Advaita Ashram Mayawati, 2005, 168.

13 Swami Tathagatananda. *Light from the Orient*. India: Advaita Ashram Mayawati, 2005, 69.

14 R. S. Sharma, *India's Ancient Past*. Delhi: Oxford University Press, 1920, 45.

15 Dr. N. K. Prinja, *Hindu Dharma*. UK: Vishwa Hindu Parishad, 1996, 159.

16 Gavin Flood, *An Introduction to Hinduism*. UK: Cambridge University Press, 2005, 158.

17 Swami Bhaskarananda. *The Essentials of Hinduism*. Seattle: Viveka Press, 1994, 18.

18 Swami Tathagatananda. *Light from the Orient*. India: Advaita Ashram Mayawati, 2005, 95.

19 Swami Tathagatananda. *Light from the Orient*. India: Advaita Ashram Mayawati, 2005, 183.

20 Gavin Flood. *An Introduction to Hinduism*. UK: Cambridge University Press, 2005, 30.

21 Gavin Flood. *An Introduction to Hinduism*. UK: Cambridge University Press, 2005, 35.

22 Swami Tathagatananda. *Journey of the Upanishads to the West*. India: Advaita Ashram Mayawati, 2005, 54.

23 15 February 2006 Global Press Conference of Maharishi Mahesh Yogi, www. excite.com

24 Navin Doshi. *Saving Us from Ourselves*, El Segundo, Calif.: BAI, 2006, 30.

25 Swami Tathagatananda. *Light from the Orient*. India: Advaita Ashram Mayawati, 2005, 19.

26 Swami Tathagatananda. *Journey of the Upanishads to the West*. India: Advaita Ashram Mayawati, 2005, 84.

27 Paramhansa Yogananda. *Autobiography of a Yogi*. Los Angeles, Calif.: SRF, 1998, 381.

28 Paramhansa Yogananda. *Autobiography of a Yogi*. Los Angeles, Calif.: SRF, 1998, 379.

29 Paramhansa Yogananda. *Autobiography of a Yogi*. Los Angeles, Calif.: SRF, 1998, 381.

30 Swami Tathagatananda. *Meditation on Swami Vivekananada*. The Vedanta Society of New York, 1994, 200.

31 "What is Hinduism?" *Hinduism Today*. Hawaii: Himalayan Academy, 2007, 83.

32 Gavin Flood. *An Introduction to Hinduism*. UK: Cambridge University Press, 2005, 85.

33 Gavin Flood. *An Introduction to Hinduism*. UK: Cambridge University Press, 2005, 35.

34 Ram A. Panjwani. Bombay, India: *Hindvasi Weekly* (Sindhi Language), 22 Apr. 2007, 5.

35 J. Jagdeesan. Kuala Lumpur, Malaysia: TRAC Publication, 2002, 32-36.

36 Swami Vivekananda. *The Complete works of Swami Vivekananda*. Calcutta, India: Advaita Ashrama, 1970–1973, 412.

37 *Srimad Bhagavad Geeta*, Ch.II Verse 3. Delhi, India: Shree Geeta Ashram, 1985.

38 Satguru Sivaya Subramuniyaswami. *Living with Siva*. Kuai, Hawaii: Himalayan Academy.

39 Talk at the Vedanta Temple. Hollywood, California.

40 Sadhu Brahmadarshandas. *Karamasddhant & Punarjanmavad, Part II.* Ahmedabad, India: Swaminarayan Aksharpith, 2003, 217–218.

41 Swami Tathagatananda. *Light from the Orient.* Mayawati, India: Advaita Ashram, 2005, 24.

42 Gavin Flood. *An Introduction to Hinduism.* UK: Cambridge University Press, 2005, 115.

43 Gavin Flood. *An Introduction to Hinduism.* UK: Cambridge University Press, 2005, 120.

44 Priya Hemenway. *Hindu Gods.* San Francisco: Chronicle Books, 2003, 65.

45 Linda Johnsen. *The Complete Idiot's Guide to Hinduism.* Indianapolis: Alpha Books, 2002, 193.

46.1 Ions Veronica, *Indian Mythology,* New York: Peter Bedrick Books, 1983

47 Gavin Flood. *An Introduction to Hinduism.* UK: Cambridge University Press, 2005, 103.

48 Swami Vivekananda. *The Complete Works of Swami Vivekananda.* Calcutta, India: Advaita Ashrama, 1970–1973.

49 Ed Viswanathan. *Am I a Hindu?* San Francisco, Calif.: Halo Books, 1992, 88.

50 Priya Hemenway. *Hindu Gods.* San Francisco: Chronicle Books, 2003, 69.

51 Chitralekha Singh, *Hindu Goddesses,* New Delhi, India: Crest Publishing House, 1995.

52 Dr. Vilas A. Sanghave. *Aspects of Jaina Religion.* New Delhi, India: Bharatiya Janpith, 2001, 24.

53 Dr. Vilas A. Sanghave. *Aspects of Jaina Religion.* New Delhi, India: Bharatiya Janpith, 2001, 15

54 John Bowker. *Cambridge Illustrated History of Religions.* Mass: Cambridge University Press, 2002. 11.

55 Vastupal Parikh. *Jainism and the New Spirituality.* Toronto: Peace Publications, 2002, 10.

56 Parikh Vastupal, *Jainism and the New Spirituality,* Toronto: Peace Publications, 2002, 10

57 Vastupal Parikh. *Jainism and the New Spirituality.* Toronto: Peace Publications, 2002, 55.

58 S. K. Aiyangar. *Ancient India.* Madras, India: Lucaz & Co, 1911, 12.

59 Smith Huston. *The World's Religions.* San Francisco: Harper, 1958, 82

60 Swami Tathagatananda. *Journey of the Upanishads to the West.* Mayawati, India: Advaita Ashram, 2005, 46.

61 Dalai Lama. *The Heart of Compassion.* Wisconsin: Lotus Press, 2002, 67.

62 Gavin Flood. *An Introduction to Hinduism.* UK: Cambridge University Press, 2005, 114

63 R. S. Sharma. *India's Ancient Past.* Delhi: Oxford University Press, 1920, 243.

64 Paramhansa Yogananda. *Autobiography of a Yogi.* Los Angeles: SRF, 1998, 81.

65 Gavin Flood. *An Introduction to Hinduism.* UK: Cambridge University Press, 2005, 133.

66 Gavin Flood. *An Introduction to Hinduism.* UK: Cambridge University Press, 2005, 134.

67 Bruce M. Sullivan. *The A to Z of Hinduism.* New Delhi, India: Vision Books, 2003, 233.

68 Gavin Flood. *An Introduction to Hinduism.* UK: Cambridge University Press, 2005, 268.

69 Swami Tathagatananda, *Light from the Orient.* Mayawati, India: Advaita Ashram, 2005, 40.

70 Swami Tathagatananda. *Global Vedanta,* Seattle: Viveka Press, Spring 2007, 2.

71 Swami Tathagatananda. *Journey of the Upanishads to the West.* Mayawati, India: Advaita Ashram, 2005, 167.

72 Swami Tathagatananda. *Light from the Orient.* Mayawati, India: Advaita Ashram, 2005, 210.

73 Gavin Flood, *An Introduction to Hinduism,* UK: Cambridge University Press, 2005, 270.

74 Ed Viswanathan. *Am I a Hindu?* San Francisco: Halo Books, 1992, 119.

75 Dr. N. K. Prinja. *Hindu Dharma.* UK: Vishwa Hindu Parishad, 1996, 155.

76 Dalai Lama. *The Universe in a Single Atom.* New York: Morgan Road Books, 2005, 75.

77 Swami Bhaskarananda. *Meditation.* Seattle: Viveka Press, 2001, 1.

78 Gavin Flood. *An Introduction to Hinduism.* UK: Cambridge University Press, 2005, 95–96.

79 Mataji's discourse. *Art of Living:* , Sanathan Dharam Temple, Los Angeles, 2/22/07.

80 Swami Sivananda. *May I Answer That?* Shivanandnagar, India: The Divine Life Society, 1999, 7–14.

81 Joel Stein. Just Say Om. *Time.* October 4, 2003, 48-52

82 Paramhansa Yogananda. *Autobiography of a Yogi*. Los Angeles: SRF, 1998, 117.

83 Tapovan Prasad, Chinmaya Mission, Chennai, India, July 2006.

84 Swami Saradananda. *Sri Ramakrishna The Great Master*. Chennai, India: Sri Ramakrishna Math, 1952.

85 Deepak Chopra. *Quantum Healing*. New York: Bantam Books, 1989

86 Editors of Hinduism Today magazine. *What is Hinduism?* Hawaii: Himalayan Academy, 2007, 348.

87 Priya Hemenway. *Hindu Gods*. San Francisco: Chronicle Books, 2003, 36.

88*Hinduism Today*. Himalayan Academy. Kapaa, Hawaii, Oct-Dec 2006, 52.

89 WWW.Beliefnet.com

90 Swami Tathagatananda. *Meditation on Swami Vivekananada*. New York:The Vedanta Society of New York, 1994, 166.

91 Priya Hemenway. *Hindu Gods*. San Francisco: Chronicle Books, 2003, 23.

92 Devdutt Pattanaik. *Indian Mythology*. Rochester, Vermont: Inner Traditions, 2003, 7.

93 Devdutt Pattanaik. *Indian Mythology*. Rochester: Vermont: Inner Traditions, 2003, 8.

94 R. S. Sharma. *India's Ancient Past*. Delhi: Oxford University Press, 1920, 101.

95 Swami Tapovan Maharaj. *Wanderings in the Himalayas*. Bombay, India: Central Chinmaya Mission Trust, 1996, 144.

96 Dr. K. Dharmaratnam. *Questions and Answers on Hinduism*. Kuala Lumpur: Visal Print Service, 1997, 53.

97 Swami Srikantananda. *Human Excellence*, Hyderabad, India: Ramakrishna Math, 2001, 29.

98 The Master Course of Himalayan Academy.

99 M. K. Gandhi. Ahmedabad, India: Navajivan Publishing House, 1927.

100 Swami Vivekananda. *The Complete Works of Swami Vivekananda*, Calcutta, India: Advaita Ashrama, 1970-1973.

101 Swami Tathagatananda. *Journey of the Upanishads to the West*. Mayawati, India: Advaita Ashram, 2005, 89.

102 Swami Tathagatananda. *Journey of the Upanishads to the West*. Mayawati, India: Advaita Ashram, 2005, 50.

103 T. L. Vaswani. *The Bhagavad Gita: The Song of the Supreme*. Poona, India: Gita Publishing House,

104 Swami Tathagatananda. *Light from the Orient*, Mayawati, India: Advaita, Ashram, 2005, 91

105 Gavin Flood. *An Introduction to Hinduism*, UK: Cambridge University Press, 2005 138

106 Gavin Flood. *An Introduction to Hinduism*, UK: Cambridge University Press, 2005, 139.

107 Mahalingum Kolapen. *Hindu Temples in North America*. Winter Park, Fla.: Titan Graphics and Publications, 2002, 31.

108 Mahalingum Kolapen. *Hindu Temples in North America*. Winter Park, Fla.: Titan Graphics and Publications, 2002, 33.

109 Mahalingum Kolapen. *Hindu Temples in North America*. Winter Park, Fla.: Titan Graphics and Publications, 2002, 21.

110 Ed Viswanathan. *Am I a Hindu?* San Francisco: Halo Books, 1992, 222.

111 Swami Sivananda. *May I Answer That?* Shivanandnagar, India: The Divine Life Society, 1999, 18.

112 Swami Tapovan Maharaj. *Iswara Darshan*, Central Chinmaya Mission Trust, Bombay, India, 1983, 199.

113 Doctor Swami. *Swaminarayan Prakash.Ahmedabad*, India: Aksharpeeth Swaminarayan, 2007.

114 Talk at Chino Hills California Swminarayan Temple on 9 Sept. 2007.

115 Swami Yatiswarananda. *Universal Prayers*. Chennai, India: Sri Ramakrishna Math, 2001.

116 Lecture by Swami Atmarupannada, Ramakrishna Monastry, Trabuco Canyon, California, on 23 Sept 2007.

117 Amrutvijaydas Sadhu, *Divine Memories (Part 3)*, Amdavad, India: Swaminarayan Aksharpith, 2003, 82.

Made in the USA
Columbia, SC
27 September 2020

This book is like a map of Hinduism, which shows from where one should start his or her spiritual journey and where the journey ends.

—**BABA HARI DASS**, *Mount Madonna Center*,
Santa Cruz, California

Your book is definitely written in a way that provides abundant of information about Hinduism in an easily readable format and style that would clearly appeal to the Hindu youth Diaspora.

—**SATGURU BODHINATHA VEYLANSWAMI**,
Hinduism Today magazine, Kauai's Hindu Monastery, USA

You have wonderfully expressed your ideas in very lucid English, which has made it more readable by those who will not otherwise read such text.

—**SWAMI SARVADEVANANDA**,
Vedanta Society of South California, Los Angeles, USA

Whosoever reads this book will surely be benefitted from its beautiful and penetrating insights. This book will also certainly do justice in imparting correct and more comprehensive view about Hinduism to those settled abroad & have forgotten its lofty principles.

— **SWAMI VAGISHANANDA**, *Ramakrishna Math*, Mumbai, India

This book is like a mini-encyclopedia of Hinduism.

— **MOHAN BADLANI**, USA

Dr. Hiro Badlani

Dr H[...] [...]thalmologist from Mumbai, India is now based in Los Angeles, USA. Dr Badlani has dedicated the later part of life what he calls the "the second inning" to the study of Hinduism and its teachings.

hgbadlani@aol.com

ISBN 9781986981651